# PE☉PLE
## in Time and Place

# COMPARING COMMUNITIES

## AUTHORS

**Dr. William W. Joyce**
Professor of Education
Michigan State University
East Lansing, MI

**Roy Erickson**
Program Specialist K–12
Social Studies and Multicultural Education
San Juan Unified School District
Carmichael, CA

## SERIES CONSULTANTS

**Dr. James F. Baumann**
Professor and Head
of the Department of Reading Education
College of Education
The University of Georgia
Athens, GA

**Dr. Theodore Kaltsounis**
Professor of Social Studies Education
University of Washington
Seattle, WA

## LITERATURE CONSULTANTS

**Dr. Ben A. Smith**
Assistant Professor of Social Studies Education
Kansas State University
Manhattan, KS

**Dr. John C. Davis**
Professor of Elementary Education
University of Southern Mississippi
Hattiesburg, MS

**Dr. Jesse Palmer**
Assistant Professor, Department of Curriculum and Instruction
University of Southern Mississippi
Hattiesburg, MS

## SILVER BURDETT & GINN

MORRISTOWN, NJ • NEEDHAM, MA
Atlanta, GA • Cincinnati, OH • Dallas, TX • Deerfield, IL • Menlo Park, CA

# SERIES AUTHORS

**Dr. W. Frank Ainsley,** Professor of Earth Science, University of North Carolina, Wilmington, N.C.

**Dr. Herbert J. Bass,** Professor of History, Temple University, Philadelphia, PA.

**Dr. Kenneth S. Cooper,** Professor of History, Emeritus, George Peabody College for Teachers, Vanderbilt University, Nashville, TN

**Dr. Gary S. Elbow,** Professor of Geography, Texas Tech University, Lubbock, TX

**Roy Erickson,** Program Specialist, K–12 Social Studies and Multicultural Education San Juan Unified School District, Carmichael, CA

**Dr. Daniel B. Fleming,** Professor of Social Studies Education, Virginia Polytechnic Institute and State University, Blacksburg, VA

**Dr. Gerald Michael Greenfield,** Professor and Director, Center for International Studies, University of Wisconsin — Parkside, Kenosha, WI

**Dr. Linda Greenow,** Assistant Professor of Geography, SUNY — The College at New Paltz, New York, NY

**Dr. William W. Joyce,** Professor of Education, Michigan State University, East Lansing, MI

**Dr. Gail S. Ludwig,** Geographer-in-Residence, National Geographic Society, Geography Education Program, Washington, D.C.

**Dr. Michael B. Petrovich,** Professor Emeritus of History, University of Wisconsin, Kenosha, WI

**Dr. Arthur D. Roberts,** Professor of Education, University of Connecticut, Storrs, CT

**Dr. Christine L. Roberts,** Professor of Education, University of Connecticut, Storrs, CT

**Parke Rouse, Jr.,** Virginia Historian and Retired Executive Director of the Jamestown-Yorktown Foundation, Williamsburg, VA

**Dr. Paul C. Slayton, Jr.,** Distinguished Professor of Education, Mary Washington College, Fredericksburg, VA

**Dr. Edgar A. Toppin,** Professor of History and Dean of the Graduate School, Virginia State University, Petersburg, VA

# GRADE LEVEL WRITERS/CONSULTANTS

**Vardreane K. Elliott,** Teacher, John B. Cary School, Richmond, Virginia

**Mary Bosser Joyce,** Educational Consultant, East Lansing, Michigan

**Suzanne Peirsel,** Teacher, Mountain Way School, Morris Plains, New Jersey

**Alfred Velasquez,** Teacher, Missouri Avenue School, Roswell, New Mexico

**Beverley Wong Woo,** Teacher, Kimball School, Seattle, Washington

# ACKNOWLEDGMENTS

Page 14: Excerpt from RAMONA AND HER FATHER Copyright © 1975, 1977 by Beverly Cleary. Used by permission of Morrow Junior Books, (A Division of William Morrow & Co.)

Page 62: Excerpt from IN COAL COUNTRY by Judith Hendershot. Text Copyright © 1987 by Judith Hendershot. Reprinted by permission of Alfred A. Knopf, Inc.

Page 232: ON THE DAY PETER STUYVESANT SAILED INTO TOWN by Arnold Lobel © 1971 by Arnold Lobel. Used by permission of Harper & Row Publishers, Inc.

# CONTENTS

# 2 COMMUNITIES AND NATURAL RESOURCES

# 4 COMMUNITIES YESTERDAY AND TODAY

# RESOURCE SECTION

# MAPS

## Atlas

## Time Lines

▲ Some people live in small towns. In this town, children often get together to enjoy outdoor activities.

▲ In this large city there are many things to do and different ways to get around. People often take a bus.

# COMMUNITIES AND MAPS

There are many kinds of communities. Some are large and busy. Others are small and quiet. People work and play in all kinds of communities.

▲ Some communities are very old. They were settled many years ago. Children had fun in the past as they do now.

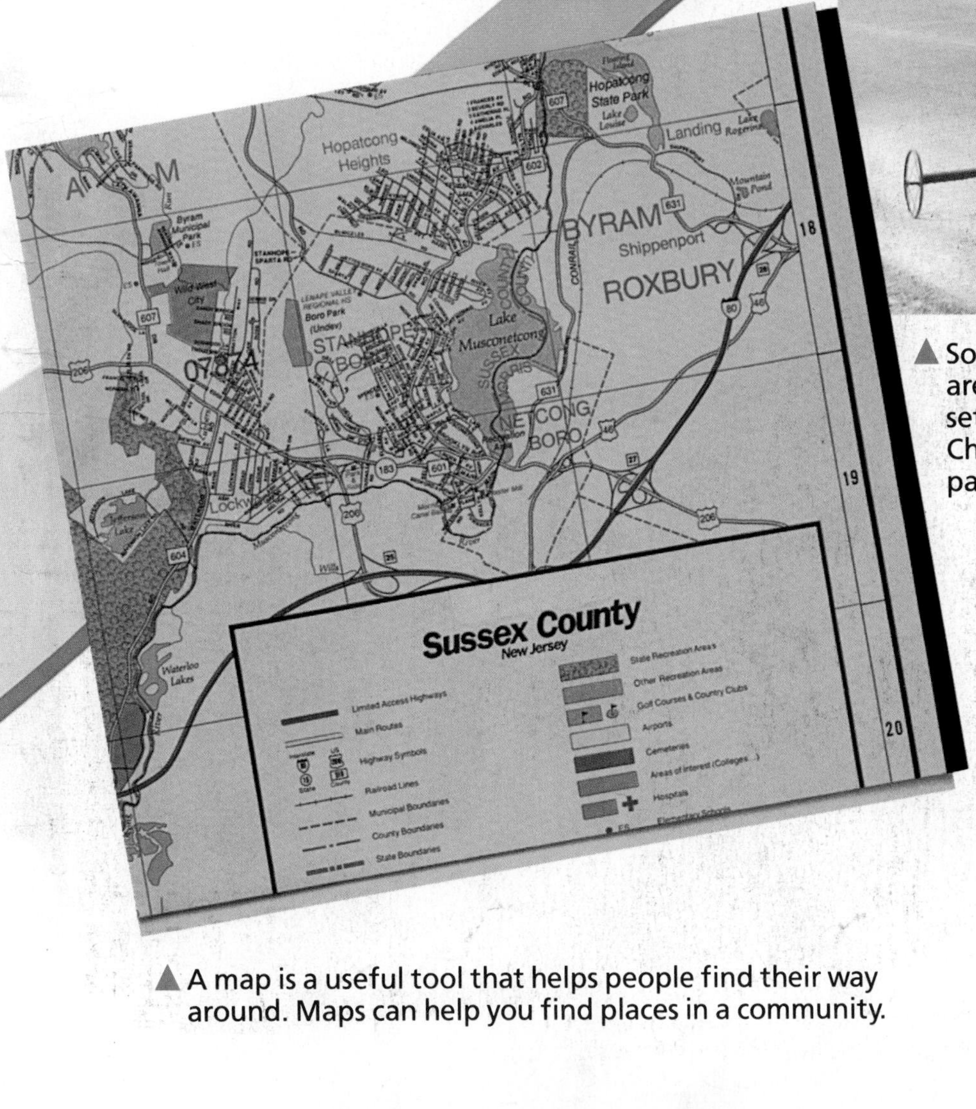

**Sussex County**
New Jersey

Limited Access Highways
Main Routes
Highway Symbols
Railroad Lines
Municipal Boundaries
County Boundaries
State Boundaries

State Recreation Areas
Other Recreation Areas
Golf Courses & Country Clubs
Airports
Cemeteries
Areas of Interest (Colleges...)
Hospitals
Elementary Schools

▲ A map is a useful tool that helps people find their way around. Maps can help you find places in a community.

CHAPTER **1** LEARNING ABOUT COMMUNITIES

People live in different kinds of communities. In all of them, people have good times together.

## Communities Are Alike and Different

**THINK ABOUT WHAT YOU KNOW**

How would you describe your community to a friend who lives far away? What would you tell your friend about some of the people and places in your community?

**STUDY THE VOCABULARY**

| | | |
|---|---|---|
| community | natural resource | suburb |
| physical feature | city | town |

**FOCUS YOUR READING**

How are communities alike and different?

---

## A. What Is a Community?

This year you will learn about many **communities**. (Words highlighted in yellow are in the Glossary, at the back of your book. The Glossary includes pronunciations.) A community is a place where people live, work, and play. You and your family, home, and neighborhood are part of a community that is special to you. It seems different from every other place. Yet in some ways your community is like most others.

For example, every community has **physical features** (FIHZ ih kul  FEE churz), which are different shapes of land and water. On the next page you will see a place with several physical features. There are hills, flat land, and a river. There is no community in this place. Suppose you decided to build one. What would this community need? How might the physical features be changed as the community grew?

Imagine the kind of community that might be built in this place. Think of some ways the land would be changed.
▶ How could the trees, water, and soil be used to begin a community?

## B. Communities and Natural Resources

The new community would need certain **natural resources**, or things in nature that are useful to people. It would need water, because no human or animal can live without it. The river in the photograph above could be a source of water.

What other natural resources do you see in the picture? There is a forest that might provide wood for building houses. The flat land might be good for farming.

To build a community on this land, people would use the earth and change it. They would cut trees and move soil. They would build houses in the forest, a bridge across the river, and perhaps even a road tunnel through the hills.

Although all communities are alike in some ways, they may appear to be very different.
▶ What are some differences between these two communities?

If you were planning the new community, would you cut down all the trees? Would you build houses or a community park near the river?

## C. How Communities Are Alike

All communities, whether they are large or small, are alike in some ways. For example, every community has a name. What do you think you would call your new community? You could name it after the river, the hills, the trees found there, or even another community. You might also want to name the new community after yourself, a member of your family, or a famous person, such as the President. No matter what communities are named, there is something special about each one.

Communities need homes, schools, stores, and places to worship. Many communities have parks, playgrounds, libraries, and other places where people play and learn. What places would you want in the new community?

Communities need jobs. In the new community, people won't want to do every kind of job for themselves. But they will need food, clothing, and homes. They will want to keep well and be safe. The children will need an education. So there will be jobs for storekeepers, builders, doctors, police officers, and teachers. Do you think the new community should have jobs for farmers and factory workers, too?

A country store, an indoor shopping mall, and a busy main street of shops are found in different kinds of communities.
▶ Where do the people of your community do their shopping?

These photographs show the city of Baltimore, Maryland (left), and a neighborhood in a suburb (right).
▶ What differences do you see between the city and the suburb?

## D. How Communities Are Different

The new community might grow to be large or medium-sized, or it might stay small. A **city** is the largest kind of community. In a city, people and buildings are close together. There are many places to live, work, and have fun.

A **suburb** is a large, medium-sized, or small community that is near a very large city. In a suburb, people often live in a one-family house with a yard. People in suburbs often travel to a city to work.

A **town** is a small community, in which most people know each other. Some towns are surrounded by farmland or forests. Others are near larger towns or cities.

How big would you want the new community to grow? Is that about the size of the community where you live?

## E. Working and Playing in Communities

Like all kinds of communities, in the new community, people will want to work and play together. They will try to improve their community by planting trees, cleaning up garbage, building a community center, or planning special activities for children and senior citizens. They will need schools, clubs, and places to worship. What kinds of meeting places do you want in the new community? How will the people work together?

These people are working hard to make their communities better.
▶ What do you think each person is doing to help his or her community?

These children are part of a community parade in Victor, Idaho.
▶ What do you think the sign on the float means?

FREEDOM IS EDUCATION

Sometimes people have fun together by planning community celebrations. Some communities have celebrations called Pioneer Days or Homecoming Days. On these days the people remember the community's history. In the next lesson, you will learn about such a celebration in a town called Jefferson.

## LESSON 1 REVIEW

### THINK AND WRITE

A. What makes a community special to the people who live there?

B. Why do all communities need water?

C. What is one way that communities are alike?

D. In your opinion, what is the best thing about a city, a suburb, and a town?

E. Why, do you think, do people try to make their communities better?

### SKILLS CHECK

**MAP SKILL**

Find the Gazetteer, at the back of your book. What kinds of places are in the Gazetteer? Write five or more kinds of places.

# Communities Celebrate Their Past

**THINK ABOUT WHAT YOU KNOW**

What do you know about your community's past?

**STUDY THE VOCABULARY**

| | | |
|---|---|---|
| settlement | museum | history |
| immigrant | Native American | gristmill |

**FOCUS YOUR READING**

What are some ways communities change and some ways they stay the same?

## A. Immigrants in America

Jennifer Anderson, Jason Williams, and Cam Tran are third graders just like you. They live in the make-believe town of Jefferson. Although the community of Jefferson in your book is a make-believe place, it is like many real communities. The town was named for Thomas Jefferson, the third President of the United States. More than 25 communities in our country were named for him.

The three children have come to the Homecoming Day celebration in the community park named Settler's Park. They want to have fun and learn about the early days of their community. Jason's father has told them that long ago, Jefferson was a farm **settlement**, or small village. It was started by **immigrants**, or people from other countries who come to live in a new country. The first immigrants came to Jefferson to farm the land because they could not raise enough food on the land in their old countries.

Cam, Jason, Jennifer, little brother Eric

## B. Learning About Work Long Ago

On Homecoming Day in Settler's Park, people can learn about old ways of doing things. Jennifer, Jason, and Cam enjoyed visiting the many displays in the park.

The children saw a woman making dolls from dried apples. They watched basket-making, quilting, and wood chopping, too. They visited a **museum**, where they could see old things, such as paintings, clothing, and tools.

"Most of the museum has Native American things," Jennifer said. "**Native Americans**, or American Indians, lived here long before the immigrant farmers came."

Making apple dolls

## C. Learning from an Older Person

After their visit to the museum, the children hurried to meet their families near the bandstand. Other people gathered near the bandstand, too. The children helped to spread blankets on the ground and to prepare a picnic lunch.

After lunch, a special program began. Several older people told about life in Jefferson when they were young. They talked about times when there were no TV sets or computers, and few cars. At last, Jennifer's grandfather walked briskly to the stage. He began his speech about the **history**, or story of the past, of the community.

Indian bowl and dolls

13

# FROM: RAMONA AND HER FATHER

**By: Beverly Cleary**
**Setting: Oregon, 1970's**

Older people like Grandpa Anderson have things to teach us. In the book *Ramona and Her Father*, Mrs. Swink, an elderly neighbor, teaches Ramona and Beezus about tin-can stilts.

*Let's see now. . . .'' Mrs. Swink looked thoughtful. "We made fudge, and—oh, I know—tin-can stilts.'' She smiled to herself. "I had forgotten all about tin-can stilts until this very minute.''*

*At last Beezus could ask a question. "How did you make tin-can stilts?''*

*Mrs. Swink laughed, remembering. "We took two tall cans. Two-pound coffee cans were best. We turned them upside down and punched two holes near what had once been the bottom of each. The holes had to be opposite one another on each can. Then we poked about four feet of heavy twine through each pair of holes and knotted the ends to make a loop. We set one foot on each can, took hold of a loop of twine in each hand, and began to walk. We had to remember to lift each can by the loop of twine as we raised a foot or we fell off—my knees were always skinned. . . .''*

"Ladies and gentlemen, boys and girls," Grandpa Anderson said. "I am going to tell you a little history of this community. This history belongs to all of us. As my mother told me, the Borg family were among the first people to settle here. They were immigrants from the faraway country of Sweden. When more and more people came to Jefferson, the Borg family gave some of their land to the community for a church and a school. Later they gave all the land that makes up this park, which many of us continue to enjoy today.

"Today in Settler's Park we can still see the old **gristmill**. There, water power once turned huge wheels to grind grains into flour. Long ago

## A GRISTMILL

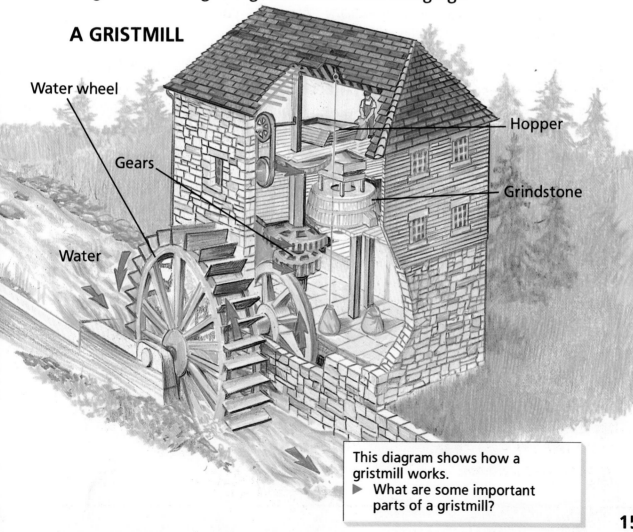

Water wheel

Gears

Water

Hopper

Grindstone

This diagram shows how a gristmill works.
► What are some important parts of a gristmill?

my great-grandparents' friends from miles around brought their corn to this mill to be ground.

"You can still see the log cabins, the old school, and the first church built in this community. When I was a child, my father told me about his visits with his grandmother Borg in a log cabin that is here in the park. The little one-room school has special meaning for me, too. My parents were students there — for all eight grades. They chopped wood for the potbellied stove inside the school. They cleaned chalkboards and erasers and did many other chores. The church? That's where Mrs. Anderson and I were married, and so were my parents."

Grandpa Anderson giving a speech

## D. Learning About Change

"I would never miss a chance to be back here in Jefferson on Homecoming Day. Each year when I return, I see more changes. Someone has moved away. Someone else has moved in. A new business has replaced an old one. Some trees have been cut down so a new house could be built. Yet somehow, for me, Jefferson remains the same. After all, the people of Jefferson still do their work, raise their children, and gather at least once a year in Settler's Park."

A crowd has gathered near the bandstand to hear a special program of music and speeches.
▶ How do you think people feel when they meet at a gathering like this?

"Now strike up the band," called Grandpa Anderson, as he rejoined his family. Homecoming Day was over for this year. Jennifer, Jason, Cam, and all the other people in Settler's Park could look forward to another Homecoming Day next year.

## LESSON 2 REVIEW

### THINK AND WRITE

A. Long ago, why did some people leave their home countries to farm the land in America?
B. In your opinion, why are museums important places?
C. What is history?
D. What changes might take place in a community?

### SKILLS CHECK

**WRITING SKILL**

Find the word *museum* in the Glossary, at the back of your book. What information is given about the word? Write a paragraph about what you would want to include in a museum that had items from your community.

## YOU DECIDE:
## SHOULD THIS BUILDING BE SAVED?

**I**n Chapter 1 you learned that communities change. Americans often welcome change, but sometimes we want to preserve, or keep, the past.

Mayor Burns wanted to build a new courthouse. He said the old courthouse was too small. He said it was run-down and needed too many expensive repairs. According to Mayor Burns, the old courthouse was too old-fashioned to save.

When Mrs. Jones heard this, she was very upset. Mrs. Jones loved the old courthouse. "Our great-grandparents built this wonderful old building," she said. "To keep this building is like giving a nice gift to our children and grandchildren."

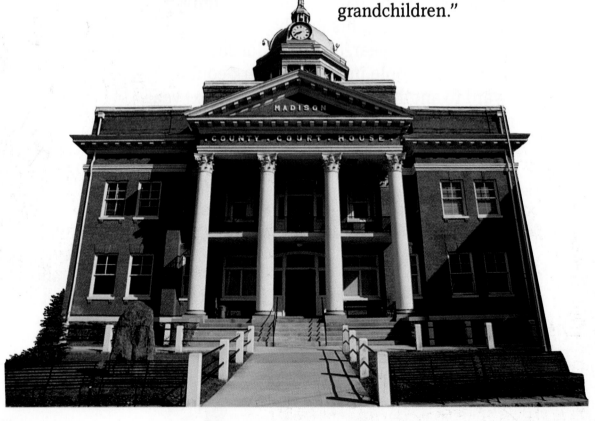

The citizens held a meeting. They discussed tearing down the courthouse; repairing it; and even moving it to a new location.

The pictures on this page show some things that can happen to an old building.

## Thinking for Yourself

1. What might Mrs. Jones do to save the courthouse?
2. How would you feel about the building being torn down?

## USING THE VOCABULARY

community
physical features
natural resources
city
suburb
settlement
immigrants
Native Americans
history
gristmill

On a separate sheet of paper, write the word or words from above that best complete the sentences.

1. A _____ is a place where people live, work, and play.
2. _____ is the story of the past.
3. Grain was once ground at a _____.
4. Things in nature that are useful to people are _____.
5. A _____ is the largest kind of community.
6. A _____ is a small village.
7. Land and water of different shapes are called _____.
8. The first people in America were _____.
9. A _____ is a community near a large city.
10. _____ are people from other countries who come to live in a new country.

## REMEMBERING WHAT YOU READ

On a separate sheet of paper, answer the questions in complete sentences.

1. What are three important things that people do in a community?
2. What is one important resource that no human or animal can live without?
3. List five places that are needed in communities.
4. What can you see at a museum?
5. How do communities change?

## TYING LANGUAGE ARTS TO SOCIAL STUDIES

Write a story about something that happened at a community celebration. The story can be about you or someone you know. Tell the story in the order that things happened. If you have time, draw a picture to go with the story.

## THINKING CRITICALLY

On a separate sheet of paper, answer the following in complete sentences.

1. Why do communities change?
2. List five important jobs in your community and tell why you think each job is important.
3. Why, do you think, do people want to celebrate the history of their community?
4. How can you learn from an older person?
5. List three changes that you think will take place over the next five years in your community.

## SUMMARIZING THE CHAPTER

**Copy this graphic organizer on a separate sheet of paper. Under the main idea for each lesson, write three facts that support the main idea.**

**CHAPTER THEME**

Communities are alike and different, and each one has its own history.

**LESSON 1**

**Communities are alike and different in many ways.**

1. _____
2. _____
3. _____

**LESSON 2**

**Communities celebrate their past.**

1. _____
2. _____
3. _____

# MAPS AND GLOBES

**M**aps and globes are used to find many different places. Learning to read them is very useful.

## Directions on the Earth

What directions would you give to help a new classmate find the school library?

**globe**       **compass rose**       **South Pole**
**direction**       **North Pole**

How can you use the North Pole and South Pole to find directions on a globe?

## A. What Is a Globe?

Globe

Jennifer, Jason, and Cam are in Mrs. Allen's third-grade class. It is the beginning of the school year. The students are reviewing what they know about a **globe**.

As you can see from the pictures on this page, a globe shows how the earth looks from space. It is a model of the earth. A model has the same shape as the real thing, but usually the model is smaller.

When Mrs. Allen was a child, she had a dollhouse that was a model of her family's house. The dollhouse stood in one corner of her bedroom.

What kinds of models do you have at home? Perhaps you build model cars, ships, or planes.

Earth from space

## B. Main and In-between Directions

The **directions** on a globe are the directions on the earth. The main directions are north, south, east, and west. The in-between directions are northeast, southeast, southwest, and northwest.

You can use the picture of the globe on this page to learn about directions. Find the drawing with eight points. It is the **compass rose**, or direction finder. The letters on the compass rose stand for directions.

The letter *N* points north, toward the **North Pole**. The North Pole is the most northern place on

Matthew Henson, an African-American explorer, went to the North Pole in 1909.
▶ Why did he dress this way?

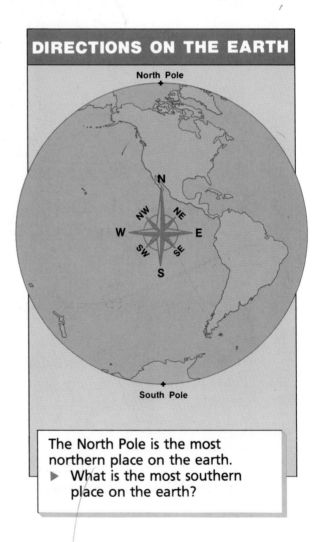

**DIRECTIONS ON THE EARTH**

North Pole

South Pole

The North Pole is the most northern place on the earth.
▶ What is the most southern place on the earth?

24

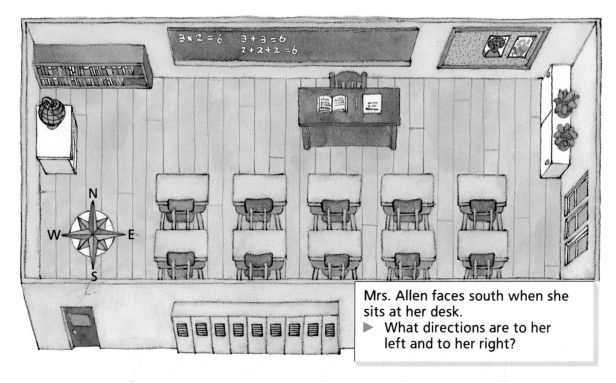

Mrs. Allen faces south when she sits at her desk.
► What directions are to her left and to her right?

the earth. The letter *S* points south, toward the **South Pole**. The South Pole is the most southern point on the earth. The North Pole and South Pole are opposite each other. Find the other directions on the globe. Use the compass rose for help.

Do you know the directions in your classroom? In the drawing of Mrs. Allen's classroom above, a compass rose shows directions. When the students sit at their desks, they face north. South is behind them. East is to their right, and west is to their left.

## LESSON 1 REVIEW

### THINK AND WRITE
A. How are a globe and a dollhouse alike?
B. How might you use the main and in-between directions?

### SKILLS CHECK
**THINKING SKILL**
The North Pole and the South Pole are opposites. List five words and their opposites. For example, you might think of *small* and *big*.

# Using Symbols on a Map

Why do people use maps? Think of at least two times you have seen someone use a map. What did the map help the person do?

**map     symbol     map key**

How does a map key help you read a map?

## A. Symbols and a Map Key

You have learned that a globe is a model of the earth. A **map** is a flat drawing that shows what the earth, or part of the earth, looks like from above. Maps can show outdoor or indoor places. You can use a map to do many things, such as to plan a trip or to find a particular store in a shopping mall.

The map on the next page shows Settler's Park, where the community of Jefferson holds its Homecoming Day celebration. You can see that the map has **symbols**, which stand for real places or things on the earth. Symbols can be different colors or shapes. They can be circles, dots, diamonds, triangles, or small pictures. The **map key** explains what the symbols on the map mean.

Find the map key on the map of Settler's Park. What is the symbol for the gristmill? Find the symbol for log cabins. How many log cabins are on the map?

Suppose you wanted to find the bandstand on the map. First you would find the symbol for the bandstand in the key. Then you would look for that symbol on the map.

Use the symbols to help you plan a walk in Settler's Park. Start at the entrance and end at the building that is farthest north in the park. The compass rose will show you which direction is north on the map. The church is the building that is the farthest north.

**SETTLER'S PARK**

THUNDER RIVER

There are many things to see and do in Settler's Park.
▶ What places could you visit west of Thunder River?

**MAP KEY**

| | | | |
|---|---|---|---|
| Ballfields | Church | General Store | Paths |
| Bandstand | Craft Areas | Gristmill | Playgrounds |
| Bridges | Entrance | Log Cabins | Schoolhouse |
| | Food Tents | Museum | Woods |

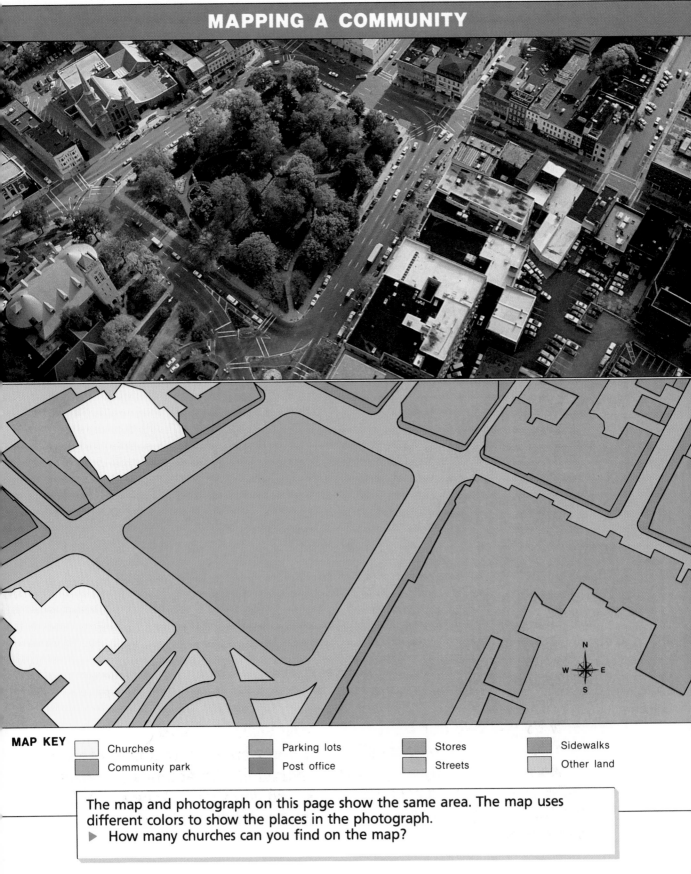

**MAP KEY**

Churches

Community park

Parking lots

Post office

Stores

Streets

Sidewalks

Other land

The map and photograph on this page show the same area. The map uses different colors to show the places in the photograph.

▶ How many churches can you find on the map?

## B. Comparing a Photograph and a Map

A map shows how the earth looks from overhead. A map shows a bird's-eye view, or what a bird would see if it looked down on the earth from high in the sky. If you were in an airplane or a helicopter, you could get this kind of view, too. The higher up you were, the more of the earth you would see. If you went high enough, you could see one half of the earth.

The photograph on the left-hand page was taken from a helicopter. The photograph and the map below show the same place. Find some unusual shapes in the photograph. Now find those same unusual shapes on the map. Next find some buildings in the photograph. Then find those same buildings on the map.

Find the color symbol for streets in the map key. Find the streets on the map. Notice that the streets are in the same places on the map as they are in the photograph.

If you went to a new community, would you rather have a photograph or a map to help you get around? What kinds of things would the photograph show that the map might leave out? What things would show more clearly on the map?

*LESSON* 2 *REVIEW*

### THINK AND WRITE

A. How do you find out what symbols stand for on a map?
B. In your opinion, why do people make maps when they could see the same places in a photograph?

### SKILLS CHECK

**MAP SKILL**

If you were making a map of your community, what kinds of places would you show? Draw symbols for five kinds of places.

## Maps of Your State and Country

**THINK ABOUT WHAT YOU KNOW**

What is your address? When do people need to know your address?

**STUDY THE VOCABULARY**

**state       state capital       border**

**FOCUS YOUR READING**

What is one difference between a community, a state, and a nation?

## A.  Where Do You Live?

You live in many places at the same time. In this lesson we will think about three places where most of you live. You live in a community, in a **state**, and in the United States.

How can you live in these three places at one time? You can do this because communities are within states, and states are within the United States. If you listed the places where you live in order of their size, your community would be the smallest, your state the next largest, and the United States the largest.

## B.  Finding Communities on a State Map

Louisiana is one of the 50 states in the United States. Look at the map of Louisiana on page 31. Find the symbol for **state capital**. A state capital is a special community where state leaders meet to make decisions for the state. Find the state capital of Louisiana.

# THE STATE OF LOUISIANA

ARKANSAS

Shreveport
Monroe

MISSISSIPPI

Ouachita River
Boeuf River
Red River
Mississippi

TEXAS

Alexandria

Pearl River

Calcasieu River
Sabine River

Lake Charles
Crowley
Baton Rouge
Lafayette

Lake Maurepas
Lake Pontchartrain

Norco
New Orleans

Calcasieu Lake
Grand Lake
White Lake

Lake Verret
Lake Salvador

Lake Borgne

Sabine Lake

Houma

Breton Sound

Vermilion Bay

Terrebonne Bay
Barataria Bay

Mississippi Sound

Gulf of Mexico

⊛  State capital
•  Other cities

This map shows the entire state of Louisiana and portions of
bordering states.
▶  What rivers form part of the border between Louisiana and
Mississippi?

Find the symbol for other cities. Count those
cities on the map. Do you think they are the only
communities in Louisiana? If you answered no, you
are correct. Most state maps do not include all the
communities of the state. The map of Louisiana
shows only the largest cities.

Sometimes a state map shows only one state.
But usually small parts of the states that **border**

the main state are shown, too. To *border* means
"to touch." Which states border Louisiana?

Find a map of your state. Is your community
on the map? If it is not, ask your teacher to tell
you about where your community would be on the
map if it were shown.

## C. Finding States and Capitals on a United States Map

Look at the states on the map below. You will
see that states are different sizes. Alaska is the

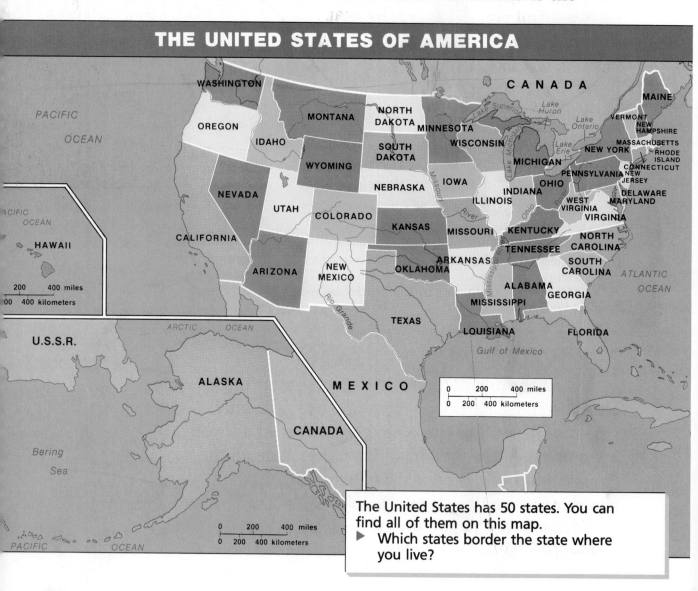

### THE UNITED STATES OF AMERICA

The United States has 50 states. You can
find all of them on this map.
▶ Which states border the state where
you live?

largest state. Rhode Island is the smallest. Does the eastern or western part of the United States have the biggest states?

Some states in the United States have a great many people. Other states have far fewer people. Isn't it strange to think that Alaska, which has the most land, has the fewest people? California has more people than any other state.

Find Louisiana on the map on page 32. Next find your state on the map.

The photograph on the right was taken in Baton Rouge (BAT un roozh), the capital of Louisiana. The photograph shows the building where Louisiana state leaders work. You will learn more about state capitals in Chapter 6.

Turn to the United States map on pages 324 and 325 of the Atlas in your book. Find Baton Rouge on the Atlas map. Now find the capital of your state. What are some other state capitals?

Baton Rouge, Louisiana

## LESSON 3 REVIEW

### THINK AND WRITE

A. Which is larger, the state of California or the United States?
B. In your opinion, why don't most state maps show every community in the state?
C. What are two ways states are different from each other?

### SKILLS CHECK

**MAP SKILL**

Find Baton Rouge in the Gazetteer, at the back of your book. Write two things you learn about Baton Rouge from the Gazetteer.

## Continents and Hemispheres

**THINK ABOUT WHAT YOU KNOW**

If you gave the most complete address for the place where you live, what would come after the United States?

**STUDY THE VOCABULARY**

**continent**    **Equator**    **hemisphere**

**FOCUS YOUR READING**

What are the seven continents and the four hemispheres of the earth?

### A. Continents on the Earth

The United States is on the **continent** of North America. A continent is a very large body of land.

Look at the map on the opposite page. You can see all the countries of North America. Canada is the country to the north of the United States. Mexico is the country to the south of the United States. The islands of the West Indies and the countries of Central America are also part of the continent of North America.

Find Puerto Rico, in the West Indies. Puerto Rico is part of the United States, although it is not a state. Now find the seven small countries of Central America.

Besides North America, there are six other continents on the earth. They are South America, Europe, Africa, Asia, Australia, and Antarctica. Find these continents on the map on page 36.

# THE CONTINENT OF NORTH AMERICA

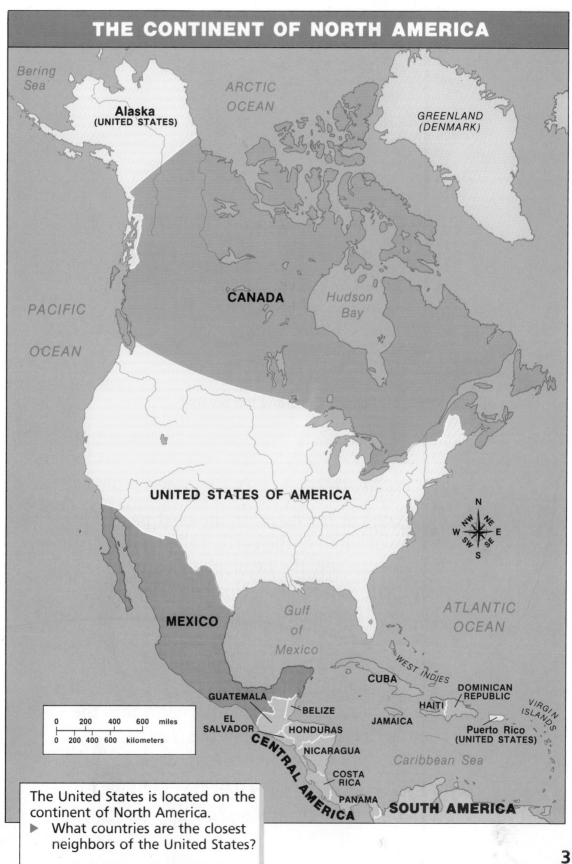

Bering Sea

ARCTIC OCEAN

**Alaska** (UNITED STATES)

GREENLAND (DENMARK)

PACIFIC OCEAN

CANADA

Hudson Bay

UNITED STATES OF AMERICA

N
NW  NE
W       E
SW  SE
S

Gulf of Mexico

ATLANTIC OCEAN

**MEXICO**

GUATEMALA

WEST INDIES

CUBA

DOMINICAN REPUBLIC

BELIZE

HAITI

VIRGIN ISLANDS

EL SALVADOR

JAMAICA

Puerto Rico (UNITED STATES)

HONDURAS

NICARAGUA

Caribbean Sea

CENTRAL AMERICA

COSTA RICA

PANAMA

**SOUTH AMERICA**

| 0 | 200 | 400 | 600 | miles |
| 0 | 200 | 400 | 600 | kilometers |

The United States is located on the continent of North America.

▶ What countries are the closest neighbors of the United States?

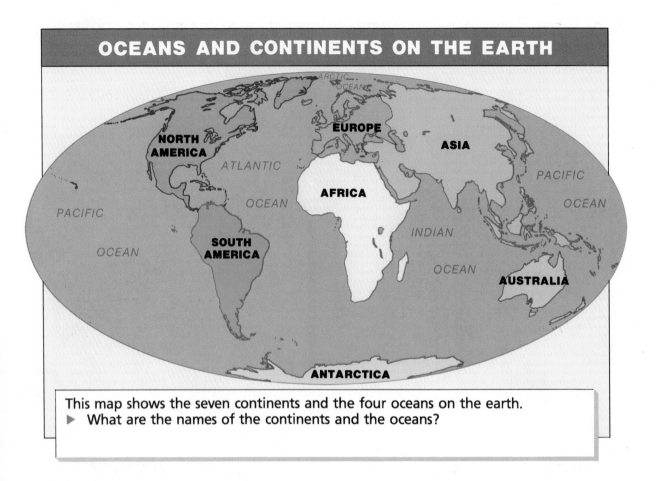

## OCEANS AND CONTINENTS ON THE EARTH

This map shows the seven continents and the four oceans on the earth.
▶ What are the names of the continents and the oceans?

## B. Hemispheres on the Earth

Look at the maps on the next page. Each map shows one half of the earth, called a **hemisphere**. As you can see, the hemispheres are named the Southern Hemisphere, Northern Hemisphere, Eastern Hemisphere, and Western Hemisphere. North America and South America are entirely within the Western Hemisphere.

The **Equator** (ee KWAYT ur) is a line that is drawn on maps. It divides the earth into the Southern Hemisphere and the Northern Hemisphere. All of North America is in the Northern Hemisphere. Which continents are entirely in the Southern Hemisphere?

# HEMISPHERES OF THE EARTH

## SOUTHERN HEMISPHERE

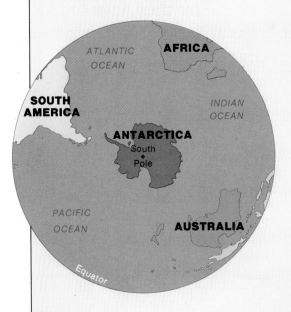

## NORTHERN HEMISPHERE

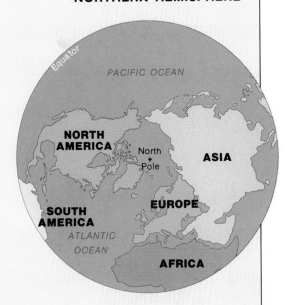

## WESTERN HEMISPHERE

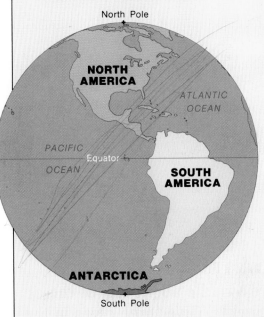

## EASTERN HEMISPHERE

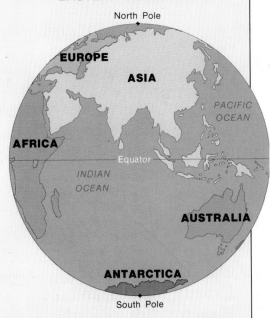

Each globe on this page shows one half of the earth. Each half is called a hemisphere.

▶ In which three hemispheres can you find all or part of South America?

It can be fun to learn about the world by finding places on a globe. The children in the photograph below are finding the countries that the Equator passes through. So far they have found Borneo, Kenya, Colombia, and Brazil. Look on a globe or in the Atlas of your book to find these countries and other countries along the Equator. See how many you can find.

These children from Mrs. Allen's class enjoy using a globe.
► How could you use a globe to review the information presented in this lesson?

---

*LESSON* **4** *REVIEW*

### THINK AND WRITE

A. On which continent are Canada, Mexico, and the United States located?

B. Why is each continent in at least two hemispheres?

### SKILLS CHECK

**WRITING SKILL**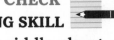

Write a riddle about one of the continents. Give three clues in the riddle. Have a clue about one hemisphere the continent is in.

## USING THE VOCABULARY

globe            state capital
directions       border
compass rose     continents
symbols          hemisphere
map key          Equator

On a separate sheet of paper, write the word or words from above that best complete the sentences.

1. The _____ is a line drawn on maps to divide the earth into the Southern Hemisphere and the Northern Hemisphere.
2. A special city where state leaders meet to decide things for all the people who live in the state is called the _____.
3. _____ on a map stand for real places or things.
4. The words *north, south, east,* and *west* name _____.
5. One half of the earth is called a _____.
6. A _____ shows how the earth looks from space.
7. The seven largest bodies of land on the earth are the _____.
8. A _____ is a direction finder.
9. Symbols on a map are explained in the _____.
10. To _____ means "to touch."

## REMEMBERING WHAT YOU READ

On a separate sheet of paper, answer the questions in complete sentences.

1. How is a model usually different from the real thing?
2. How is the North Pole different from the South Pole?
3. How is a map like a globe?
4. How can you compare a photograph and a map?
5. How can you live in three places at one time?
6. What is the largest state?
7. What is the smallest state?
8. What are the seven continents?
9. How many states are in the United States?
10. What are the names of the four hemispheres?

## TYING ART TO SOCIAL STUDIES

Draw a map of your classroom. Label each wall with a main direction. Label each corner with an in-between direction. Remember to use symbols on your map. Show the symbols in the map key.

## THINKING CRITICALLY

On a separate sheet of paper, answer the following in complete sentences.

1. Explain why you think it is important to know the in-between directions, such as northeast, southeast, southwest, and northwest.

2. Why do we need symbols on a map?
3. Why, do you think, is Alaska the state with the least number of people?
4. When might a map save a person's life?
5. If you traveled to the Equator, would you be able to see the line on the earth?

## SUMMARIZING THE CHAPTER

Copy this graphic organizer on a separate sheet of paper. Under the main idea for each lesson, write three facts that support the main idea.

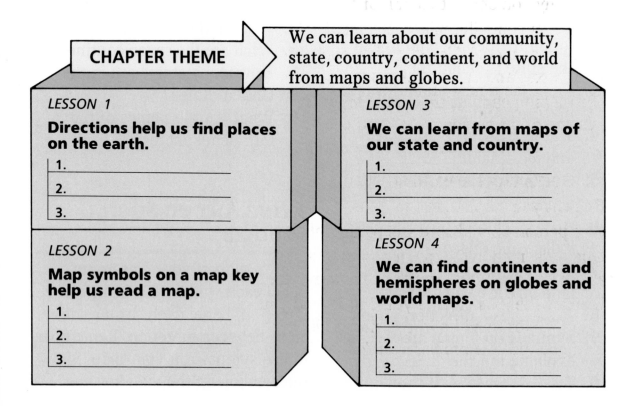

CHAPTER THEME

We can learn about our community, state, country, continent, and world from maps and globes.

LESSON 1

**Directions help us find places on the earth.**

1. _____
2. _____
3. _____

LESSON 2

**Map symbols on a map key help us read a map.**

1. _____
2. _____
3. _____

LESSON 3

**We can learn from maps of our state and country.**

1. _____
2. _____
3. _____

LESSON 4

**We can find continents and hemispheres on globes and world maps.**

1. _____
2. _____
3. _____

# REVIEW

## COOPERATIVE LEARNING

In this unit you learned about several kinds of communities. You learned that all communities have buildings such as homes and stores. In this activity you will make a model of a building in your community.

### PROJECT

- Work with a partner for this activity. Make a model of a building in your community and write a paragraph about that building. Tell why it is important or interesting.
- Look over the unit to review the kinds of buildings that most communities have.
- Choose a building in your community.
- One of you should write the paragraph about why you chose this building.
- Plan how you will build your model.
- Build your model. Use materials such as empty boxes and cardboard tubes.
- One person can put the model together while the other person draws and colors windows, doors, chimneys, or decorations.

### PRESENTATION AND REVIEW

- Present your project to the class.
- One person should read the paragraph.
- One person should explain how the model was built and what its important features are.
- Discuss the jobs each of you did. Would you divide the work and build the model the same way if you did this project again?

## A. WHY I NEED THIS SKILL

As you have already learned, a map is much smaller than the real place that is shown on the map. By using the map scale, you can find out how big the real place is. You can also use the scale to measure distances between places on the earth.

## B. LEARNING THE SKILL

Look at the map scale below. Each inch on the scale stands for 100 miles. To find the number of miles that 2 inches represents, add 100 + 100. How many miles does 3 inches represent?

## C. PRACTICING THE SKILL

The Virginia maps on page 43 are drawn to different scales. On Map A the scale is 1 inch = 100 miles. What is the scale on Map B?

Find the distance between Roanoke and Richmond. First use a strip of paper and make a scale of your own. Your scale should match the Map A scale. It should be the same size, and it should be marked in the same way. Next place your scale with one end at Richmond and the other end at Virginia Beach. You will see that the distance between these two cities is a little less than 100 miles.

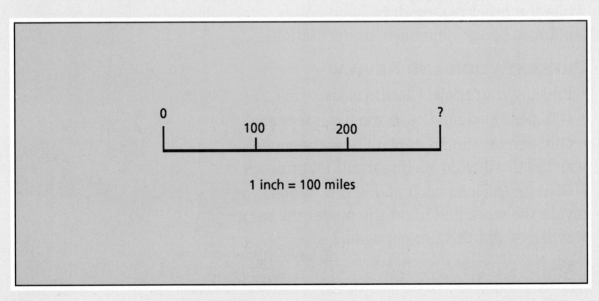

0    100    200    ?

1 inch = 100 miles

Now make your own scale to match the scale on Map B. Use your scale to measure the distance between Richmond and Virginia Beach on Map B. Even though the two maps use different scales, the distance between Richmond and Virginia Beach measures the same on both maps.

## D. APPLYING THE SKILL

If you and your family were traveling to another community, you might use a map. How would you know the distance to the new place? You might use a map and a map scale to measure the distance.

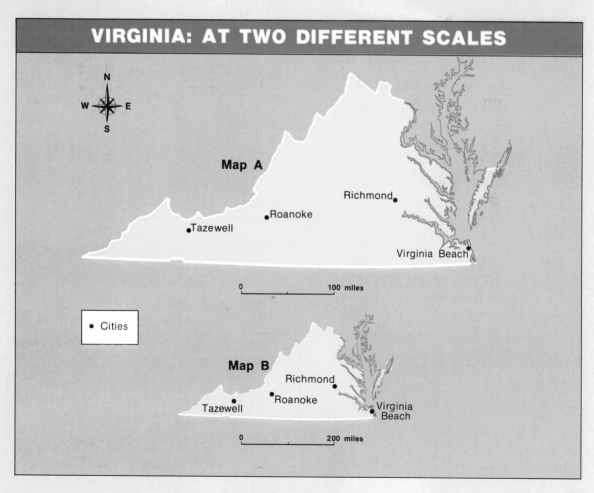

VIRGINIA: AT TWO DIFFERENT SCALES

## A. WHY I NEED THIS SKILL

Sometimes people write about things that happen in their lives. For example, explorers might write about the places they have visited and the people they have met. You might write about a vacation.

Such writings are called journals. Writing a journal is a good way to keep a record of what happens in your life. Later on it will be interesting to reread your journal and remember events.

You can write about exciting times, such as your birthday, in a journal. But even an ordinary day can seem interesting when you read about it years later.

## B. LEARNING THE SKILL

A journal can be kept in a notebook or on several sheets of paper stapled together. Each time you write in a journal, you are making a journal entry. When you begin an entry, write the date at the top of the page.

Look at Jennifer's journal entry on this page. Here, Jennifer has written about Homecoming Day in Settler's Park. She has described some of the things she and her two friends did to celebrate that important day. She has described how she felt about the celebration by using the words *fun* and *interesting*. Jennifer began her entry by writing the date.

Notice the kinds of things Jennifer included in her journal entry. She named the friends who were with her. She told what they did, and she also described the way people felt.

> September 15, 1991
>
> Cam, Jason, and I had fun today. We went to Settler's Park and did many things. It was interesting to see a woman making dolls from dried apples. Jason and Cam were excited when they saw many things from the museum. I especially liked the tools that the Native Americans used.

## C. PRACTICING THE SKILL

Pretend you are Jennifer. Complete the entry for September 19 that Jennifer began. Write down the things you think Jennifer might have written in her journal. If you cannot remember what happened on Homecoming Day, reread Lesson 2.

You might begin your entry this way.

September 19, 1991

Today was Homecoming Day. Jason, Mom, Dad, and I all went together to Settler's Park. We

## D. APPLYING THE SKILL

Start to keep your own journal. In your journal write about things that are important to you. You might write about events that happened at school. Or you might write about something special, such as a day your family spent at a beach. Reread your journal once in a while. It's interesting to recall the things you did and when you did them.

▶ These men are moving lumber down a river. This wood will be used for many different things.

▲ People catch fish in oceans, lakes, and rivers. Fish provide a healthful food for people all around the world.

▶ Farming is an important way to use the land. Farmers need to know how to grow good crops and raise healthy animals.

# COMMUNITIES AND NATURAL RESOURCES

Natural resources are important
to the growth of many communities.
We all depend on natural
resources for things we need.

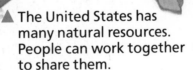

▲ The United States has
many natural resources.
People can work together
to share them.

# CHAPTER 3

# FINDING AND USING NATURAL RESOURCES

People use the earth in many ways. Sometimes a hike in the woods is the best way to spend a winter day.

# Physical Features of the Earth

How would you describe the land where you live?
What is the nearest body of water?

| | | | |
|---|---|---|---|
| geography | desert | ocean | peninsula |
| mountain range | river | coast | |
| plain | lake | island | |

Describe ten physical features of the earth.

## A. What Is Geography?

Have you ever built a sand castle at the beach? Have you skated on a frozen pond or sledded down a snow-covered hill? Maybe you have gone climbing, camping, or boating. If you have done any of these things, you have used the earth to have fun. Can you think of some other ways people use the earth for fun?

**Geography** is the study of the earth and the ways people use it. In this chapter you will study the geography of the United States. In this lesson, you will review some physical features, or parts, of the earth. In Lessons 2 and 3, you will learn about some ways people use the earth to get what they need or want.

Turn the page to see pictures and descriptions of some physical features in the United States. Which of them have you seen?

Mountain

Plain

## B. Mountains, Plains, and Deserts

A mountain is land that rises high above the land around it. In the United States there are several **mountain ranges**, or mountain groups. The Appalachians are in the eastern part of the United States. The Rocky Mountains and the Sierra Nevada (see ER uh nuh VAD uh) are in the west. The Appalachians are very old mountains. Their tops are worn and rounded, and the range is not as high as the western mountain ranges. The Rockies and Sierra Nevada are newer mountains, and their tops are still pointed.

A **plain** is flat land. In the middle of our country there is a large area called the Great Plains. The Great Plains reaches north into Canada and south into Mexico.

Lake

Desert

River

A **desert** (DEZ urt) is land where little rain falls and few plants grow. Some deserts are seldom visited by people. Others, such as the Mojave (moh HAH vee), in California, have towns, mines, and recreation areas.

## C. Bodies of Water

A **river** is a long, flowing body of water. The Mississippi River and the Missouri River are the two longest rivers in the United States.

A **lake** is a body of water with land all around it. The Great Lakes are Lake Superior, Lake Michigan, Lake Huron, Lake Erie, and Lake Ontario. They are the largest group of freshwater lakes in the world.

Homes

Ocean

Island

Coast

Peninsula

**Oceans** are the largest bodies of water in the world. Ocean water is saltwater. The world has four oceans, named the Atlantic Ocean, Pacific Ocean, Indian Ocean, and Arctic Ocean.

The United States borders the Atlantic, Pacific, and Arctic oceans. The land that borders an ocean is called a **coast.**

## D. Islands and Peninsulas

An **island** is a body of land with water all around it. One of our states is made up entirely of islands. That state is Hawaii.

A **peninsula** has water almost all the way around it. Our states of Florida, Michigan, and Alaska are peninsulas.

## A PAINTING BY GEORGIA O'KEEFFE

**G**eorgia O'Keeffe painted many pictures of flowers, animal bones, and desert landscapes. She did not paint things as you might see them in a photograph. Instead, she used some details and left out others. She chose colors and shapes that would show how she felt about an object in nature. The painting below is called "The Grey Hills."

### Understanding Source Material

1. How does the painting make you feel?
2. In your opinion, why didn't the artist include a person or an animal in the painting?

© 1989 Indianapolis Museum of Art, Gift of Mr. and Mrs. James W. Fesler.

A map can show where certain physical features are located. Study the map below to find some of the physical features that were described in this lesson. Use the colors and symbols in the key for help. The photograph on the next page shows one of the physical features you can find on the map.

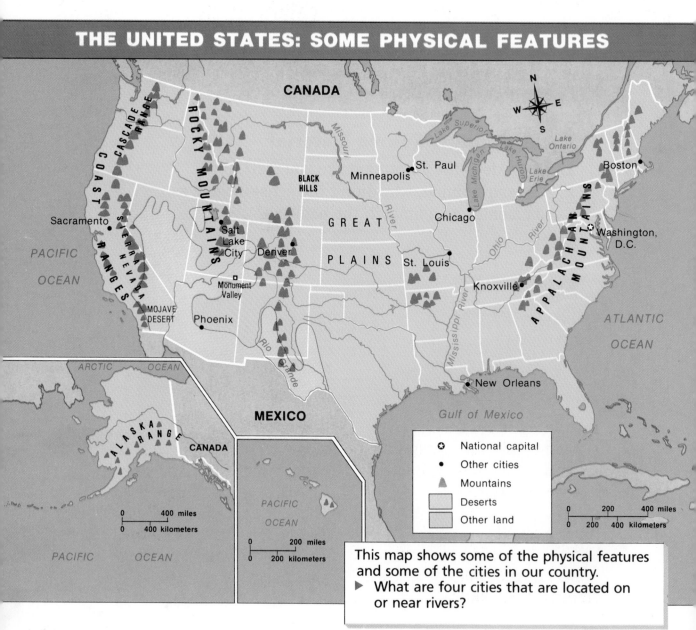

## THE UNITED STATES: SOME PHYSICAL FEATURES

CANADA

CASCADE RANGE

COAST RANGES

ROCKY MOUNTAINS

SIERRA NEVADA

BLACK HILLS

Minneapolis

St. Paul

Lake Superior

Lake Michigan

Lake Huron

Lake Ontario

Lake Erie

Boston

Sacramento

Salt Lake City

Denver

GREAT

PLAINS

Missouri River

Chicago

St. Louis

Ohio River

Knoxville

APPALACHIAN MOUNTAINS

Washington, D.C.

PACIFIC OCEAN

Monument Valley

MOJAVE DESERT

Phoenix

Rio Grande

Mississippi River

ATLANTIC OCEAN

New Orleans

MEXICO

Gulf of Mexico

ARCTIC OCEAN

ALASKA RANGE

CANADA

PACIFIC OCEAN

| ⊙ | National capital |
| • | Other cities |
| ▲ | Mountains |
| | Deserts |
| | Other land |

0     400 miles
0     400 kilometers

0    200 miles
0    200 kilometers

0    200    400 miles
0    200    400 kilometers

PACIFIC OCEAN

This map shows some of the physical features and some of the cities in our country.
▶ What are four cities that are located on or near rivers?

54

This desert scene is in Monument Valley Navajo Tribal Park, in Arizona.
▶ How would you describe the rock formations that can be seen in this photograph?

## LESSON 1 REVIEW

### THINK AND WRITE

A. In your opinion, why is studying geography important?

B. How are mountains, plains, and deserts alike?

C. How are rivers, lakes, and oceans alike?

D. Which three of these states are peninsulas: Florida, Michigan, Nebraska, Alaska?

### SKILLS CHECK

**THINKING SKILL**

Make a chart of physical features. Write the words *Land* and *Bodies of Water* as headings on your paper. Under the headings, list the physical features from this lesson and other physical features that you know.

55

## Two Important Underground Resources: Oil and Coal

### THINK ABOUT WHAT YOU KNOW

Important natural resources are under the surface of the earth. How do you think people get these natural resources?

### STUDY THE VOCABULARY

| mineral | petroleum | mining |
|---------|-----------|--------|
| fuel | coal | county |

### FOCUS YOUR READING

Why do people want to get oil and coal from underground?

## A. Important Underground Resources

What do people use that they cannot make? "Natural resources" is the answer to that question. People cannot make the air, water, and soil that are needed for life. We cannot make the resources we get from underground.

Many natural resources are found underground. Some of them, such as gold, silver, salt, iron, and diamonds, are **minerals.** Rocks and soil on the earth's surface contain minerals, too.

A **fuel** is anything that is burned to produce heat or provide power for running machines. In this lesson, you will learn about two important fuels that are found underground.

**Petroleum** (puh TROH lee um) and **coal** were formed in the earth from things that were once living. Coal is a black or brown rock. Petroleum, which is usually a liquid, comes out of the earth and is often called oil. On the map on this page, you can see where coal and petroleum are found in the United States.

## B. Some Uses of Coal and Oil

Coal has two very important uses. It is used to make steel, which is a strong metal, and to produce electricity at some power plants.

Like coal, oil can be used to make electricity. So when you turn on a light or use your TV set or computer, you may be using coal or oil.

Oil is also used to make many everyday things. Ink, plastic, phonograph records, some medicines, and some clothing are just a few of the things that

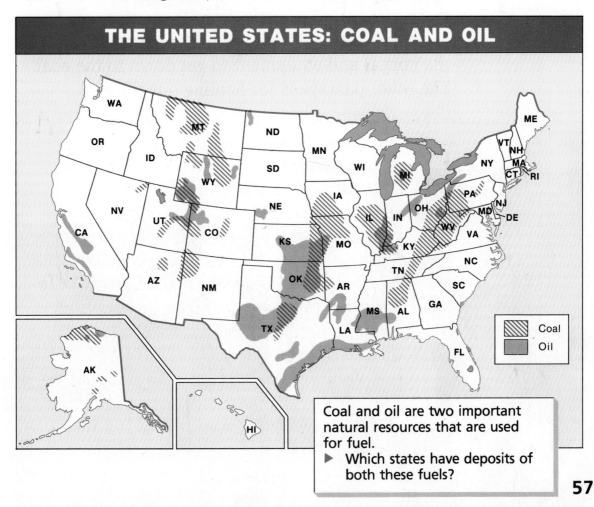

THE UNITED STATES: COAL AND OIL

Coal and oil are two important natural resources that are used for fuel.
▶ Which states have deposits of both these fuels?

contain oil. The gasoline that makes cars, buses, trucks, and planes run is made from oil. Oil is burned in some furnaces to keep homes, schools, and places of business warm.

## C. Mining Coal

**Mining** is the way many resources are taken from underground. Coal, which is usually found in mountainous places, is mined in two main ways.

Surface mining is used to get the coal that is quite close to the surface of the ground. Big machines with shovels or buckets dig or scoop the coal out. Underground mining is used to get the coal that is deep in the ground.

In underground mining, the miners usually dig two passages, or tunnels, from the surface of the ground to the coal underground. One passage is for the miners and equipment to get down to the coal. The other passage is for hauling out the coal.

After surface mining, (left), coal is moved by train (right).
▶ What should be done to land when the mining is over?

These coal miners work in an underground mine, where they use machines to help them do the work.
► How do you think it would feel to work underground?

Long ago, miners dug coal with picks and shovels. Today they use machines. In an underground mine, the miners operate machines that dig the coal and load it onto a moving belt. The belt takes the coal to the mine train, which carries it to an elevator. The elevator with the coal moves up the passage to the surface of the earth. There it is loaded onto trains, trucks, or barges.

## D. Williamson, West Virginia: A Coal-Mining Community

Coal is often found in places that are far away from large cities. Williamson, West Virginia, is a coal-mining community of about 5,000 people in the Appalachian Mountains. It is the county seat, or government center, of Mingo County. A **county** is part of a state.

West Virginia

During the 1800s, the first coal mines opened near Williamson. Today millions of tons of coal are mined in the area each year. Many people in

Williamson work for coal-mining companies. Many more people work for the railroad that carries the coal to other parts of the United States.

People in Williamson are proud of the part that coal has played in the development of their town. Williamson has the only house in the United States that is built entirely of coal. This house was built to remind people of the importance of coal in the Williamson area.

### E. Drilling for Oil

Oil is found in many places, including under deserts and under the sea. Oil is usually taken from underground by drilling a well and then pumping the oil to the surface of the earth.

From left to right, these photographs show oil derricks, an offshore oil platform, an oil pipeline, and an oil tanker.
► In the small picture, what do you think the worker is doing?

You can see an oil derrick on page 60. A derrick is a steel tower that holds the drilling equipment. The drill is a pipe with a bit, or cutting tool, on the end of it. A motor turns the drill as it goes deep into the ground. The drilling is stopped when oil is reached or the decision is made that the well is dry. A pump may be needed to bring the oil to the surface of the ground.

People drill for oil on land and in lakes and oceans. To reach oil that is under the sea, oil workers often live and work on an offshore oil platform. This large structure has a derrick and living space for the workers.

Oil must be moved to a refinery, which is a building where the oil is made pure or changed into useful products. You may wonder how oil is

# FROM: IN COAL COUNTRY

**Author: Judith Hendershot**
**Setting: A Small Coal Mining Town**

The author of *In Coal Country* grew up in a mining area. Her father and grandfathers were miners. Read the selection below. How do you think the author felt about their work?

*Papa dug coal from deep in the earth to earn a living. He dressed for work when everyone else went to bed. He wore faded denims and steel-toed shoes and he walked a mile to his job at the mine every night. He carried a silver lunch bucket and had a light on his miner's hat. It was important work. He was proud to do it.*

*In the morning I listened for the whistle that signaled the end of the hoot-owl shift. Sometimes I walked up the run to meet Papa. He was always covered with grime and dirt, but I could see the whites of his eyes smiling at me. He let me carry his silver lunch bucket.*

*We lived in a place called the Company Row. The ten white houses sat in a straight line. They were built by the people who owned the Black Diamond Mine. Two miners' families lived side by side in each two-story house. Seventy-five children lived and played there in the row. We had many friends.*

moved. Often it goes through pipelines above or below the ground. Oil can also be moved by trucks, railroad tank cars, and large ships called tankers.

## F. Tulsa, Oklahoma: An Oil Community

Natural resources, such as oil and coal, create jobs in a community. Sometimes when a resource is discovered, a community grows quickly and attracts other kinds of businesses, too. That is what happened in Tulsa, Oklahoma.

Oklahoma

During the early 1900s, oil was discovered near Tulsa. Many people moved to the area to find jobs in the oil business. By the 1930s, the oil business was so big in Tulsa that the city was often called the Oil Capital of the World. As years passed, factories making many kinds of products, such as airplanes, metal, and machinery, began to move to Tulsa. Today, Tulsa is a city of more than 360,000 people. It is still an oil business center. More than 850 oil companies have offices there.

*LESSON* **2** *REVIEW*

### THINK AND WRITE
A. What are fuels?
B. In your opinion, how might your life be different if there were no coal or oil?
C. What are two of the ways coal is mined?
D. Why, do you think, are people in Williamson proud of the history of coal in their area?
E. In what way is most oil taken from the earth?

F. How did the discovery of oil affect the growth of Tulsa, Oklahoma?

### SKILLS CHECK
**WRITING SKILL**
Think of some ways your family might help to save oil. Write a paragraph about one way. Draw a picture to go with your paragraph.

## Resources of Land and Sea: Forests and Fish

Lumberjack contest, Albany, Oregon

Timber Carnival Association

### THINK ABOUT WHAT YOU KNOW

Why do many people enjoy camping and fishing?

### STUDY THE VOCABULARY

| | | |
|---|---|---|
| lumbering | wood pulp | renewable |
| lumberjack | trawler | resource |
| | shellfish | pollute |

### FOCUS YOUR READING

How do we use and save our trees and fish?

### A. Lumbering

Cutting trees and preparing the logs for sale is called **lumbering**. Jim Walters is a **lumberjack**, or logger. He works in a forest, cutting trees and removing the branches from the tree trunks. The trunks without their branches are called logs. The logs are loaded onto trucks and taken to a sawmill, where they are cut into boards and other big pieces of wood called lumber. From the sawmill, the lumber is taken to a lumberyard, where people buy the lumber to build things.

Maybe you have been to a lumberyard, where lumber is sold. You might have seen people buying lumber to add a room to their house or to make shelves. But have you thought of all the things you use that are made from lumber? Houses, furniture, baseball bats, bowling pins, muscial instruments, and telephone poles may be made from lumber. Can you think of other things?

# THE UNITED STATES: FORESTS

Albany

Willamette National Forest

Forests

Some things that are made from wood do not look like wood at all. Many of these things are made from **wood pulp**, which is a mixture of cooked wood chips and water. Paper and cardboard are two things that are made from wood pulp.

## B. Lumbering in Oregon

Oregon is a state that is famous for its great forests and its lumbering industry. Many Oregon communities have factories that manufacture wood products. Albany, Oregon, is a city of about 29,000 people. Find it on the map on this page.

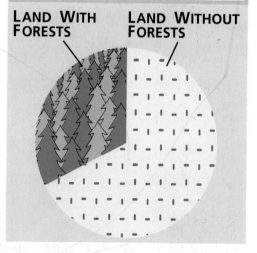

Both the map and the pie graph give information about forests.
▶ What does the map show about forests that the pie graph does not show?

LAND WITH FORESTS

LAND WITHOUT FORESTS

Albany has many businesses, but lumbering provides the most jobs. A number of people who live in Albany are lumberjacks. Others make wood products, such as paper. Still other workers sell lumber and wood products.

Every July 4, Albany has a big festival. Lumberjacks from all over the world come to find out who is the best at rolling logs, chopping wood, climbing trees, and cutting the tops from trees.

## C. Fishing

Liz Murphy fishes from a **trawler** on the Atlantic Ocean, off the coast of North Carolina. A trawler is a boat that uses a net, or trawl, to catch fish and **shellfish**. Shellfish are sea animals that have a shell. You can see a picture of one kind of trawler below.

This trawler pulls a net behind it.
▶ Would an otter trawl catch fish that live near the surface or the bottom of the sea?

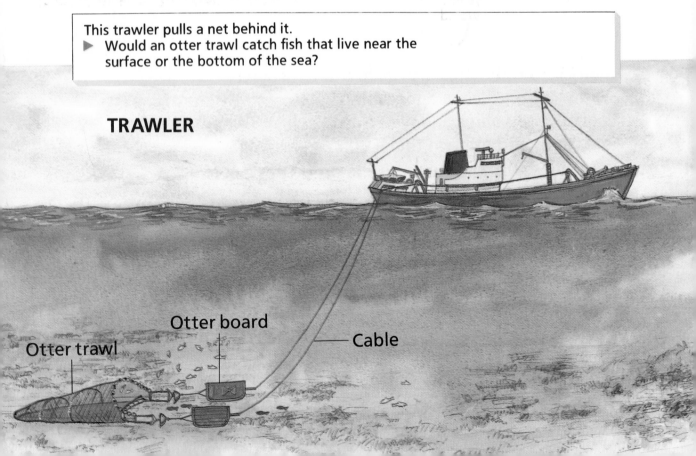

**TRAWLER**

Otter board

Cable

Otter trawl

Ice fishing (left), trawling for shrimp (upper right), and trapping lobster (lower right) are three ways to fish.
▶ Which of these would you like to do?

Fish is a healthful food, and fishing is an important business in the United States. More fish are caught in Alaska and in Louisiana than in any other states.

Many different methods are used to catch fish. Liz Murphy uses nets. Hooks and traps may also be used to catch fish. Native Americans sometimes use spears to catch fish for their families.

Fishing boats may be small or large. Huge factory ships can stay at sea for months at a time. On these ships, after the fish are caught, they are cleaned and prepared for sale. The fish may even be canned or frozen on a ship while it is far out to sea.

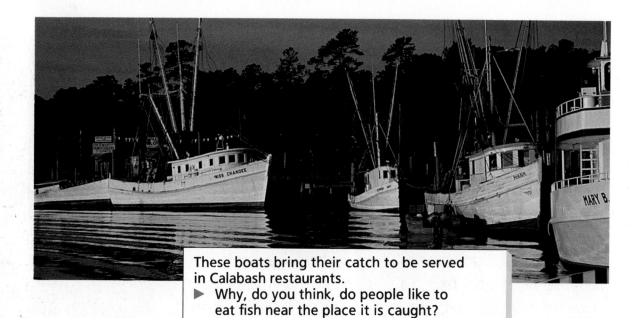

These boats bring their catch to be served in Calabash restaurants.
▶ Why, do you think, do people like to eat fish near the place it is caught?

## D. Calabash, North Carolina: A Small Fishing Community

North Carolina

Calabash, North Carolina, is a small community near the border between North Carolina and South Carolina. Find it on the map in the Atlas of your book.

Calabash is a fishing village with a difference. The community has more than 24 restaurants, and all of them serve fresh seafood. People travel long distances to eat seafood in Calabash. The town has become so well known for its seafood that restaurants in other parts of the state advertise that they have Calabash-style seafood.

## E. Saving Renewable Resources

You have learned that people cannot make natural resources. However, some natural resources, called **renewable resources**, can be replaced if they are not used too quickly or completely. Trees and fish are renewable resources.

Michelle Smith plants trees on her tree farm. She starts with young trees called seedlings. As the trees grow, smaller trees are cut to allow bigger ones to grow faster. After more than 30 years, some trees are big enough to cut for lumber.

Ted Sugarman raises fish in a lake on his fish farm. He feeds the fish and keeps the water clean. He makes sure that the fish are not taken from the lake while they are too young.

Michelle Smith and Ted Sugarman help to replace trees and fish. But all people can help to save renewable resources. We can be careful to put out campfires safely in the forests. We can clean up our trash when we go camping or boating.

If we do not cut down too many trees too fast, we can replace them. If we do not **pollute**, or dirty, the air and water, we can help to save our trees and fish. Polluted air can hurt and even kill trees and other plants. Polluted water can kill fish and shellfish. We can all work together to use our natural resources wisely.

Small trees at a tree farm

## LESSON 3 REVIEW

### THINK AND WRITE

A. What does a lumberjack do?
B. Why, do you think, does Albany have a lumberjack contest?
C. Would fishing with a hook or a net catch more fish?
D. How has Calabash used its natural resource?
E. Why, do you think, do we need laws against polluting?

### SKILLS CHECK

**MAP SKILL**

Make a list of the places in this lesson. Find these places in the Gazetteer of your book. Using the facts from this chapter and the Gazetteer, tell how these places are alike and different.

## USING THE VOCABULARY

| | |
|---|---|
| plain | petroleum |
| island | coal |
| peninsula | lumbering |
| mineral | trawler |
| fuel | renewable resources |

On a separate sheet of paper, write the word or words from above that best complete the sentences.

1. Cutting trees and preparing logs for sale is called _____.
2. A _____ is a substance, such as gold, that is often found underground.
3. Flat land is a _____.
4. A _____ is a boat that uses a net to catch fish and shellfish.
5. A body of land with water all around it is an _____.
6. A _____, such as coal and oil, can be burned to produce heat.
7. Some natural resources called _____ can be replaced if they are not used too quickly or are not completely used up.
8. *Oil* is another name for _____.
9. A _____ has water almost all the way around it.
10. A black or brown rock that is used for fuel is called _____.

## REMEMBERING WHAT YOU READ

On a separate sheet of paper, answer the questions in complete sentences.

1. Name the two longest rivers in the United States.
2. What state is made up entirely of islands?
3. Name five minerals.
4. What are two important uses of coal?
5. What two states catch the most fish?

## TYING SCIENCE TO SOCIAL STUDIES

Bring in a rock from your collection or from your community. Label the rock with its name or a special fact.

## THINKING CRITICALLY

On a separate sheet of paper, answer the following in complete sentences.

1. Compare a lake to an ocean. How are they alike and different?
2. Why is Williamson, West Virginia, an important community?
3. Why is Tulsa, Oklahoma, an important community?
4. How can you and your family help to save our forests?
5. How can you and your family help to prevent or stop pollution in your community?

## SUMMARIZING THE CHAPTER

Copy this graphic organizer on a separate sheet of paper. Under the main idea for each lesson, write three facts that support the main idea.

**CHAPTER THEME**

The earth has natural resources that people use.

*LESSON 1*
**We can study the earth and the ways people use it.**
1. _____
2. _____
3. _____

*LESSON 2*
**Oil and coal are valuable resources for our communities.**
1. _____
2. _____
3. _____

*LESSON 3*
**Resources of the land and sea must not be wasted.**
1. _____
2. _____
3. _____

# CHAPTER 4

# USING RESOURCES IN RURAL COMMUNITIES

To raise their crops and animals, farmers need to know about the land and weather. Farm children sometimes help with the care of animals.

## Farming in the United States

Draw a picture of something that is raised on a farm. What are some other plants or animals that are raised on farms?

| | | |
|---|---|---|
| **livestock** | **soil** | **temperature** |
| **crop** | **weather** | **thermometer** |
| **bar graph** | **climate** | **precipitation** |

What are some different kinds of farms?

## A. Farms Today

Tomatoes

Did you have a toy farm set when you were younger? Was it the kind that had a farmhouse, a barn, and a few cows, horses, pigs, and chickens? Perhaps there were figures of a mother, father, boy, girl, and baby, too. A tractor and a pickup truck might have completed the farm set. A farm set like this shows what many farms were like years ago, when a family could do most of the work with a few machines.

There are still small farms like this in the United States. But today many farms are very large. The company or family that owns the farm probably raises a great number of **livestock** or a huge **crop**. Livestock are farm animals. Crops are plants that can be grown and picked to eat or to sell. On a large farm today, the livestock might be all of one kind, such as pigs, or the crop might be all corn or all wheat.

On some large farms, many hens live close together in long rows (right).
A machine gathers the eggs the hens have laid (left).
▶ What do you think the farm worker is doing?

## B. Why Farms Are Important

Farms are important because they produce
most of our food and many of the other things we
need. Fruits, vegetables, and grains are some
healthful foods that come from farms. Milk comes
from cows that are raised on dairy farms. Most of
the meat we eat comes from cattle, turkeys,
chickens, and pigs that are raised on farms.

Many farm animals and crops are not used for
food. For example, cotton is a plant that is raised
on farms. Cotton is used to make cloth. Sheep are
animals that may be raised for their wool coat, as
well as for meat. The sheep's coat is cut off and
used to make cloth.

## C.  A Bar Graph of Farm Animals

You can learn something about farm animals by reading the **bar graph** below. A bar graph is one of the most useful kinds of graphs. It shows information in bars. On this graph, bars are used to answer the question *How many?*

The bottom of the graph is marked *Kinds of Animals*. Each bar stands for one kind of animal. The left side of the graph is marked *Millions of Animals*. Each line stands for a number.

Read the graph to find out how many cattle were raised in the United States in one year. First find the bar for cattle. Next put your finger at the top of this bar. Then move your finger to the number on the left. You will see that more than 100 million cattle were raised in one year.

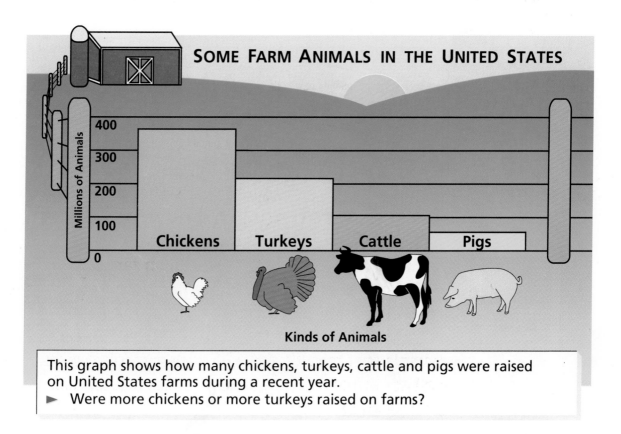

**SOME FARM ANIMALS IN THE UNITED STATES**

Millions of Animals

400
300
200
100
0

Chickens   Turkeys   Cattle   Pigs

Kinds of Animals

This graph shows how many chickens, turkeys, cattle and pigs were raised on United States farms during a recent year.

► Were more chickens or more turkeys raised on farms?

## D. Farming and Natural Resources

To raise animals and crops, farmers need natural resources. They need water and good **soil**, which is the upper layer of earth where plants grow.

**Weather** and **climate** are natural resources. Weather is the way the air is at a certain time. It may be hot or cold, wet or dry. When you say, "It's too hot today," you are talking about the weather. Climate is the way the weather is in one place over a long time. If you said, "The summers here are very hot," you would be talking about climate.

Different crops need different climates. Imagine that you are going to grow corn, which needs a warm summer and plenty of rain. But, you live in a climate that is cold and dry. Would you still grow corn?

Corn is raised on this farm. Most corn is used to feed farm animals.
▶ What do the photographs show about a corn field and corn plants?

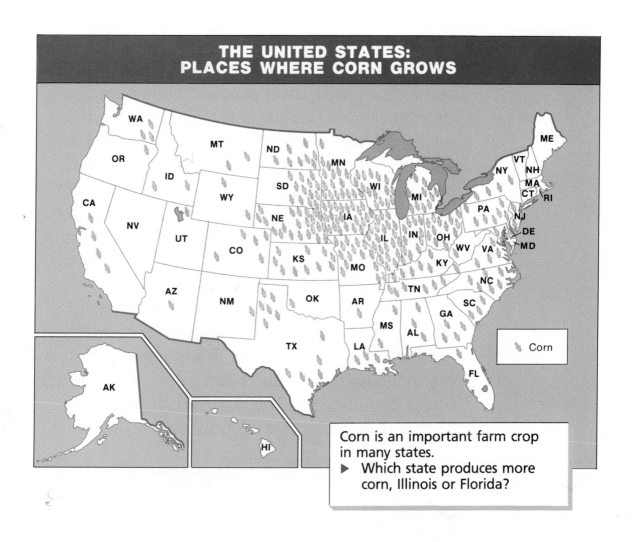

**THE UNITED STATES: PLACES WHERE CORN GROWS**

Corn

Corn is an important farm crop in many states.
▶ Which state produces more corn, Illinois or Florida?

Maps provide many kinds of information. Look at the map above. This map shows where corn is raised in the United States. The states with the most corn symbols grow the most corn. As you can see, corn is grown in many states. However, Illinois, Indiana, Iowa, Michigan, Minnesota, Missouri, Nebraska, Ohio, South Dakota, and Wisconsin raise lots of corn. They are sometimes called the Corn Belt states.

What kind of summers do you think the Corn Belt states have? Do you think these states have a wet or dry climate?

## E. Measuring Temperature and Precipitation

Farmers learn about the weather in their area the same ways as other people. They watch weather reports on television and read about the weather in the newspaper. They measure the **temperature**, or how hot or cold the air is, with a **thermometer**. They might even use a rain gauge (GAYJ) to measure **precipitation**. Precipitation includes all forms of water that fall to the earth, such as rain, snow, sleet, and hail.

Look at the diagram of an outdoor thermometer on this page. This is a Fahrenheit (FER un hyt) thermometer, named for Gabriel Fahrenheit, a scientist who lived long ago. Notice the numbers next to the black lines along the side of the thermometer. The numbers show the temperature in degrees, or units in which

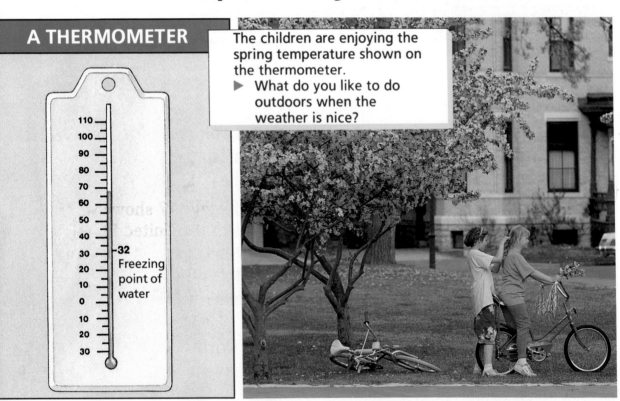

**A THERMOMETER**

110
100
90
80
70
60
50
40
30 — 32
20    Freezing
10    point of
0     water
10
20
30

The children are enjoying the spring temperature shown on the thermometer.
▶ What do you like to do outdoors when the weather is nice?

temperature is measured. The degrees on this thermometer are called degrees Fahrenheit.

The red line in the middle of the thermometer shows the liquid inside the glass tube. When the air gets colder, the liquid falls in the glass tube. When the air gets warmer, the liquid rises in the tube. The temperature on this thermometer is 68 degrees Fahrenheit.

The rain gauge at the right is a jar and a ruler. The numbers on the ruler measure the amount of water in the jar. Each number represents one inch. You can make a rain gauge like this to measure the precipitation where you live.

In the next lesson, you will learn how wheat farmers in the United States depend on climate and weather for growing their crop.

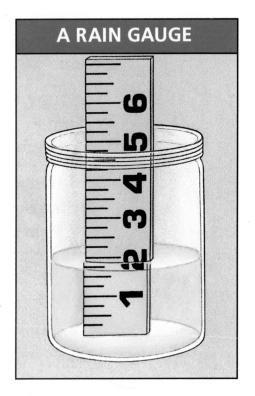

**A RAIN GAUGE**

---

## LESSON *1* REVIEW

### THINK AND WRITE

A. In your opinion, why were many farms quite small long ago?
B. Why are farms important?
C. What is one question a bar graph can answer?
D. Why are natural resources important to farmers?
E. What are some reasons people want to know what temperature it is outside?

### SKILLS CHECK

**MAP SKILL**

The map on page 77 shows where corn grows in the United States. Corn is a good food for pigs. Do you think a map showing where pigs are raised would look like a map showing where corn is grown? Tell why or why not.

## Raising Winter Wheat

**THINK ABOUT WHAT YOU KNOW**

Have you ever helped to bake something good to eat? What ingredients did you use?

**STUDY THE VOCABULARY**

| | | |
|---|---|---|
| **grain** | **drill** | **combine** |
| **line graph** | **harvest** | **grain elevator** |

**FOCUS YOUR READING**

How is winter wheat planted and harvested?

## A. Wheat, an Important Crop

Many things you like to eat are made from wheat, which is the **grain** that is used in most kinds of flour. Grains are the seeds of certain grasses, such as wheat, rye, oats, and corn. The word *grains* can also mean the plants themselves.

Hundreds of millions of people eat wheat in some form each day. They may eat breads, cakes, muffins, or other baked goods made from wheat flour. Spaghetti, macaroni, noodles, breakfast cereal, animal feed, and many other foods are made from wheat, too.

Wheat is an important crop in the United States and in many countries in the world. During most years, Kansas farmers grow more wheat than farmers in any other state in the United States. Find Kansas on the map of the United States on page 82. The abbreviation for Kansas is *KS*.

## WHEAT PLANT

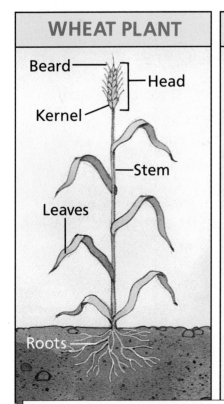

Beard
Head
Kernel
Stem
Leaves
Roots

## WHEAT PRODUCTS

Flour
Breakfast cereal
Pasta
Animal feed
Strawboard
Baked goods

Many foods are made from wheat flour. The entire kernel of the wheat plant is ground into whole wheat flour. Only part of the kernel is used in white flour.
▶ In which part of the wheat plant are the kernels?

## LEADING WHEAT-GROWING STATES

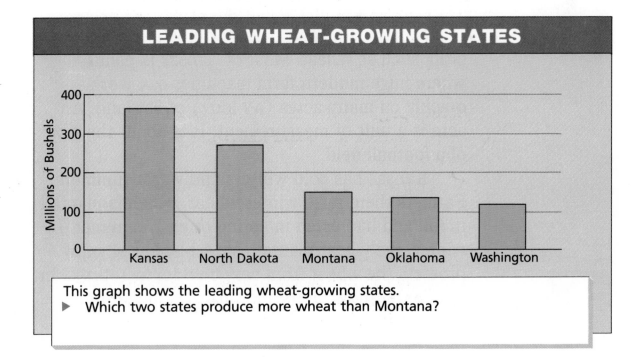

Millions of Bushels

400
300
200
100
0

Kansas   North Dakota   Montana   Oklahoma   Washington

This graph shows the leading wheat-growing states.
▶ Which two states produce more wheat than Montana?

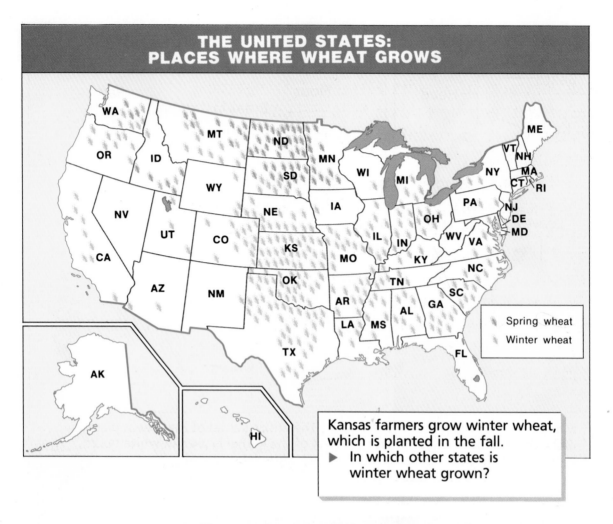

## THE UNITED STATES: PLACES WHERE WHEAT GROWS

Spring wheat
Winter wheat

Kansas farmers grow winter wheat, which is planted in the fall.
▶ In which other states is winter wheat grown?

Kansas is a good place for growing a large crop, such as wheat. Most of Kansas is plains, where huge modern farm machines can work quickly on many acres (AY kurz) of flat land. An acre is a unit of measurement. It is about the size of a football field.

Kansas has cold winters and warm summers. Farmers there raise winter wheat, which is planted in fall and harvested in spring or early summer. In winter, the wheat plants rest. A blanket of snow protects the wheat from very cold temperatures. In spring the snow melts and provides moisture for the growing wheat plants.

# B. Temperature and Precipitation on Graphs

The **line graph** on this page shows temperatures in Wichita, Kansas. A line graph helps you see change over time. When do the temperatures in Wichita begin to get lower? During which month is the lowest temperature?

The bar graph shows the amount of water in all forms of precipitation in Wichita, Kansas, during a year. This graph compares information. In winter months there is more snow than you would think from what you see on the graph. That is because 6 inches of heavy wet snow, the kind that makes good snowmen, has only 1 inch of water in it. Thirty inches of dry squeaky snow also has only 1 inch of water.

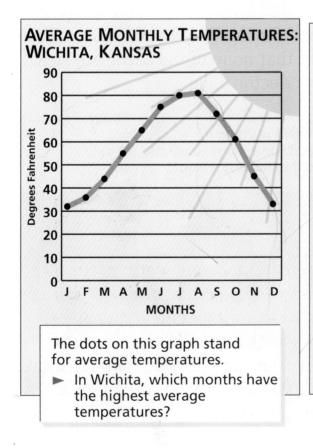

**AVERAGE MONTHLY TEMPERATURES: WICHITA, KANSAS**

The dots on this graph stand for average temperatures.

▶ In Wichita, which months have the highest average temperatures?

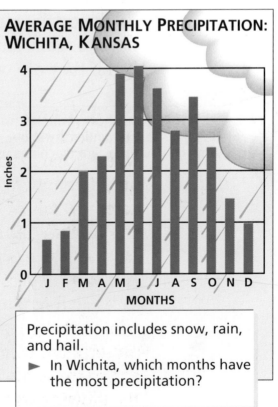

**AVERAGE MONTHLY PRECIPITATION: WICHITA, KANSAS**

Precipitation includes snow, rain, and hail.

▶ In Wichita, which months have the most precipitation?

## C. Fall and Winter on a Wheat Farm

In late summer or early fall, Kansas farmers get ready to plant winter wheat. First they prepare the fields. They might use a tractor pulling a plow or disk harrow to turn the soil or break it into pieces.

Then the wheat seeds are planted with a machine called a **drill**. The drill makes a long ditch and drops the seeds into it.

When the wheat plants come up out of the ground, they look like grass. By the time the first frost comes, they are about 6 inches tall. During the fall, cattle graze on the wheat fields. The cattle eat some of the wheat but not all of it. The winter wheat keeps growing.

One Kansas farm child described fall and winter on the farm this way.

"I go with my dad a lot after school to check on the cattle, mend fences, and do the chores. We have to make sure that none of the cattle are sick, and if they are, we doctor them.

These photographs show (from left to right) planting the wheat, the wheat plants resting under the snow, and harvesting the wheat.
▶ Why, do you think, are machines used to harvest wheat?

When it gets colder and the snow comes, we take the cattle away from the wheat. The wheat is resting now and would be hurt if the cattle continued grazing."

## D. Spring and Summer on a Wheat Farm

In spring the snow melts and gives the wheat lots of moisture. The wheat grows quickly to about 2 or 3 feet high. The plants form heads with grain in them.

This is the way another farm child described the wheat **harvest**, when the grain is picked by a machine called a **combine** (KAHM byn).

"Wheat harvest is here! Hot, dry weather came and the wheat has turned golden brown. It's ripe and ready to harvest! Harvest time is a busy time for all wheat farmers. Dad's in a real hurry in case of bad weather, which could destroy the crop. Our whole family helps with the harvest and with feeding the hired help.

At the grain elevator

We use a combine to cut the grain. The combine cuts the grain-filled heads off the stalks. The grain is separated from the stalks in the combine. The grain goes into the grain tank in the combine, and the straw or stalks go out the back of the combine onto the ground.

When the grain tank is full, we dump the wheat into our trucks. Then we take the wheat to the **grain elevator** in town. The elevators are those tall buildings that store grain. The elevator will then sell the wheat to the mill, where it is made into flour. We can also store our wheat on our farm in grain bins."

In the next lesson you will learn more about living on a farm where wheat is raised. You will also learn about a farming town.

---

LESSON *2* REVIEW

## THINK AND WRITE

A. In your opinion, why is wheat an important crop?
B. Using information on the graphs, how would you describe the climate in Kansas?
C. What happens on a wheat farm during fall and winter?
D. In your opinion, what might make the harvest an exciting time on a farm?

## SKILLS CHECK

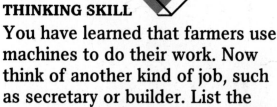

**THINKING SKILL**
You have learned that farmers use machines to do their work. Now think of another kind of job, such as secretary or builder. List the machines needed in that job. How do these machines help to get the work done?

## Living in a Rural Area

What is it like to grow up where you live? What kinds of things do you enjoy doing at home, at school, and in your community?

**STUDY THE VOCABULARY**

**rural area     conservation     service**

**FOCUS YOUR READING**

What is it like to grow up on a farm?

## A. What Is a Rural Area?

Jeff, Kristy, and Lexy live on Kansas farms. They live in a **rural area**, where communities are far apart and surrounded by farms and open land. There are few tall buildings, and neighbors may be miles away.

This rural area is like many others in the middle of our country.
► How would you compare this place with the place where you live?

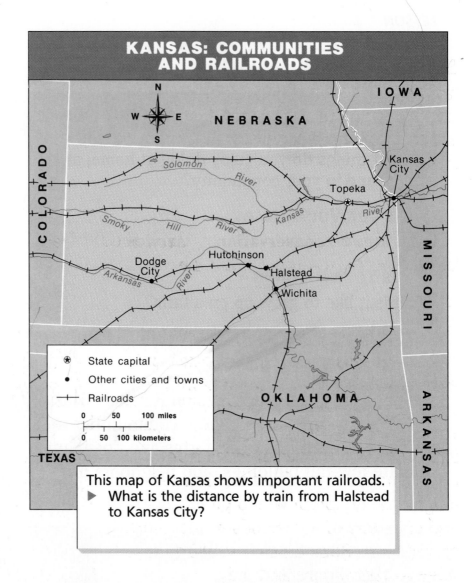

## KANSAS: COMMUNITIES AND RAILROADS

This map of Kansas shows important railroads.
▶ What is the distance by train from Halstead to Kansas City?

Look at the map of Kansas on this page. You can see the states that border Kansas. They are Nebraska, Missouri, Oklahoma, and Colorado. You can see some communities in Kansas. Wichita is the largest city in the state. The second largest city is Kansas City.

The Kansas map shows some railroad routes, which are important to rural areas. Farm crops may go by train from a grain elevator in a small town to factories far away. Find the route that grain travels from Halstead to Kansas City.

In this lesson you will read parts of letters that were written by Jeff, Kristy, and Lexy. They wanted you to know what it is like to live in a rural area today. At the end of the lesson, you will learn about a farming community that is the center of one rural area.

## B. Kristy's Summer

As you read Kristy's letter, think about what kinds of things you do during the summer.

Dear Students,

I had a busy summer. I took swimming lessons and gymnastics and rode my bike at home. My dad built Josh (my four-year-old brother) and me a treehouse. It's really neat. We played in it a lot. We live seven miles from town, and since we don't have next-door neighbors, my mom would go to town and get some of my friends to play here on the farm. Sometimes I would go to town to their house and play.

There's always a lot to do on a farm. I have the same jobs as my friends in town. I have to make my bed, clean my room, help in the kitchen, and feed the dog and cats. We have some new baby kittens that are really cute and fun to play with.

Love,
Kristy

Fun and work on a farm

## C. Lexy and Nicholas's 4-H Project

Have you ever helped to take care of an animal? Read Lexy's letter about caring for two calves, or young cattle.

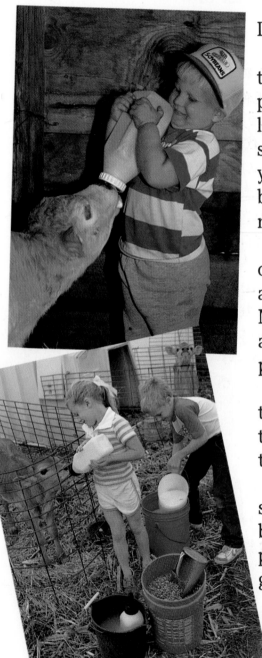

Dear Students,

My brother Nicholas and I belong to a 4-H Club. We have different projects each year. Each project has a leader or teacher so we can learn about something we are interested in. This year Nicholas and I have bucket or bottle calves for 4-H projects. Their names are Stevie and Milt.

Bucket or bottle calves are usually orphans. They have to be fed milk from a bucket or bottle. When Stevie and Milt were old enough, we took the milk away and gave them alfalfa and starter pellets.

I was glad when the calves got off the bottle. It was lots of work to feed them three times a day and check on them at least two more times a day.

At the county fair in August, we showed Stevie and Milt. Then we brought them home and put them in the pasture, where they will stay until they grow bigger. Then we will sell them.

Your friend,
Lexy

Feeding time

## D. Jeff's Ride with Dad

Like children everywhere, farm children learn from their parents. One Saturday Jeff learned about **conservation**, or saving natural resources, from his dad.

Dear Students,

We try to practice good soil conservation on our land. I got to ride with Dad last Saturday to look at our terraces. Terraces are rows of earth ridges, or raised strips of soil, that hold the land in place. Terraces also keep the water on the land so it can soak into the soil for the crops to use.

Dad only found one terrace that needed some work. He said he would take a tractor and dozer blade to the field and push up more dirt to repair the break in the terrace. He wants to do that before the ground freezes this winter. Then the terrace will be in good repair in case we get heavy rains in the spring or a quick thaw of heavy snow cover. When the ground is frozen and the snow melts fast, the soil runs off if there are no terraces to stop it.

Your friend,
Jeff

Saving the soil

Hertzler Clinic and Halstead Hospital was started in 1902 by a doctor who visited his patients in a horse and buggy.
▶ Why would a small farming community have such a large hospital?

## E. A Farming Community

Children who live on farms usually go to school in town. They may ride for many miles on a school bus to get there. Farm families go to town to buy food and seed, borrow books from the library, or attend a movie or worship service.

Halstead, Kansas, is a farming community of about 2,000 people, located on the Little Arkansas River. Find Halstead on the map on page 88.

Although Halstead is a small town, it is an important center for a rural area. There are stores and other businesses that make or sell things people need. The community provides many **services** for farmers and other people, too. A service is work that helps people, such as work a firefighter does to prevent and put out fires.

The grain elevators in Halstead provide an important service to farmers. The grain is weighed and stored there. Afterward, it may be sold and transported by train to other parts of Kansas and the United States. On the map on page 88, you saw the railroad route through Halstead.

Other important services in Halstead are health care, education, and recreation. For health care, there is the Hertzler Clinic and Halstead Hospital. It is a well-known medical center, where people with serious health problems can get help. Health education is provided at the Kansas Learning Center in Halstead, where adults and children can learn how to keep well. Children of the area are taught in the Halstead schools, which have about 600 students. For recreation, Halstead has parks, ballfields, a swimming pool, a golf course, and a teen center. In spring there is an art fair, and in August an Old Settler's Celebration.

Kansas Learning Center

## LESSON 3 REVIEW

### THINK AND WRITE

A. How would you describe a rural area?
B. How might some farm children spend the summer?
C. What, do you think, did Lexy and Nicholas learn from their 4-H project?
D. How do terraces keep soil from running off when it rains?
E. Which services found in Halstead are also available in your community?

### SKILLS CHECK

**WRITING SKILL**

Imagine that you live on a farm and that you keep a day-by-day journal. Today you went into town. What were some things you enjoyed doing? Were you happy to get back home? Why or why not? Answer these questions in your journal entry.

## PIONEER CHILDREN

In this chapter you have learned about farm families and children who live in rural Kansas today. They, like the pioneer families before them, believe in working hard for the things they need and want.

Pioneers first came to Kansas in the 1800s. They brought with them their courage and their dream for a better life. But a better life did not come easily. Each member of a pioneer family had to work hard. Children worked with their parents. The men and older boys built the sod house. Sod is a layer of earth with grass plants and their roots. A sod house is pictured on page 95.

Boys also helped their father fish, hunt, and trap animals. It was a boy's job to tend the farm animals and cut wood for the fire. Older girls and women did the housework. This included making clothing, cooking, and caring for the babies. Girls were also responsible for the family's vegetable

garden. Even the small children helped in the garden. They could pick the vegetables and pull out the weeds.

With all their chores, few children had time for school. Some were taught at home by a mother or an older girl. As more people moved in the area, they began to build one-room schoolhouses. The teacher might be a girl of 14 or 15. The picture on page 94 shows a young teacher and her students.

## Thinking for Yourself

1. In what ways did the pioneer children help their families?
2. How is your school different from the schools the pioneer children attended?
3. What are some inventions that make life easier today?

## USING THE VOCABULARY

| | |
|---|---|
| weather | combine |
| climate | grain elevator |
| precipitation | rural area |
| grain | conservation |
| harvest | service |

On a separate sheet of paper, write the word or words from above that best complete the sentences.

1. _____ is the way the air is at a certain time.
2. The seeds of certain grasses, such as wheat, rye, oats, and corn, are called _____.
3. A _____ is a place where communities are far apart and are surrounded by farms and open land.
4. The way the weather usually is in one place over a long time is called _____.
5. _____ is saving natural resources.
6. A _____ is some kind of work that helps people, such as the work a firefighter does to prevent and put out fires.
7. _____ includes all the forms of water that fall to the earth: rain, snow, sleet, and hail.
8. The _____ is the time when the grain is picked.
9. A _____ is a place where grain is stored.
10. A _____ is used to cut grain.

## REMEMBERING WHAT YOU READ

On a separate sheet of paper, answer the questions in complete sentences.

1. Why are farms important?
2. Why do we use a bar graph?
3. Name five things made from wheat.
4. Why is a line graph important?
5. Where do children who live on a farm usually go to school?

## TYING ART TO SOCIAL STUDIES

Look in a magazine for pictures of things that are made from wheat. Cut out several pictures and paste them on a piece of colored paper to make a collage.

## THINKING CRITICALLY

On a separate sheet of paper, answer the following in complete sentences.

1. Why, do you think, is it important for farmers to learn about the weather in their area?
2. Why is the state of Kansas one of the top states in wheat production?
3. List the four steps needed to grow winter wheat.
4. What could happen if there was a mild snowy season on a wheat farm?
5. What are two ways conservation is important in your community?

## SUMMARIZING THE CHAPTER

Copy this graphic organizer on a separate sheet of paper. Under the main idea for each lesson, write three facts that support the main idea.

LESSON 1

**There are different kinds of farms in our country.**

1. _____
2. _____
3. _____

LESSON 2

**Wheat is raised on some farms in the United States.**

1. _____
2. _____
3. _____

CHAPTER THEME — Farming is important in the United States.

LESSON 3

**Rural areas are good places to live.**

1. _____
2. _____
3. _____

CHAPTER **5**

# USING RESOURCES IN URBAN AREAS

People make things at work and at home. All these things are made from the resources of the earth.

# Manufacturing in the United States

Do you enjoy making things? What kinds of things do you like to make?

**STUDY THE VOCABULARY**

| | | |
|---|---|---|
| **manufacture** | **goods** | **population** |
| **raw material** | **urban area** | **flowchart** |

**FOCUS YOUR READING**

Why are natural resources needed to manufacture goods?

## A. What Is Manufacturing?

When something is **manufactured**, it is made by people using their hands or using machines. Your bed, books, clothes, bike, and the family television set were all manufactured.

Long ago most things were manufactured at home by hand. They were made by the family to use. Today, most things are made in factories by machine. They are made to be sold.

Factories use natural resources, usually called **raw materials**, to make things. As you have learned, cloth might be made from raw materials such as cotton or wool. Paper is made from wood. Even plastics are made of raw materials such as coal, oil, salt, and water. Natural resources, such as coal, oil, or water, are also used to make the electricity that runs machines and provides light in factories.

## B. Goods Made in the U.S.A.

Things that are made and offered for sale are often called **goods,** or products. Many kinds of goods, such as transportation products, food products, and machines, are made in the United States. Cars, computers, tractors, frozen dinners, clothing, furniture, toys, crayons, paper, and thousands of other things are made here.

Read the labels on the products you use. See if the things you buy were made in this country. Some labels say *Made in the U.S.A.* or give the name of the city where the product was made. Other labels provide important information about the product, such as how to wash a sweater. Still others tell how to use the product safely.

Labels

MACHINE WASH WARM
TUMBLE DRY
WASH SEPARATELY
MADE IN U.S.A.

DRY CLEAN ONLY

"Faribault Woolen Mill Company, Faribault, MN."

These photographs show cloth being made on a hand loom at home (left) and on power looms in a factory (right).
▶ Why, do you think, do some people like to make cloth on a hand loom?

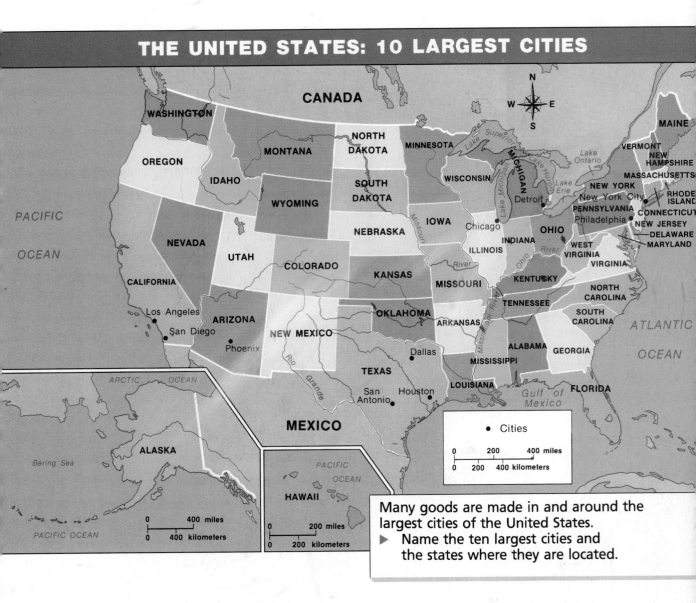

# THE UNITED STATES: 10 LARGEST CITIES

Many goods are made in and around the largest cities of the United States.
▶ Name the ten largest cities and the states where they are located.

## C. Making Things in Urban Areas

The United States has many manufacturing centers. Most of them are in **urban areas**, sometimes called metropolitan areas. An urban area includes a city and its suburbs. The largest manufacturing centers are in the urban areas of Los Angeles–Long Beach, Chicago, New York, Philadelphia, and Detroit. You can find these cities on the map above.

## Making a Birthday Card

1. Planning the card

2. Finding the materials

When you have a project to do, following the steps on this flowchart can help you.
▶ In step 4, what will the children look for on their card?

Urban areas have a large enough **population** to do the work in big factories. Population is the number of people in a certain place. Urban areas are usually transportation centers, too. Good transportation is needed to carry raw materials and manufactured goods to and from factories.

Today some companies are building factories in rural areas, where there is more space. These areas often grow quickly and become more urban.

3. Putting the card together

4. Inspecting the card

5. Packaging the card

## D. Using a Flowchart to Make Things

Manufacturers follow many of the same basic steps to make goods. You follow these steps, too, whenever you make something, such as a cake, a model, or a project for school.

A **flowchart** can show how something is done or how it works. The flowchart above shows the steps in making a birthday card. The steps are in order. The numbers and the arrows help you know what happens next.

Sometimes the steps in manufacturing are a little different from those on the flowchart for making a birthday card. For example, when automobiles are manufactured, all the steps on the flowchart on pages 102 and 103 are followed except one. Which step do you think car-makers would leave out? You will be able to answer this question when you learn, in the next lesson, how cars are made.

This auto worker works on an assembly line in a factory today.
▶ What might make a person feel good about this kind of work?

LESSON 1 REVIEW

## THINK AND WRITE

A. Why, do you think, are more natural resources used in manufacturing today than when things were made by hand?

B. When you buy something, how can you tell where it was made?

C. Why are many big factories located in urban areas?

D. How might a flowchart help you to make something?

## SKILLS CHECK

**THINKING SKILL**

Study the flowchart on pages 102 and 103. It shows five steps in manufacturing. Make a flowchart that shows how to make or do something. Write five steps. Draw a picture for each step.

# Manufacturing Automobiles

**THINK ABOUT WHAT YOU KNOW**

What is your favorite kind of car? How do you think that car will change in the future?

**STUDY THE VOCABULARY**

| | | |
|---|---|---|
| **assembly line** | **designer** | **test driver** |
| **consumer** | **prototype** | **robot** |

**FOCUS YOUR READING**

What are the main steps in manufacturing cars?

## A. Early Automobile Manufacturing

Can you imagine your community without cars, trucks, or buses? How would people get from place to place?

Until about 100 years ago, there were no cars in everyday use. To travel long distances, most people rode in carriages pulled by horses. Then during the late 1800s, a few cars were made in different parts of the world. The first cars were made one at a time and by hand. Making cars was very slow and expensive, and not many people could afford to buy them.

Faster ways of building cars began in Detroit, Michigan, in 1901. Find Detroit on the map on page 113. In Ransom Olds's factory, car parts were wheeled from one worker to another to be put together. This was the first automobile **assembly line**.

In 1908, Henry Ford's factory began building a car called the Model T. The Model T's

A Model T

In 1896, Henry Ford built his first automobile, shown here.
▶ In your opinion, how does the horse add interest to the picture?

were built on a moving assembly line. A line of workers added a part to the car body as it passed by on a moving belt. This is the way cars are put together today.

## B. Planning New Cars Today

Although cars are still built on moving assembly lines, many other ways of doing things have changed. For example, Henry Ford decided what kind of car he thought people needed, and then he built it. Today many workers take as long as four years to plan a new car.

To help in the planning of new cars, a car company today asks **consumers** what kinds of cars they like and might want to buy. A consumer is a person who buys goods and services.

**Designers** help to plan the new cars. They use computers to show what the new cars might be like. They draw pictures and build models of clay, paper, plastic, and wood to show how the cars might look and work.

Finally several metal **prototypes** (PROHT oh typs) are built by hand. Prototype cars are full-size models that can be driven. The prototypes must pass many tests before the company manufactures new cars for consumers to buy.

First the prototype cars are tested in the car factory. Testers heat the cars in a huge oven and freeze them in a huge freezer. They blast the cars with terrible winds and soak them with pouring rains. The prototype cars, without drivers, are put on a track and crashed into steel poles.

These workers are making a full-size clay model of a car.
▶ What could this kind of model show that a drawing of the car might not show?

It's easier to check the inside of a car on a model like this.
▶ What do you think car designers would be concerned about when they design the inside of a new car?

Next, **test drivers** take the prototype cars out onto sand and gravel roads. The drivers speed the cars through water, race them up and down hills, and turn them around sharp curves. They drive the prototype cars 24 hours a day, 7 days a week, in the coldest and the hottest places in the United States.

When all the tests are finished and the test drivers have written their reports, the prototype cars are examined carefully. Have the tests shown that the cars are strong and safe in all kinds of driving conditions? This is the main question that must be answered.

## C. Gathering Raw Materials and Parts

If the prototype cars have passed all their tests, the car company gets ready to make many cars like them. Then all the raw materials and parts that are needed to build the new cars must be gathered or made. Steel, made from iron, is needed for the car bodies. Glass, made from sand, must be obtained for the windows. Plastic, made from oil or coal, will be used for the dashboards. Rubber for the tires, and cotton, wool, or leather for the seat covers will be needed, too.

Cars have more than 18,000 parts today, many more than Henry Ford's Model T. Some of these parts will be made in smaller factories far away from the huge factory where cars will be put together. New machines will be built to work on the cars, and workers will be trained to run these machines.

| AUTOMOBILE MANUFACTURING: WHICH STATES MAKE THE MOST CARS? | | |
|---|---|---|
| **States** | Michigan | 🚗🚗🚗🚗🚗🚗🚗🚗🚗🚗🚗🚗🚗🚗🚗🚗🚗🚗🚗 |
| | Missouri | 🚗🚗🚗🚗🚗🚗🚗🚗🚗🚗 |
| | Ohio | 🚗🚗🚗🚗🚗🚗🚗🚗🚗🚗 |
| | Georgia | 🚗🚗🚗🚗🚗🚗 |
| | Illinois | 🚗🚗🚗🚗🚗 |
| | Delaware | 🚗🚗🚗🚗🚗 |
| | New Jersey | 🚗🚗 |
| 🚗 Stands for 100,000 cars | | |

Cars and car parts are manufactured in many states. This graph shows the states where most cars are made.
▶ Which are the top two states in car manufacturing?

# Manufacturing Cars

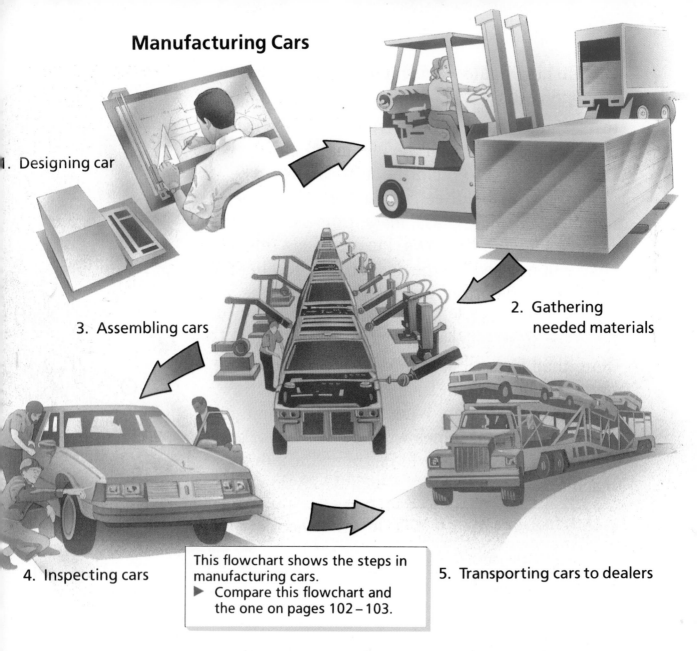

1. Designing car

2. Gathering needed materials

3. Assembling cars

4. Inspecting cars

5. Transporting cars to dealers

This flowchart shows the steps in manufacturing cars.
▶ Compare this flowchart and the one on pages 102–103.

## D. Assembling, Inspecting, and Transporting

Imagine that all the planning has been done now. Raw materials and parts have been gathered. New machines have been built.

The workers take their places along several assembly lines. They work in a factory that is five or six stories high. The factory has a door so big that trucks or trains can come inside to deliver raw materials and parts as they are needed.

The car bodies move along the big belts, through the factory and past workers and **robots**. A robot is a machine that does work that a person usually does. Some of these human workers and robots paint the car bodies. Other human workers are inspectors. They check to see that work has been done correctly.

A human worker or robot puts the seats, radio, clock, speedometer, and other parts into the body. Then the windows are attached.

The car body is given a 4-minute shower to check for water leaks. The inside stays dry, so the auto body continues to the next stop on the line.

The gas hoses, tail pipe, bumpers and other parts are attached. Then the engine is put in. The last parts to be added are the wheels and tires.

Finally the new cars are inspected and driven out of the factory onto a huge parking lot. From the lot the cars are taken by carrier or train to a car dealer, where they are sold to consumers.

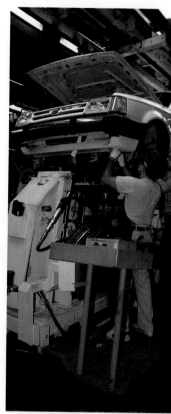

Auto workers

## LESSON 2 REVIEW

### THINK AND WRITE

A. How were Olds's and Ford's assembly lines different?

B. In your opinion, why didn't Henry Ford have to do as much planning as car companies do today?

C. What are some raw materials used in making cars?

D. Why, do you think, are robots used for some work in an automobile factory?

### SKILLS CHECK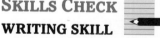
### WRITING SKILL

Write an advertisement for a worker in automobile manufacturing. Choose one of the jobs from this lesson, such as designer or test driver. In your ad, tell what kind of person is needed for the job.

## Living in an Urban Area

### THINK ABOUT WHAT YOU KNOW

Think of the adults you know. Do most of them live and work in the same community?

### STUDY THE VOCABULARY

**chamber of**
    **commerce**     **commuter**     **mural**
**freighter**     **custom**     **inventor**

### FOCUS YOUR READING

What are some advantages of living in or near a large city?

## A. Learning About Detroit

Meet Mr. and Mrs. Elliott and their two children, Erin and Mike. The Elliotts have lived in a rural area for many years. They like living in their small town, where they know almost everyone.

Imagine the children's surprise one summer evening as the Elliotts sat down to dinner. "Mother and I have an announcement to make," said Mr. Elliott. "Our company is sending us to Detroit, Michigan, to work. We are all going to move there."

The Elliott children did not know much about Detroit. They did not know what it would be like to live in an urban area. But their parents had maps and folders about the Detroit area. They helped Erin and Mike write to the Detroit Chamber of Commerce for more materials, too. A **chamber of commerce** is a group of business people who help their community.

Moving to Detroit

## B. Size and Location

More than 1 million people live in Detroit, which is in southeastern Michigan. Detroit is the seventh largest city in the United States. The Detroit River separates Detroit from Windsor, a city in Canada. The two cities are opposite each other. People use the Windsor Tunnel or the Ambassador Bridge to travel between these two cities. Find Detroit, Windsor, and the Detroit River on the map below.

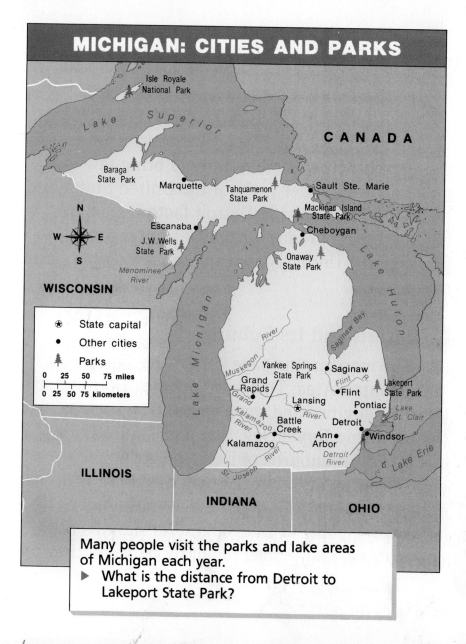

**MICHIGAN: CITIES AND PARKS**

Isle Royale National Park

Lake Superior

CANADA

Baraga State Park

Marquette

Tahquamenon State Park

Sault Ste. Marie

Mackinac Island State Park

Escanaba

Cheboygan

J.W. Wells State Park

Onaway State Park

Menominee River

Lake Huron

WISCONSIN

Lake Michigan

Saginaw Bay

Muskegon River

Yankee Springs State Park

Grand Rapids

Grand River

Kalamazoo River

Lansing River

Battle Creek

Kalamazoo

Saginaw

Flint R.

Flint

Lakeport State Park

Pontiac

Lake St. Clair

Detroit

Ann Arbor

Windsor

Detroit River

Lake Erie

St. Joseph River

ILLINOIS

INDIANA

OHIO

State capital
Other cities
Parks

0  25  50  75 miles
0  25  50  75 kilometers

Many people visit the parks and lake areas of Michigan each year.
▶ What is the distance from Detroit to Lakeport State Park?

The Detroit River is a busy place. Visitors to Belle Isle Park often see freighters such as this one passing by.
► Why, do you think, are these freighters important to Detroit?

Large ships called **freighters** carry goods on the Detroit River. Some freighters bring raw materials from other parts of the United States and the world to be used in Detroit factories. Some freighters take products from Detroit to other places in the United States and to many other parts of the world.

## C. Detroit and Its Suburbs

The map on this page shows the Detroit Metropolitan Area. This area includes Detroit and the smaller cities and towns around it, such as Dearborn and Royal Oak. The smaller cities and towns are the suburbs of Detroit. They have their own governments, schools, police and fire departments, parks, libraries, and museums.

Many people in Detroit and its suburbs are **commuters**. They travel regularly between the city and the suburbs. A great number of people who live in the suburbs work in Detroit. They may also go to Detroit to shop, to have fun, and to learn. On the other hand, some people who live in the city work in the suburbs. They might travel to the suburbs for many other reasons, such as shopping in a mall, attending a football or basketball game, or picnicking in a park. This travel between city and suburbs happens in urban areas everywhere.

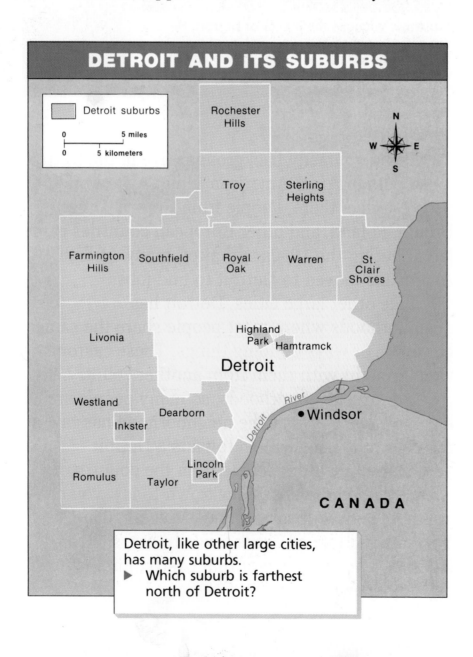

## DETROIT AND ITS SUBURBS

Detroit suburbs

0       5 miles
0       5 kilometers

Rochester Hills

Troy

Sterling Heights

Farmington Hills    Southfield    Royal Oak    Warren    St. Clair Shores

Livonia    Highland Park   Hamtramck

Detroit

Westland    Dearborn    Detroit River   ●Windsor

Inkster

Romulus    Taylor    Lincoln Park

CANADA

Detroit, like other large cities, has many suburbs.
▶ Which suburb is farthest north of Detroit?

Coleman Young is the mayor of Detroit. Here he gives a speech at a workers' meeting.
▶ What do you think the mayor would talk about at a meeting like this?

### D. People in Detroit

People of many backgrounds live in the Detroit Metropolitan Area. American Indians were the first people to live there. People from France, Great Britain, Poland, and other European countries came later. During the 1940s and after, many African Americans moved to Detroit to find jobs.

Like other large cities, Detroit has neighborhoods where most people share the same **customs**, or ways of doing things. These customs were brought with them from another country.

In some neighborhoods, so many people are from one country that the neighborhood has taken the country's name. Greektown is a Detroit neighborhood where people from the country of Greece came to live. In Greektown today, you can still hear people speaking the Greek language. You can find lots of Greek foods to eat, such as baklava, a desert made of thin pastry, nuts, butter, cinnamon, and honey.

## E. Interesting Places in Detroit

Besides its neighborhoods, Detroit has many interesting places. Belle Isle (bel EYE ul) Park is on an island in the Detroit River. The park has a zoo, an aquarium, and a museum.

Detroit has huge buildings where large groups of people come to special events. People watch sports at the Joe Louis Sports Arena and at Tiger Stadium. The arena is named for Joe Louis, an African American boxer who was heavyweight champion of the world. Tiger Stadium is the home of Detroit's baseball team, the Detroit Tigers. At Cobo Hall and the Fox Theater, there are special shows.

Detroit is a center for the arts. For example, there are many museums. The great **murals** of Diego Rivera (de AY goh ree VE rah), a Mexican painter, are at the Detroit Institute of Arts. Murals are large paintings. Rivera's murals show workers in Detroit's automobile factories. The Detroit

Belle Isle Park has many things to see and do during all four seasons of the year.
▶ What activities are shown in the photographs below?

Historical Museum features a walk through an earlier time in an exhibit called "Streets of Old Detroit." Arts and crafts by African Americans and other groups can be seen at Your Heritage House.

Detroit is a center for shopping and eating out, too. The Renaissance (REN uh sahns) Center is a group of skyscrapers with offices, shops, theaters, restaurants, and the world's tallest hotel. At the Eastern Market, farmers bring their vegetables, fruits, and fresh flowers to sell.

In cities large numbers of people get around better if they can travel above or below the busy streets. In Detroit, the People Mover is an elevated railroad that moves people high above the traffic.

A 73-story hotel is the tallest building in Renaissance Center, pictured here.
▶ What do huge buildings like this tell about a city?

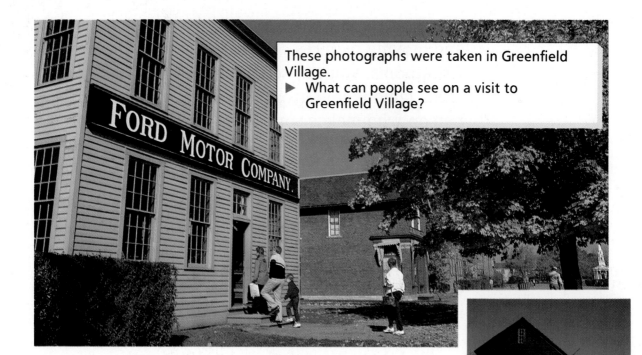

These photographs were taken in Greenfield Village.
▶ What can people see on a visit to Greenfield Village?

## F. An Interesting Place in the Suburbs

Suburbs have interesting places, too, such as sports arenas. Amusement parks and shopping malls are often located in suburban areas, where more land is available than in a city.

Greenfield Village and Henry Ford Museum is an interesting place to visit in Dearborn, a Detroit suburb. Find Dearborn on the map on page 115.

Greenfield Village and Henry Ford Museum was started by Henry Ford and his wife in 1929. You will remember that Henry Ford was the man who used the moving assembly line to make Model T's. The Fords wanted everyone in America to see how people lived long ago.

In Greenfield Village, you can see Henry Ford's first workshop. You can also see the workrooms of the Wright brothers and Thomas Edison. Orville and Wilbur Wright made the first flight in an airplane. Mr. Edison invented many things, including the electric light, the phonograph, and moving pictures. When you go into these workrooms, you can see the tools and machines these famous **inventors** used. An inventor is a person who makes something that has never been made before. Sometimes there are drawings that show their ideas.

The Henry Ford Museum has collections of old cars, trains, farm equipment, cameras, furniture, toys, phonographs, music boxes, and much more. All of the things you see were once owned and used by Americans. Many were made in the United States.

Do you remember the Elliott children? They decided that although they would miss their friends when they moved, living in the Detroit area would be exciting. In the city and its suburbs, they would see and do many things they had never done before. They were eager to visit Windsor, too, and to be in Canada for the first time.

## LESSON 3 REVIEW

**THINK AND WRITE**

A. What materials do you think a person might receive from a chamber of commerce?

B. Why is the Detroit River important?

C. How do the people who live in Detroit and its suburbs depend on each other?

D. Explain why you think it is a good or a bad idea to name a neighborhood for another country.

E. What place in your community is most like a place in Detroit?

F. In your opinion, what is the most important invention that you use today?

**SKILLS CHECK**

**MAP SKILL**

Study the map of Michigan on page 113. Use the scale to find the distances between Detroit and Ann Arbor, Grand Rapids, and Sault Ste. Marie.

## USING THE VOCABULARY

manufactured
flowchart
urban area
consumer
designer
prototype

chamber of commerce
freighter
commuters
inventor

On a separate sheet of paper, write the word or words from above that best complete the sentences.

1. A person who makes something that has never been made before is called an _____.
2. _____ travel regularly between the city and the suburbs.
3. A _____ is a large ship.
4. A group of business people who help their community are called the _____.
5. _____ cars are full-size models that can be driven.
6. A _____ makes pland and models to show how a new product might look and work.
7. A person who buys goods and services is called a _____.
8. An _____ includes a city and the suburbs around it.
9. A _____ can show how something is done or how it works.
10. When something is _____, it is made by people using their hands or using machines.

## REMEMBERING WHAT YOU READ

On a separate sheet of paper, answer the questions in complete sentences.

1. List five goods that are made in the United States.
2. Where are three large manufacturing centers in the United States?
3. Who was Henry Ford?
4. Why is the Detroit River important?
5. What kinds of interesting places might be found in a large city?

## TYING MATH TO SOCIAL STUDIES

List some products that you use. Find out where they were made. Write a fraction to show what part of the list of products was made in the United States.

## THINKING CRITICALLY

On a separate sheet of paper, answer the following in complete sentences.

1. Why, do you think, are machines used to manufacture many products?

2. Why, do you think, does planning a new car take as long as four years?

3. What are two customs that are special in your community?

4. What kinds of things might you see in the Henry Ford Museum?

## SUMMARIZING THE CHAPTER

Copy this graphic organizer on a separate sheet of paper. Under the main idea for each lesson, write three facts that support the main idea.

**CHAPTER THEME**

Urban manufacturing centers use natural resources to make products.

*LESSON 1*

**Manufacturing, which follows five basic steps, is an important business in the United States.**

1. _____
2. _____
3. _____

*LESSON 2*

**Many kinds of workers are needed to manufacture automobiles.**

1. _____
2. _____
3. _____

*LESSON 3*

**An urban area can be a good place to live.**

1. _____
2. _____
3. _____

## COOPERATIVE LEARNING

In this unit you learned about physical features and natural resources. In this activity you will work with two other classmates to prepare a TV advertisement about your community. In your ad, include a physical feature or natural resource that is well known in your community.

**REMEMBER TO:**
- Give your ideas.
- Listen to others' ideas.
- Plan your work with the group.
- Present your project.
- Discuss how your group worked.

### PROJECT

One person in your group should write down what the ad will say. One person should make things such as pictures or signs to be used in the ad. Another person should direct the practice for presenting the ad.

• Choose a physical feature or natural resource in your community that you will include in your ad.

• Plan your TV ad. It should tell why your community is a good place to visit or to live. Mention the physical feature or natural resource you have chosen.

• Practice presenting your ad. The director should give suggestions for making the ad better.

### PRESENTATION AND REVIEW

• Present your ad so that everyone can hear. Pretend you are trying to get people to visit or live in your community.

• With your group, discuss what you would do differently if you planned another ad.

# Using SKILLBUILDER Grids

## A. WHY I NEED THIS SKILL

Have you ever seen people looking all over a map trying to find a place? That would not have happened if they had used a grid. Using a grid is an easy way to locate places on a map.

## B. LEARNING THE SKILL

Look at the map on this page. As you can see, there are some lines on the map going from left to right and from top to bottom. Lines cutting across each other like this make what is called a grid. As the lines cut across, they form a number of boxes. These boxes are named using the letters along the left side of the map and the numbers along the top of the map. For example, the name of the box in the top left corner is A-1. The name of the top middle box is A-2. The name of the bottom middle box is C-2.

It is easy to find something on the map if you know in which box it is located. Let's try to find box B-3. Put one finger from your left

hand on the letter *B*. Then put one finger from your right hand on the number 3. Move the finger on *B* across and the finger on 3 down. The box where they meet is B-3. What do you see in this box?

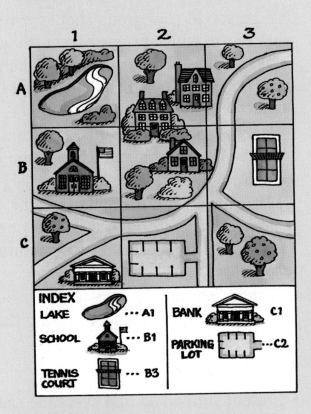

## C. PRACTICING THE SKILL

On page 125 there is a treasure map. A treasure hunter looking for a hidden treasure approached the island from the direction shown by

**124**

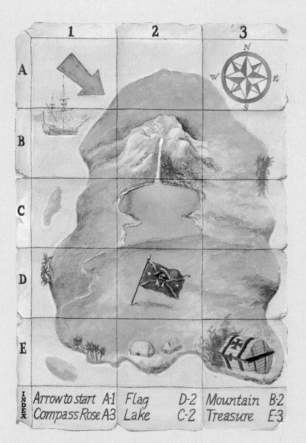

| INDEX | | | |
|---|---|---|---|
| Arrow to start A-1 | Flag | D-2 | Mountain B-2 |
| Compass Rose A-3 | Lake | C-2 | Treasure E-3 |

## D. APPLYING THE SKILL

The maps you have used in this lesson are quite small. Even without the index and grid, you could have found all the places and objects on each map. But when a map is large, an index and a grid are needed.

Has your family ever used a road map on a long car trip? A road map sometimes looks like the map shown here. Find a road map at home or at school. Use the index and the grid to find five cities on the map.

the arrow. He followed the path across the island to the place where the treasure was hidden. Using the grid, answer these three questions.

1. How would you use the index to find the compass rose?
2. What is located in box D-2?
3. In which box is the treasure located?

## A. WHY I NEED THIS SKILL

Do you ever have trouble remembering what you have read? If you can learn to find the main ideas in what you read, remembering will be easier. Main ideas are a writer's most important points.

## B. LEARNING THE SKILL

A paragraph usually has a main idea. Sometimes the main idea is stated in one sentence. This *main idea sentence* tells what the whole paragraph is about. Main idea sentences are often found at the beginning or end of a paragraph. *Details* are used to tell about and support the main idea.

The Main-Idea-Pede below shows how main ideas and details work together in a paragraph. The body is the most important part of the Main-Idea-Pede, so the main idea sentence is on the body. The legs hold up and support the body, so the details that support the main idea sentence are on the legs. A Main-Idea-Pede can have as many legs as there are details in a paragraph. Can you imagine one with ten legs?

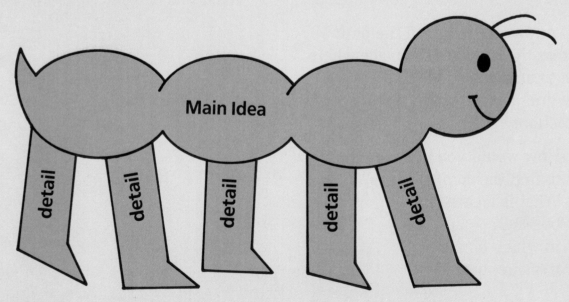

Main Idea

detail  detail  detail  detail  detail

## C. Practicing The Skill

Read the paragraph below. Find the main idea sentence and the details that support it.

Living on a farm can be fun. You can take long walks on your family's land. You can have a pet and raise a farm animal. You can belong to 4-H and go to the county fair. On Saturdays a trip to town can be fun, too.

On a sheet of paper, draw a Main-Idea-Pede like the one below. Write the main idea sentence on the body. Did you select the first sentence? If you did, you are correct. Now draw six legs on your Main-Idea-Pede. Write a detail on each leg. Remember that a Main-Idea-Pede can have as many legs as you need.

## D. Applying The Skill

Use the skill of finding main ideas as you read the next chapter, which is about community and state government. See if you can find the writer's main ideas. Remember that the main idea is not always in the first or last sentence of a paragraph. Use the Main-Idea-Pede to help you remember main ideas and details.

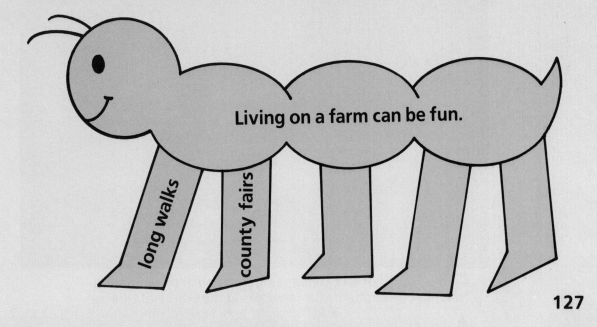

Living on a farm can be fun.

long walks

county fairs

In the United States people choose leaders who meet to make laws and plans. This photograph shows a meeting of the Navajo Tribal Council, in Arizona.

▲ On the Fourth of July, we remember the birth of our nation. New York celebrated with fireworks at the Statue of Liberty.

▶ The United States has had some great leaders. Abraham Lincoln was a President who kept this country together in hard times.

▼ Helping others is something everyone can do. It makes us good members of our community.

UNIT 3

# GOVERNMENT AND CITIZENSHIP

People do many things to make their communities, states, and countries good places to live. Leaders work to make communities succeed.

CHAPTER

# 6

# COMMUNITY AND STATE GOVERNMENT

**P**eople in states and communities choose leaders to make laws and provide services. People can visit their mayor.

MAYOR WILLIAMS

130

# Community Government

## THINK ABOUT WHAT YOU KNOW

What rules do you have in your family and at school? Who makes these rules?

## STUDY THE VOCABULARY

| | | |
|---|---|---|
| law | vote | council |
| government | elect | tax |
| town meeting | mayor | |

## FOCUS YOUR READING

What do community governments do?

## A. What Is Community Government?

Most people like to live near other people, in communities. People living in communities need **laws**, or rules that everyone must follow. They need **government**. A government is a group of people who make laws and provide services for a community, county, state, or nation.

Communities in the United States have different kinds of government. In some very small communities all the adults participate directly in the government. They go to a **town meeting**, where people make decisions for the community. For example, they might decide to buy a new fire engine or allow a new restaurant to be built on Main Street. At the meeting, everyone **votes** on what to do. To vote means "to tell in some way what your choice is." A voter might raise a hand or mark a piece of paper with his or her choice.

Police, who help us obey laws

**131**

At a town meeting, everyone has a chance to talk and to vote.
▶ What are the people doing in the photograph at left?

In larger communities leaders are **elected**, or chosen by vote, to make decisions for everyone. Many communities elect a **mayor**, or leader who helps make laws and also sees that these laws are carried out. Many communities also have a **council**, which is a group of men and women who make laws and plans for the community.

A mayor and council have meetings so that people in the community can give their ideas. But the mayor and council actually make the decisions. For example, the mayor and council might want to allow a builder to put up a 10-story building on Main Street. Many townspeople might be against this. However, the mayor and council may still allow the new building.

## B. Community Laws

Some laws are the same in all communities in the United States. For example, in all communities a red traffic light means cars must stop. Other laws are different in different communities. For example, in some towns, cars cannot park on the streets overnight. In other towns, there is no law against overnight parking.

Do you think your community has laws that you must obey? Your community might have a law about where you can ride your bike or use your skateboard. There might be a law against jaywalking, or crossing the street illegally. There might be laws against writing on buildings and about where and how loud a radio can be played.

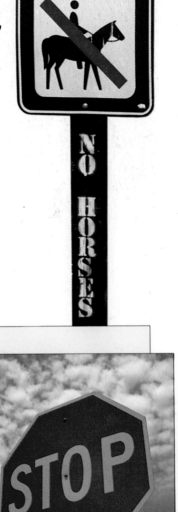

Signs use words and symbols to help us know what to do and what not to do.
▶ What is the message on each of these community signs?

133

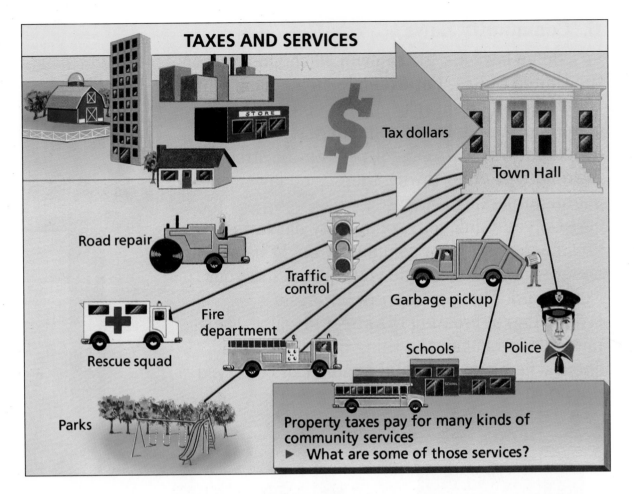

**TAXES AND SERVICES**

Tax dollars

Town Hall

Road repair

Traffic control

Garbage pickup

Rescue squad

Fire department

Schools

Police

Parks

Property taxes pay for many kinds of community services
▶ What are some of those services?

## C. Community Services

All community governments provide some services for people. Community governments run schools and provide fire and police protection. These services cost money. To pay for the services, the government collects money from the people. This money is called a **tax**. Everyone who owns property in the community, such as land, a house, or a store, must pay a property tax.

Your community might have special services for children. There might be a recreation program, so that children can swim and play baseball or soccer in summer. There might be holiday celebrations for all the children of the community.

## D. Learning About Your Community

You can find out about the government in your community. Writing letters is a good way to learn. You might write to the mayor, the fire chief, and the police chief. You might arrange to visit the town hall to talk with the workers there. You can ask a school or town librarian to help you find information. Your town might even have a public information telephone number you can call.

Maria and Alfred live in Roswell, New Mexico. Their class made a booklet about their town. Maria and Alfred made a map for the cover. The booklet included letters from government workers and photographs of special places and events.

Writing a book like this one can be a good way to learn about your community. What would you like to find out about the town where you live?

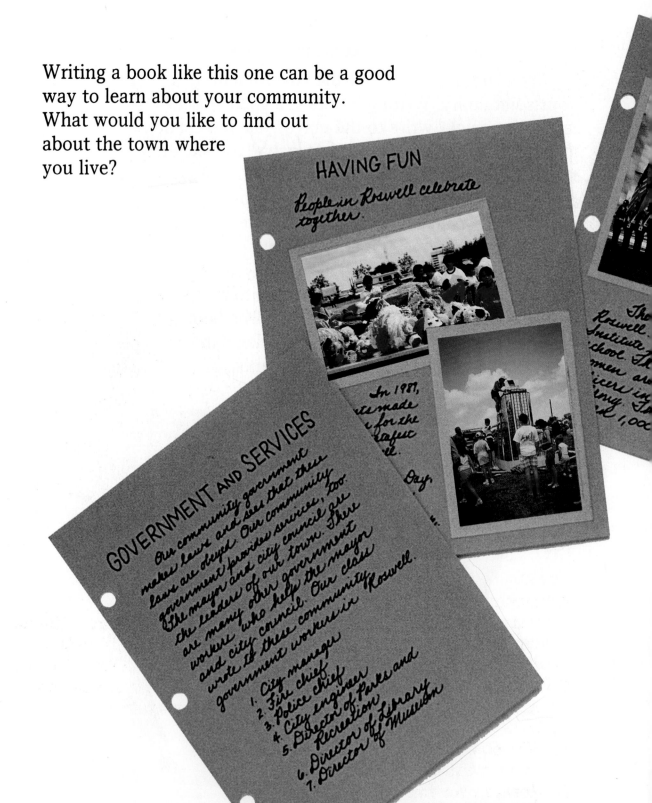

HAVING FUN

People in Roswell celebrate together.

In 1987, ...te made ...e for the ...afest ...l.

Day.

GOVERNMENT AND SERVICES

Our community government makes laws and sees that these laws are obeyed. Our community government provides services, too. The mayor and city council are the leaders of our town. There are many other government workers who help the mayor and city council. Our class wrote to these community government workers in Roswell.

1. City manager
2. Fire chief
3. Police chief
4. City engineer
5. Director of Parks and Recreation
6. Director of Library
7. Director of Museum

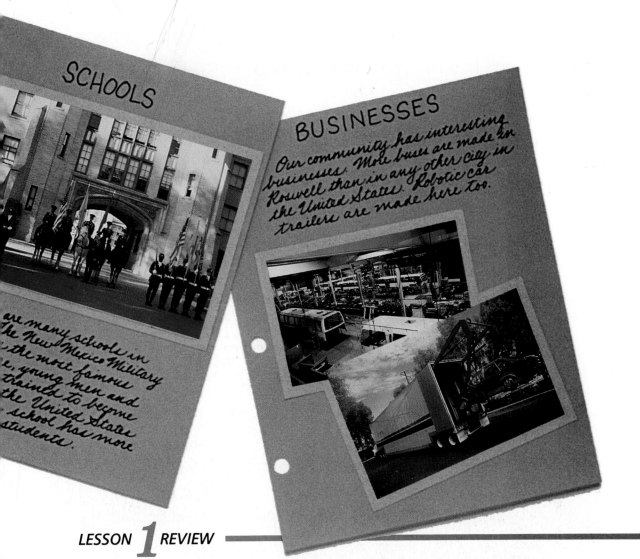

SCHOOLS

BUSINESSES

Our community has interesting businesses. More buses are made in Roswell than in any other city in the United States. Robotic car trailers are made here too.

...are many schools in ...The New Mexico Military ...e, the most famous ...e, young men and ...trained to become ...the United States ...school has more ...students.

## LESSON 1 REVIEW

### THINK AND WRITE

A. In your opinion, what can voters do when they are unhappy with the decisions that elected leaders make?

B. Why, do you think, do many communities have the same laws?

C. Why do community governments collect taxes?

D. How can you find out about the government in your community?

### SKILLS CHECK

**MAP SKILL**

Make a map of your state like the one Maria and Alfred made of New Mexico. On the map of your state, show the capital city and your own community.

## State Government

**THINK ABOUT WHAT YOU KNOW**

What is the name of your state? Have you always lived there? What do you like best about the state or states where you have lived?

**STUDY THE VOCABULARY**

**governor**  **capital**  **capitol**

**FOCUS YOUR READING**

How does state government help the people of the state?

## A. States Have Government

You have learned that communities have their own government. Each of the 50 states in our country has its own government, too. The **governor** is the most important leader in state government. He or she is elected by the people of the state.

The governor works in the state **capital**. A capital is a city where the government of a state or country is located. The governor and other state leaders work in a building called the state **capitol**.

What is the name of your state capital? Find your state capital on a map. How far is it from your community?

## B. State Laws and Services

The governor and other state leaders make laws for the whole state. These laws must be obeyed in every community in the state. All states have laws about certain kinds of things, such as who can drive a car. Only people who have reached a certain age and who have passed a driving test are allowed to drive in the state.

Some state laws are especially for children and young people. Your state has a law that sets the number of days in the school year. There may also be a state law about the number of days you must be in school to pass to the next grade.

Like communities, states collect taxes to pay for services they provide for people. If you look around you, you will see your state at work to provide services for you. Notice police cars with the words STATE POLICE, and look for signs in stores and restaurants that say STATE BOARD OF HEALTH.

This girl is obeying a state safety law.
▶ What do you think that law is?

An American flag frames this photograph of the domed capitol in Tallahassee.
► Compare your state capitol to the one pictured here.

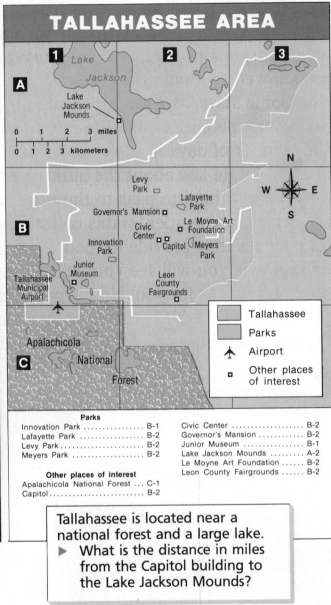

## TALLAHASSEE AREA

### Parks

| | |
|---|---|
| Innovation Park ............... B-1 | Civic Center ................... B-2 |
| Lafayette Park ................ B-2 | Governor's Mansion ........... B-2 |
| Levy Park .................... B-2 | Junior Museum ............... B-1 |
| Meyers Park .................. B-2 | Lake Jackson Mounds ........ A-2 |
| | Le Moyne Art Foundation ...... B-2 |
| **Other places of interest** | Leon County Fairgrounds ...... B-2 |
| Apalachicola National Forest ... C-1 | |
| Capitol ....................... B-2 | |

Tallahassee is located near a national forest and a large lake.
► What is the distance in miles from the Capitol building to the Lake Jackson Mounds?

## C. A State Capital Is a Special City

Tallahassee is a special city. It is the state capital of Florida. Find Tallahassee on the map on page 141. It is located in the northern panhandle of Florida. A panhandle is a narrow piece of land sticking out from a bigger piece of land. Can you see the reasons for the name *panhandle*?

Tallahassee became the capital of Florida in 1823. It was chosen because of its location between the two most important cities in Florida at the time. These cities were St. Augustine and Pensacola. Find them on the map below.

The first capitol building in Tallahassee was a small log cabin. You can still see it today. In 1826 the log cabin was replaced by a 2-story wooden building. In 1845 a 3-story building with a dome was built. Today the domed building and a 22-story building are the capitol. Both are pictured on the previous page.

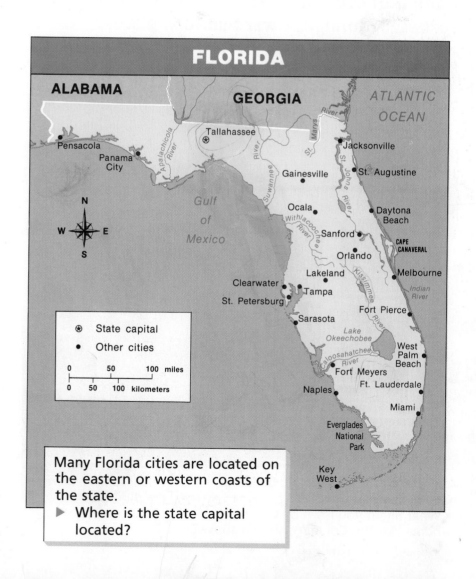

## FLORIDA

Many Florida cities are located on the eastern or western coasts of the state.

▶ Where is the state capital located?

## D. Visiting a State Capital

Marilyn and Jeff live in Florida. When they visited Tallahassee last summer, they felt proud of the city and their state.

They visited a 150-year-old house called The Columns. This house looks just as it did 150 years ago. Even the furniture, pictures, and wallpaper are the same.

Marilyn and Jeff also visited the Natural Bridge Historic Site, near Tallahassee. A historic site is a place where something important happened. An important battle was fought near Natural Bridge. This battle took place about 130 years ago, during the war that took place

Florida State Archives

Many state capitals have old buildings that you can visit.
▶ What might you learn by visiting a home like The Columns, shown above?

between the northern and southern states of the United States. The war lasted for four years.

Marilyn and Jeff visited two museums to learn about Florida history. At the Museum of Florida History, they saw a mastodon skeleton. Mastodons were huge creatures that lived in Florida millions of years ago. At the Tallahassee Junior Museum they learned about farming in Florida long ago.

Perhaps you can visit your state capital. You can learn about the history of your state. You can learn other special things about your state, too, from places such as the capitol building, historic sites, and museums. Visiting your state capitol can be fun and educational.

Courtesy Tallahassee Junior Museum

Tallahassee Junior Museum

## LESSON 2 REVIEW

### THINK AND WRITE

A. How many state governors are there in the United States?
B. In your opinion, why do all states have laws governing who is allowed to drive an automobile?
C. Why, do you think, did Florida need to build new capitol buildings?
D. How can a person learn about the history of a state and its capital?

### SKILLS CHECK

**THINKING SKILL**

Draw a circle on a separate sheet of paper. Write the word *states* inside the circle. Draw at least five lines coming from the circle. On each line write one fact that is true about all the states in the United States.

# CHAPTER 6 PUTTING IT ALL TOGETHER

## USING THE VOCABULARY

government     capital
town meetings    capitol
elected

On a separate sheet of paper, write the word or words from above that best complete the sentences.

1. A _____ is a group of people who make laws and provide services for a community, county, state, or nation.
2. A _____ is a city where the government of a state or country is located.
3. The governor and other state leaders work in a building called the state _____.
4. In larger communities and in counties, states, and nations, leaders are _____, or chosen, to make decisions for everyone.
5. At _town meeting_ people gather to learn about what is happening in the community.

## REMEMBERING WHAT YOU READ

On a separate sheet of paper, answer the questions in complete sentences.

1. What do people do at a town meeting?
2. What is the job of a mayor?
3. Why does the government collect taxes from the people in the community?
4. How can you find out about your community government?
5. How many states have their own government?
6. Where does a governor work?
7. Who must obey the laws in a state?
8. What is a panhandle?
9. How did Florida choose its capital?
10. What is a historic site?

## TYING LANGUAGE ARTS TO SOCIAL STUDIES

Describe a rule that you would like to have in your community. In a paragraph, explain the rule and tell why it is needed in your community.

## THINKING CRITICALLY

On a separate sheet of paper, answer the following in complete sentences.

1. Why do we need rules in our community?
2. Why is it important to vote?
3. Why don't all communities have the same laws?
4. If a community or state did not collect any taxes, what might happen?
5. Why do many people like to visit their state capital?

## SUMMARIZING THE CHAPTER

Copy this graphic organizer on a separate sheet of paper. Under the main idea for each lesson, write three facts that support the main idea.

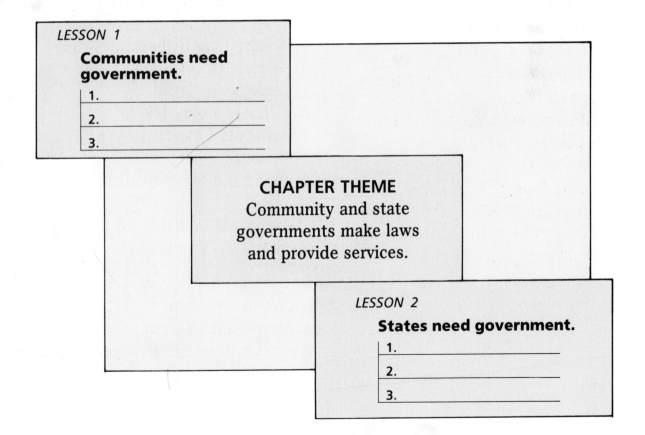

LESSON 1

**Communities need government.**

1.
2.
3.

CHAPTER THEME
Community and state governments make laws and provide services.

LESSON 2

**States need government.**

1.
2.
3.

# CHAPTER 7
# OUR NATIONAL GOVERNMENT

Our country has a national government. We vote for people to be our leaders. They go to our capital city, Washington, D.C., to make laws that will help our country.

## Choosing Our Leaders

### THINK ABOUT WHAT YOU KNOW

Do you belong to a club or sports team? Does your club or team have leaders? Tell how the leaders are chosen.

### STUDY THE VOCABULARY

| election | candidate | debate |
|----------|-----------|--------|
| ballot   | citizen   |        |

### FOCUS YOUR READING

How do we choose the leaders of the United States?

---

### A. A Class Election

Mrs. Allen's class was holding an **election**. An election is one way leaders are chosen. The students were voting for class president and vice president. The new leaders would plan a parents' day program. But first, the election had to take place.

On Mrs. Allen's desk there were enough **ballots** for each class member. Each ballot listed all the people who wanted to be leaders. You can see a copy of the ballot on the bulletin board on the next page. You can read the rules the students wrote for the election.

"You may vote anytime during the school day today," said Mrs. Allen. "Put a check mark next to your choices. Remember to vote for the people who will do the best job as president and vice president. You can vote for yourself if your name is on the ballot. I hope all of you will vote, but you are not required to do so."

Running for president  **147**

ELECTION DAY SEPTEMBER 10

Pat for President

Rules for Voting
1. You must be a class member.
2. You may vote only once.
3. Nobody can tell you how to vote.
4. All votes are secret.

BALLOT ★ ☆ ★
Check one for President
☐ Ramon
☐ Jennifer
☐ Pat
Check one for Vice President
☐ Don
☐ Laura
☐ Mike

I LIKE MIKE
For VICE PRESIDENT!

VOTE For DON He's #1

This bulletin-board display provides information to help students vote wisely in a class election.
► Which part of the display do you think is the most helpful?

## B. Learning About Elections

On class election day, Mrs. Grove came to give a talk. She came to tell the students about United States elections.

Mrs. Grove is a member of the League of Women Voters. The league is made up of groups of women all over the United States. These groups help voters learn about the **candidates** for community, state, and national offices. A candidate is a person who is trying to be elected to an office.

"I see that you are having a class election," Mrs. Grove began. "Your election will help you understand how people vote for government leaders in our country.

"Communities, states, and nations hold elections. Today we are going to discuss national elections, when people vote for leaders of a whole nation. We vote for President and Vice President in the United States.

"Your bulletin board shows rules for your class election. They are almost like the rules for national elections."

Mrs. Allen's class learned that only United States **citizens** who are at least 18 years old can vote in a national election. A citizen is a member of a nation. A person becomes a citizen of the United States by being born in the United States or by law. In the United States, each citizen can vote only once in each election. No one can tell a voter how to vote, and all votes are secret.

New voters must register with the government. After they complete a form, their names are added to a list of people who can vote.
▶ Why, do you think, does the government need a list of voters?

Conventions, or meetings, and campaign buttons are part of an election for President. Many Americans learned about George Bush by watching the convention pictured above on television.
▶ What do people learn from campaign buttons?

Campaign buttons

## C. Learning About Candidates

"The President of the United States is our most important leader. The Vice President must be ready to take over if the President becomes sick or dies," said Mrs. Grove.

"It is important for voters to learn about candidates for President and Vice President. Voters must know what the candidates believe and what they want to do for our country. How do people learn about candidates?" Mrs. Grove asked.

"They learn from signs and speeches that the candidates make," said Ramon.

"And from newspapers and magazines, too," added Cam.

"From news and **debates** on TV," said Jason.

"That's right. In a debate, people with different ideas discuss the same topics and answer the same questions," Mrs. Grove said.

## D. What Happens on Election Day?

During the school day, Mrs. Allen's students filled out their ballots. They made a check mark beside the names of the candidates they wanted. Each student folded his or her ballot so that the vote was hidden. The students put their ballots through the slit in the ballot box on Mrs. Allen's desk. By the end of the day, all the students in the class had voted.

Mrs. Allen told the students that she would count the ballots and tell them in the morning who had won. "If this had been an election for President of the United States," Mrs. Allen said, "you would see the results on television tonight. And probably you would have voted by pulling handles on a big voting machine. When you pull the handles of a voting machine, an *X* appears next to your choice."

"I can't wait until I am 18 years old and I can vote for the President and Vice President of the United States," Jennifer said.

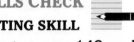

Voting machine

LESSON *1* REVIEW

**THINK AND WRITE**
A. What is a ballot?
B. Who can vote in a national election?
C. How can people learn about candidates in a national election?
D. Why should people vote?

**SKILLS CHECK**

**WRITING SKILL**
Turn to page 148 and read the rules for Mrs. Allen's class election. Write a paragraph about one rule. Tell why that rule was needed.

## Our National Government at Work

### THINK ABOUT WHAT YOU KNOW

What do you think the President and Vice President of our country do? Where did you learn about what they do?

### STUDY THE VOCABULARY

**Congress**     **representative**     **Supreme Court**

### FOCUS YOUR READING

What are some jobs of the President and Vice President, Congress, and Supreme Court of the United States?

## A. Our President and Vice President

The President of the United States lives and works in our national capital, Washington, D.C. You have probably seen the President and Vice President on television. They may have been getting on an airplane, giving a speech, talking with the leader of another country, or shaking hands with people. Maybe you have wondered what kind of work the President and Vice President do when they are not having their pictures taken.

Visiting places in our country as well as in the rest of the world is one part of the job of these two leaders. But much of the time the President and Vice President are reading reports and attending meetings to learn about what is happening in our country and the world. An important job of the President is signing new laws that everyone in the nation must obey.

The President commands the armed forces of the United States and helps to keep our country strong. The President meets with leaders of other countries to talk about world problems and to try to find ways to solve them. Sometimes the President helps other countries work out disagreements between them.

From time to time the President gives a speech on televison to explain something that has happened. Once a year, in the State of the Union speech, the President talks about plans for our country. The President might talk about how to solve problems such as people taking drugs or being without a home.

Presidents often travel. Here, President and Mrs. Bush have arrived in Maine by helicopter.
▶ Who came with them?

## B. The Congress of the United States

The Senate and the House of Representatives make up the **Congress** of the United States. The main job of Congress is to make laws and send them to the President to sign. Members of Congress meet in our national Capitol building.

Each state elects members to Congress. They speak for their state at meetings. For example, think of a member of Congress from a state where there are many farmers. He or she will want to have laws that help farmers. All the members of Congress work hard for their states, but they also make laws for the good of the whole United States.

Members of Congress often receive letters, telephone calls, and even visits from the people of their home state. The people may want to tell about

Members of Congress applaud President Bush as he is about to speak to them.
► What do you think the President would talk to Congress about?

Congress makes laws against polluting the air (small photograph).
▶ What kinds of laws are needed to make all factories as clean as the one in the large photograph?

problems in the state and ask for help. Often members of Congress receive letters asking them to vote for or against new laws. If you were writing to a member of Congress from your state, what would you write about?

## C. How Congress Works

You can learn how Congress works by thinking about what once happened at Mrs. Allen's school. The school needed new rules for recess. Many students were complaining that they hardly ever had a chance to use the slides or swings.

The principal of the school decided to have students make new rules for recess. He asked each class to choose one student **representative** to go to a meeting about new rules. A representative is a person who acts or speaks for others.

Jennifer was the representative from Mrs. Allen's class. She asked the class what new rules there should be. Jennifer wrote down the rules the class suggested.

Then Jennifer went to the meeting of class representatives. They discussed the rules each class had suggested. They made new rules for taking turns on the slides and swings. One of these new rules had been suggested by Jennifer's class. Now it became the rule for all the students in the school whenever they used the playground.

Good rules can help to make a playground safe and fun. In the three photographs below, several rules are being followed.
▶ What do you think the rules are?

## D. The Supreme Court

Many people in our national government were not elected to office. They were named to their jobs by the President or another leader.

The nine judges on the **Supreme Court** are appointed by the President of the United States. The Supreme Court is the highest court in the United States. When the Supreme Court decides whether a law is fair, all the other courts in our country must follow that decision.

From 1779 to 1981, all the Supreme Court judges were men. Then in 1981, Sandra Day O'Connor became the first woman Supreme Court judge. She was appointed by President Ronald Reagan. O'Connor was 51 years old when she became a Supreme Court judge. Like the other Supreme Court judges, she can stay on the court for the rest of her life. A Supreme Court judge can have an effect on the people of our country for a long time. That is why a President must think carefully about whom to appoint.

Sandra Day O'Connor

*LESSON 2 REVIEW*

### THINK AND WRITE

A. What are some jobs of the President and Vice President of the United States?

B. What is the main job of Congress?

C. How were the class representatives at Mrs. Allen's school like members of Congress?

D. In your opinion, what does it mean to say that the Supreme Court is the highest court in the United States?

### SKILLS CHECK

**THINKING SKILL**

Make a chart about our national government. On your chart, show some of the jobs of the President, Vice President, Congress, and Supreme Court.

## A Tour of Washington, D.C.

**THINK ABOUT WHAT YOU KNOW**

You have learned about interesting places in a state capital. What places do you think will be found in our national capital, Washington, D.C.?

**STUDY THE VOCABULARY**

| planned | White House | monument |
| community | | |

**FOCUS YOUR READING**

What can the famous places of Washington, D.C., teach about our country?

## A. A Planned Community

Washington, D.C., our national capital, is important to all people of the United States. It is the place where our leaders meet to make laws and plans. It is also the place where we can learn about our government and remember our country's history.

Do you know what D.C. means? It means "District of Columbia." The city of Washington covers the same area as the District of Columbia.

In 1791, George Washington chose the exact place for the capital of the United States. He hired a planner to decide where the streets and buildings should be. Andrew Ellicott and Benjamin Banneker laid out the boundaries of the city. Washington, D.C., is a **planned community**. Look at the map on page 159. Find The Mall, which was in the first plan for Washington. The Mall is a grassy place where people can walk.

## B. The White House

There are many interesting and important buildings in Washington, D.C., but the **White House** is probably the most famous. All our Presidents except George Washington have lived there. When the house was first built, it was called the President's House, but later its name was changed to the White House.

Do you know how the White House got its name? This is what some people think. A long time ago the President's house was damaged in a fire.

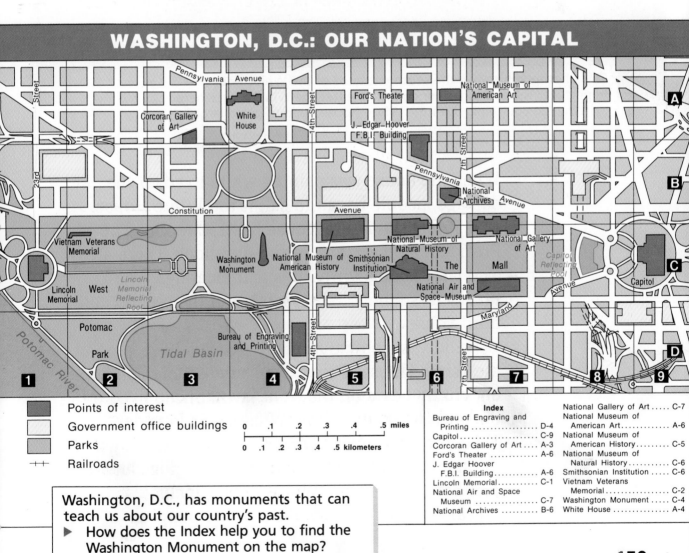

WASHINGTON, D.C.: OUR NATION'S CAPITAL

**Points of interest**
**Government office buildings**
**Parks**
+++ **Railroads**

0   .1   .2   .3   .4   .5 miles
0   .1   .2   .3   .4   .5 kilometers

Washington, D.C., has monuments that can teach us about our country's past.
► How does the Index help you to find the Washington Monument on the map?

This photograph shows the south entrance of the White House. Important visitors from other countries enter the White House here.
► Why, do you think, does the White House need to be so large?

When the house was painted white to cover the damage, people began to call it the White House.

Today the White House has 132 rooms. The President's offices are on the first floor. There are also large rooms for parties and meetings. The President's family lives upstairs on the second and third floors.

Did you know that many animals have lived at the White House? President Thomas Jefferson kept big grizzly bears on the front lawn. Sheep lived on the lawn when Woodrow Wilson was President. Theodore Roosevelt's sons once trotted a pony up to their sick brother's bedroom. Many dogs and cats have lived at the White House, including President Bush's dog Millie and her puppies.

This photograph shows the United States Capitol, which is located on Capitol Hill.

▶ How would you describe the Capitol building?

## C. The United States Capitol Building

You have learned that each state has a building called a capitol, where the state lawmakers do their work. You have also learned that Congress works in the United States Capitol. The United States Capitol is a domed building with 540 rooms. A small subway runs underground between the Capitol and other office buildings nearby.

Sometimes, Congress works late into the night. When that happens, a special light shines at the top of the Capitol building to show that Congress is still meeting.

Many people visit the Capitol. They study the beautiful paintings that tell about our history. Some people go to the meetings of Congress.

Many people visit the Vietnam Veterans Memorial. They look for the name of a relative or friend on the long wall. Sometimes touching the name makes them feel closer to the one who died.

▶ What is the monument in the background of the photograph?

## D. Monuments and Memorials

Washington has many **monuments** and memorials that help us remember an important person or event. A monument usually a building or stone. A memorial might a building or stone, or another kind of ce, such as a garden.

Some monuments and memorials in Washington, D.C. built in memory of Presidents. Others help us to remember people who died in wars.

The Vietnam Veterans Memorial and the Washington Monument are shown on this page. Find the Lincoln Memorial on the map of Washington, D.C., on page 159.

## E. National Museums

Washington, D.C., has many museums. The biggest museum was started by Congress with money from a British scientist named Smithson. The Smithsonian Institution is really 12 museums plus a zoo. The zoo, called the National Zoological (zoh uh LAHJ ih kul) Park, has more than 2,000 animals. Find the Smithsonian Institution building on the map on page 159. This is the oldest part of the Smithsonian.

The National Air and Space Museum is part of the Smithsonian Institution, too. There you can see some famous airplanes and rockets. At the National Museum of American History, you can see old cars and trains and everyday things that people used long ago. The National Museum of Natural History has models of animals from around the world. The museums of Washington, D.C., can teach us about our country and the world.

Space shuttle

---

LESSON 3 REVIEW

### THINK AND WRITE

**A.** What makes Washington, D.C., a planned community?

**B.** What makes the White House an important building?

**C.** How is the Capitol building in Washington, D.C., like the capitol buildings of the states?

**D.** Why are monuments and memorials built?

**E.** Why is the Smithsonian Institution an important place?

### SKILLS CHECK

**MAP SKILL**

Find Washington, D.C., on the United States map in your Atlas. Use the scale to find the distance from Washington, D.C., to a city close to your home.

## USING THE VOCABULARY

election     representative
ballot     Supreme Court
candidate     planned community
citizen     monument
Congress     White House

On a separate sheet of paper, write the word or words from above that best complete the sentence.

1. A ____ is a person who acts or speaks for others.
2. A person who is trying to be elected to an office is called a ____.
3. A community, such as Washington, D.C., that was built according to plans is a ____.
4. An ____ is one way leaders are chosen.
5. The ____ is the place where the President of the United States lives.
6. A ____ is usually a building or stone that helps people remember an important event.
7. A ____ lists the people who want to be leaders.
8. A member of a nation is called a ____.
9. The main job of the ____ is to make laws and send them to the President to sign.
10. The ____ is the highest court in the United States.

## REMEMBERING WHAT YOU READ

On a separate sheet of paper, answer the questions in complete sentences.

1. Who can vote in national elections in the United States?
2. Who is the most important leader of our country?
3. Who appoints the judges to the Supreme Court?
4. Where does Congress work?
5. What are some important monuments and memorials in Washington, D.C.?

## TYING LANGUAGE ARTS TO SOCIAL STUDIES

What do you think is the President's most important job? Write a report with three paragraphs. Tell what job is most important. Tell why it is important. End the report by telling how you would do this job if you were President.

## THINKING CRITICALLY

On a separate sheet of paper, answer the following in complete sentences.

1. Why do elections take place?
2. How do Congress and the President of the United States work together?
3. Why, do you think, was a woman, Sandra Day O'Connor, appointed to the Supreme Court?
4. What are two other ways to remember important people besides visiting monuments and memorials?
5. Why are museums important?

## SUMMARIZING THE CHAPTER

**Copy this graphic organizer on a separate sheet of paper. Under the main idea for each lesson, write three facts that support the main idea.**

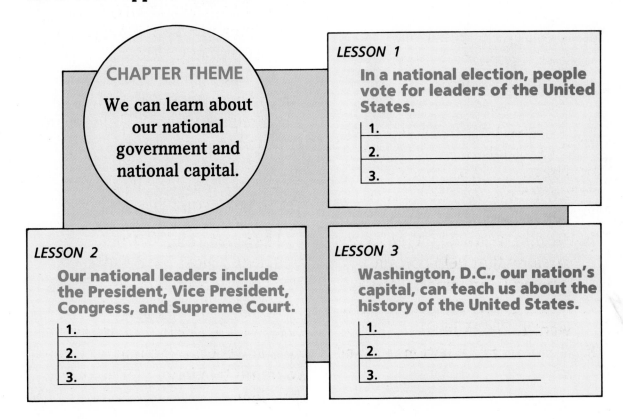

CHAPTER THEME

We can learn about our national government and national capital.

LESSON 1

In a national election, people vote for leaders of the United States.

1. _____
2. _____
3. _____

LESSON 2

Our national leaders include the President, Vice President, Congress, and Supreme Court.

1. _____
2. _____
3. _____

LESSON 3

Washington, D.C., our nation's capital, can teach us about the history of the United States.

1. _____
2. _____
3. _____

# CHAPTER 8

# CITIZENSHIP

Good citizens care about each other and their world. They are loyal to their community, state, and country.

# Rights and Responsibilities

### THINK ABOUT WHAT YOU KNOW

Pretend that you have promised to go right home after school. On the way home, your best friend asks you to come to her house to see her new puppy. What will you do?

### STUDY THE VOCABULARY

**rights**    **responsibility**    **property**

### FOCUS YOUR READING

What are some ways children can take responsibility?

## A. Rights and Responsibilities in Groups

You belong to different groups. You are a member of a family. You are a member of a class at school. You may also belong to a sports team or to a club such as the Brownie Scouts or Cub Scouts.

In every group, you have certain **rights**. A right is something that is owed a person. Think about some rights you have. In a family, you have the right to be loved and cared for. At school, you have the right to learn. On a team, you have the right to play. In a club, you have the right to take part in meetings and other activities.

Along with rights, people in groups have **responsibilities.** A responsibility is something a person must do. Rights and responsibilities go together. For example, the right to ride your bike to your friend's house might depend on how responsible you are at following safety rules.

## B. Responsibilities at Home

Most people have responsibilities at home. Eight-year-old Beverley lives with her mother in a small apartment. Beverley's mother has to work at two jobs to make enough money for rent, food, clothes, and Beverley's music lessons.

Every morning, while her mother makes breakfast, Beverley sets the table. She also feeds the cat and gives him fresh water. Every evening, Beverley does her homework. She also practices her trombone with her friend Lucas.

"I know I can count on Beverley to do her homework and her chores," her mother says. "There is another way Beverley is helpful. She remembers to write a telephone message when I cannot come to the phone. She writes the caller's name, number, and message on a pad by the phone."

What chores do you have at home? Can you be counted on to do them?

Beverley and Lucas practice for their music lessons.
► Why do they need to practice for their lessons?

Jessica wants to use Amanda's crayons to finish her work.
▶ Why doesn't Jessica just take the crayons and use them?

## C. Responsibilities at School

Children have many chances to act responsibly at school. They follow school rules. Some rules, such as "Raise your hand before talking," help keep the school orderly so students can work. Other rules, such as "No talking during fire drill," help keep students safe.

Sometimes taking responsibility means thinking before acting. Jessica is a good student in her third-grade class. However, sometimes she wants things other people have. Jessica wanted a new box of crayons like the box Amanda had just brought to school. Jessica asked her mother for new crayons, but her mother said, "Not until next week." When Amanda was absent, Jessica felt like borrowing the crayons in Amanda's desk.

"The crayons belong to Amanda," Jessica thought. "Even though I want to use them, I can't take them without asking."

Do you think before you act? Next time you want to do something that makes you feel uncomfortable, think about it first. Be sure your action will not hurt you or someone else.

## D. Responsibilities on Teams and in Clubs

Good members of teams and clubs take their responsibilities seriously. Joel is a member of the Mountain View Soccer Team. His team has a rule that team members must not miss practice unless they are sick.

On Saturday morning, Joel's friend Adam called Joel on the phone. Adam said, "My dad and I will pick you up for soccer practice. Remember, we have to be there early to take all the equipment to the field." Joel did not want to practice. He wanted to stay home and watch cartoons on TV.

"All right," Joel said. "I'll be ready."

Why did Joel say he would go to practice when he wanted to watch cartoons? Would you have done the same thing?

These children and their coach are getting ready for Saturday morning soccer practice.
▶ What will the children need to remember when practice is over?

## E. Caring for Others

Beverley, Jessica, and Joel are alike in many ways. Sometimes they think about doing things that they should not do. But they usually decide to do the things that show they care for their family, classmates, and fellow team and club members. They take good care of their pets, too. They show respect for other people's **property**, or things people own.

Think of the ways you can show other people that you care about them. Some children walk their younger brothers or sisters to and from school. At school, they lend a pencil when another child needs one. They help a friend to visit the school nurse when the friend is hurt. Children who care say *thank you, excuse me,* and *I'm sorry.* These words make life more pleasant for everyone.

Walking to school

---

*LESSON* **1** *REVIEW*

### THINK AND WRITE

**A.** What is the difference between rights and responsibilities?

**B.** What responsibilities do Beverley and her mother have?

**C.** Why is it important to think before acting?

**D.** In your opinion, why must a team member attend practice regularly?

**E.** What are some ways you can show that you care about other students in your class?

### SKILLS CHECK

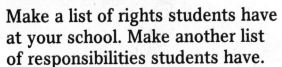

**THINKING SKILL**

Make a list of rights students have at your school. Make another list of responsibilities students have.

## Community Volunteers

### THINK ABOUT WHAT YOU KNOW

Have you ever offered to help somebody? Why did you do it?

### STUDY THE VOCABULARY

**citizenship**   **recycle**   **volunteer**

### FOCUS YOUR READING

What are some ways that volunteers help their communities?

## A. Learning About Volunteers

**Citizenship** is the way the members of a group use their rights and carry out their responsibilities. For example, members of a community might show good citizenship by becoming community **volunteers**. A volunteer chooses to do important work that is needed. Volunteers are not paid for their work.

In many communities, most or all of the firefighters are volunteers. So are the ambulance drivers. In many communities, children are volunteers, too. They visit older people who do not

172

have family nearby. They collect food or clothing for poor people and collect bottles, cans, and newspapers for **recycling** (ree SYE kling). A thing that is recycled is used again in some way.

Look at the photographs at the bottom of these pages. The people are volunteers in their communities. How are they helping to improve their communities?

## B. Volunteer Organizations

Volunteers work in many organizations. They are leaders in Boy Scouts, Girl Scouts, and other clubs. Teenagers work as candy stripers in hospitals. Parents are volunteers in organizations such as the Parent Teacher Association (PTA) and the Home and School Organization. People of all ages work in their churches or synagogues (SIHN uh gahgz).

Some organizations are very big. These organizations are at work in communities all over the world. The Red Cross and the Salvation Army help people in wartime or after an earthquake, flood, or other disaster.

The volunteers in these photographs are working outdoors, in a hospital, and in a school for adults.
► How do you think these volunteers feel about their work?

173

## C. Volunteers Who Make a Difference

Volunteers often make a real difference in their communities. They make people's lives better. This is what happened in 1989 in Harlem, a neighborhood of New York City. For 20 years, Harlem had no Little League baseball teams. There were few places in this crowded neighborhood where children could play.

Like many other children his age, nine-year-old Joshua Raiford wanted to play Little League baseball. Joshua's mother promised to bring Little League baseball back to Harlem. She knew she

The Harlem Little League season opened with a parade. The small picture shows the first game.
▶ Why, do you think, was there a parade?

couldn't do that alone. She would need other parents to volunteer to do some of the work.

A group of Harlem parents met. They asked the city government to make a ball field in Colonel (KUR nul) Charles Young Playground. They asked Harlem businesses for money for uniforms, bats, and balls. They found coaches for teams.

Joshua's father became a coach. His mother became president of the new league. All the parents worked very hard because they wanted something for the children in their community.

At last, opening day came. The new Harlem Little Leaguers paraded down 145th Street to the playground. When the first ballgame in 20 years began in Harlem, everybody was happy and proud. Once again, the people of a community had volunteered their time and given their money to create something good. They had made a difference.

Do you know any stories about volunteers in your community? Ask your family about volunteers who have made a difference.

## LESSON 2 REVIEW

### THINK AND WRITE

A. Why, do you think, do people become volunteers in their communities?

B. In your opinion, why are some volunteer organizations so big?

C. What were some jobs the volunteers in Harlem had to do to start a Little League?

### SKILLS CHECK

**WRITING SKILL**

Write a paragraph that tells what kind of volunteer you want to be when you are older. Would you like to be a firefighter, an ambulance driver, a scout leader, a Little League coach, or a candy striper in a hospital? Explain the reasons for your choice.

## Becoming a Naturalized Citizen

### THINK ABOUT WHAT YOU KNOW

In Chapter 7 you learned what a citizen is. Do you think every person who lives in a country is a citizen of that country?

### STUDY THE VOCABULARY

**naturalized citizen**
**resident**

**Oath of American Citizenship**

### FOCUS YOUR READING

How do immigrants become naturalized citizens of the United States?

### A. Two Ways to Citizenship

Each year millions of babies are born in the United States. As soon as they are born, they become United States citizens.

However, many other people become citizens of our country in a different way. These people were born in another country. They are immigrants who become **naturalized citizens** of the United States by choice. To become a naturalized citizen, a person must do many things that are required by United States laws.

### B. Preparing to Become a Naturalized Citizen

Nine-year-old John came to the United States from Poland when he was three years old. For almost five years, John and his parents lived in the United States. But they were not citizens of this country. They had permission from our government to live and work here, but they could not vote. John's father and mother wanted to become citizens of the United States. John did, too.

When John's family had been **residents** of the United States for five years, they were allowed to apply to become citizens. A resident is a person who lives in a place and is not a visitor. John's parents filled out many papers for the United States government. The government fingerprinted John's parents and took their pictures.

Then John's parents had to take a test on the history and government of the United States and show that they could speak and write simple English. They had to show that they were people who obey the laws of the United States.

Long ago these immigrants came to the United States from Europe. They arrived on a boat at Ellis Island, in New York City.

▶ What statue did the immigrants see as they came close to land?

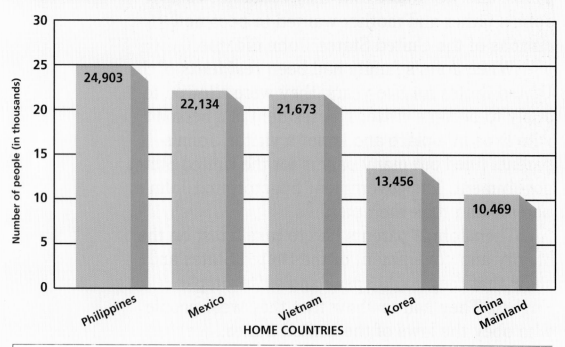

## NATURALIZED CITIZENS: WHERE ARE THEY FROM?

Number of people (in thousands)

- Philippines: 24,903
- Mexico: 22,134
- Vietnam: 21,673
- Korea: 13,456
- China Mainland: 10,469

HOME COUNTRIES

In a recent year, 242,063 people became naturalized citizens of the United States. More of them came from one of these five countries than from any other country.
► Which country did the most people come from?

## C. The Naturalization Ceremony

Finally the day came for John's parents to become naturalized citizens. John would become a citizen along with them. At last, John and his parents would each receive a paper that said they were citizens.

The family became citizens at a ceremony at the courthouse. One hundred people became naturalized citizens that day. A high school band played, and the chorus sang. A judge gave a welcoming speech about good citizenship. John's parents said the **Oath of American Citizenship**. By saying this oath, they promised to give up their

Taking the Oath of Citizenship is one of the last steps to becoming a United States citizen.
▶ What people must take this oath?

loyalty to their old country. They promised to be loyal to the United States. And, finally, each new citizen was called up in front of the room to get a certificate of naturalization. This certificate shows that the person is a naturalized citizen.

LESSON 3 REVIEW

THINK AND WRITE

A. What are two ways to become a United States citizen?
B. What is one thing that a person living in the United States cannot do until he or she becomes a citizen?
C. How do you think people feel when they become United States citizens at a naturalization ceremony?

SKILLS CHECK

MAP SKILL

Look at the graph on page 178. Which countries are on the graph? Find these countries on the world map in the Atlas at the back of your book. On which continent are most of these countries located?

# Important Writings and Symbols of the United States

## THINK ABOUT WHAT YOU KNOW

What are some symbols of the United States? Where do you see these symbols?

## STUDY THE VOCABULARY

**Declaration of Independence**
**Constitution**

**Bill of Rights**
**Pledge of Allegiance**
**national anthem**

## FOCUS YOUR READING

What are some important writings and symbols of the United States?

## A. Many Differences, But One People

The United States is a big country with many people. Some of us were born here. Some of us were born in other countries.

The people of our country come from many backgrounds, live in different kinds of places, and do different kinds of work. But, as Americans, we share many important things. The more you know about the things we all share, the more you will feel like a member of the big community that is the United States.

## B. Important Writings We Share

The people of the United States share knowledge of their country's history. Adults who become naturalized citizens pass a test that shows they know important writings of our country. But all citizens of the United States must know about these writings. The originals are in the National Archives (AHR kyvz), in Washington, D.C.

In 1776, men of the colonies that became the first states of our country wrote the **Declaration of Independence**. This was a message written to the king of Great Britain. It gave the reasons that the colonies no longer belonged to Great Britain.

Some years later the **Constitution** was written. It is the basic set of laws of the United States. The Constitution of the United States tells what powers our national government has.

The **Bill of Rights** is the first ten additions to the Constitution. These additions tell what rights belong to the citizens of the United States. For example, citizens are free to talk or write about their own ideas. They are free to meet together.

This painting shows Thomas Jefferson (seated at left) who wrote most of the Declaration of Independence. Benjamin Franklin (standing at left) and John Adams (standing at right) helped with the work.
► What do you think the artist wanted to show about these men?

## C. The Pledge of Allegiance

A pledge is a promise. The word *allegiance* means "loyalty." When you say the **Pledge of Allegiance**, you are promising to be loyal to your country and its flag.

Read the Pledge of Allegiance below. Find the words *Republic*, *indivisible*, *liberty*, and *justice*. These are important words. A republic is a nation where people vote for leaders. When something is indivisible, it cannot be divided. *Liberty* means "freedom." *Justice* means "fairness."

Think of the Pledge of Allegiance. Say it to yourself in your own words.

*The Pledge of Allegiance
to the Flag
of the United States*

*I pledge allegiance to
the flag of the
United States
of America and
to the Republic
for which it stands,
one Nation under God,
indivisible, with liberty
and justice for all.*

This class always begins the school day by saying the Pledge of Allegiance.
► What does the pledge help us remember?

After this battle at Fort McHenry, in Baltimore, Maryland, Francis Scott Key wrote the words to the "Star-Spangled Banner."
▶ Describe the flag that Key saw flying, shown at top left.

## D. Our National Anthem

Francis Scott Key wrote the words to "The Star-Spangled Banner" during the War of 1812. This war was between the United States and Great Britain. Key wrote the words that begin "Oh, say, can you see, by the dawn's early light," when he saw the United States flag still flying after a battle. The flag meant that the United States had won.

"The Star-Spangled Banner" became the **national anthem** of the United States in 1931. A national anthem is the official song of a country. It is sung at all special events.

Francis Scott Key

**183**

You can go to see the Liberty Bell at the Liberty Bell Pavilion in Philadelphia, Pennsylvania.
▶ Why, do you think, do people go to see the bell?

Bald eagle

### E. Symbols That Make Us Proud

You know about some symbols of the United States, such as the Statue of Liberty. Our most important symbol is our flag. The stripes stand for the 13 states that made up our country when it began. In the beginning the flag also had 13 stars, one for each state. Today the flag has 50 stars, one for each of our 50 states. When new states became part of our country, new stars were added.

The Liberty Bell is another important symbol of the United States. This bell rang out when the Declaration of Independence was signed in Philadelphia in July of 1776. The bell was rung every July from 1776 to 1835, when it cracked.

The bald eagle is another symbol of the United States. This eagle is not really bald at all, but the white feathers on its head make it appear to be bald. The bald eagle is found only in North America, which is one reason it was chosen as a symbol of our country.

The bald eagle became part of the Great Seal of the United States in 1782. The Great Seal is used on important papers. But you can see a copy of both sides of the seal if you look at a dollar bill. The bald eagle is on the front of the seal. The eagle holds an olive branch, which stands for peace. The eagle also holds a bundle of arrows. The arrows stand for war. The Great Seal shows that the United States wants peace but is prepared for war if it is necessary.

Great Seal

"Diplomatic Reception Rooms, Department of State" United States

## LESSON 4 REVIEW

### THINK AND WRITE

A. How is the United States like one big community?

B. Why, do you think, do many people visit the National Archives, in Washington, D.C.?

C. When you say the Pledge of Allegiance, what promise are you making?

D. In your opinion, why did Francis Scott Key write "The Star-Spangled Banner"?

E. In your opinion, why does your book say the flag is the most important symbol of our country?

### SKILLS CHECK

**THINKING SKILL**

What would you choose as a symbol for your class? Design a symbol that represents your class. Include an animal in your symbol. Include something that shows how many students are in the class.

## UNCLE SAM

You have learned about some important symbols of the United States. Uncle Sam is a symbol for our country, as well as a nickname. You know what nicknames are, and you may even have one yourself. But do you know how the United States got the nickname Uncle Sam?

To know how the symbol and nickname Uncle Sam came to be, you must know something about the War of 1812. This war was fought between the United States and Great Britain. One cause of the war was that the British were stopping and searching American ships at sea. Some Americans thought the British also were causing trouble between the Indians and settlers in the West. Not everyone in the United States was in favor of the War of 1812. Many westerners and southerners wanted it, but many northerners did not.

It was during the war that northerners began calling our government and our country Uncle Sam.

New cartoons appeared in newspapers, showing the United States as Uncle Sam.

He was a human figure wearing a suit of red, white, and blue with stars and stripes. At first these cartoons were made by people who did not like what the United States was doing during the war. But soon, just about everyone called the United States Uncle Sam.

In 1836 a newspaper reported that the term *Uncle Sam* was given to the United States because of the initials *U.S.* on government wagons. After a while, even the government made posters of Uncle Sam to represent the United States. The most famous poster is shown below.

In 1961, Congress gave a man named Samuel Wilson of Troy, New York, credit for starting the nickname Uncle Sam. During the War of 1812, Wilson had supplied the army with barrels of supplies stamped *U.S.*

## Thinking for Yourself

1. To whom is Uncle Sam pointing, and saying, "I WANT YOU"?
2. President Kennedy said, "Ask not what your country can do for you, but what you can do for your country." Why is it important to serve your country?
3. Do you think Uncle Sam is a good symbol to represent our country? Explain your answer.

## USING THE VOCABULARY

rights       **Bill of Rights**
recycle      **national**
naturalized     **anthem**
    citizen

Number your paper from *1* to *5*. Read each question and choose the correct answer from the underlined words.

1.  A <u>resident</u>, <u>right</u>, or <u>responsibility</u> is something that is due a person.
2.  "The Star-Spangled Banner" is our <u>national anthem</u>, <u>Oath of American Citizenship</u>, or <u>national pledge</u>.
3.  <u>Recycle</u>, <u>volunteer</u>, or <u>property</u> means "to be used again in some way."
4.  To become a <u>writer</u>, <u>volunteer</u>, or <u>naturalized citizen</u>, a person must do many things that are required by United States laws.
5.  The <u>Bill of Rights</u>, <u>Oath of American Citizenship</u>, or <u>property</u> tells what rights citizens of the United States have.

## REMEMBERING WHAT YOU READ

On a separate sheet of paper, answer the questions in complete sentences.

1.  What rights do you have at school?
2.  What are some words that let others know you care about them?
3.  How can a member of a community show good citizenship?
4.  When can a person living in the United States become a naturalized citizen?
5.  What is the Declaration of Independence?

## TYING ART TO SOCIAL STUDIES

Make a colorful chart to help you remember rules and responsibilities. Make the chart for one week. Design stickers to put on the chart every time you remember to do the right thing. See how many stickers your chart has at the end of the week.

## THINKING CRITICALLY

On a separate sheet of paper, answer the following in complete sentences.

1. When a friend is sick, how can you act responsibly?
2. How can you show respect for other people's property?
3. What things do you do that show you care about yourself?
4. What might be hard about leaving one country to become a citizen of another country?
5. What does the Pledge of Allegiance mean to you?

## SUMMARIZING THE CHAPTER

**Copy this graphic organizer on a separate sheet of paper. Under the main idea for each lesson, write three facts that support the main idea.**

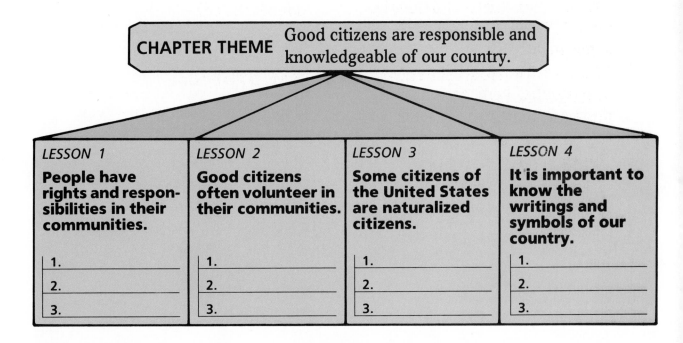

**CHAPTER THEME** Good citizens are responsible and knowledgeable of our country.

| LESSON 1 | LESSON 2 | LESSON 3 | LESSON 4 |
|---|---|---|---|
| **People have rights and responsibilities in their communities.** | **Good citizens often volunteer in their communities.** | **Some citizens of the United States are naturalized citizens.** | **It is important to know the writings and symbols of our country.** |
| 1. _____ | 1. _____ | 1. _____ | 1. _____ |
| 2. _____ | 2. _____ | 2. _____ | 2. _____ |
| 3. _____ | 3. _____ | 3. _____ | 3. _____ |

# OUR NATIONAL HOLIDAYS

**W**hen we celebrate national holidays, we can learn about and remember events that are important to our country.

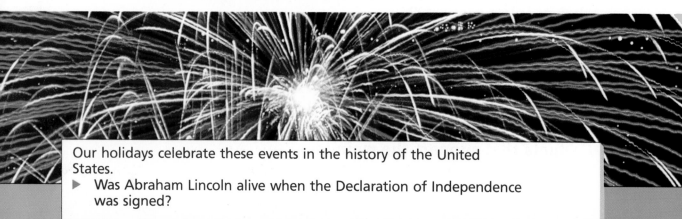

Our holidays celebrate these events in the history of the United States.

▶ Was Abraham Lincoln alive when the Declaration of Independence was signed?

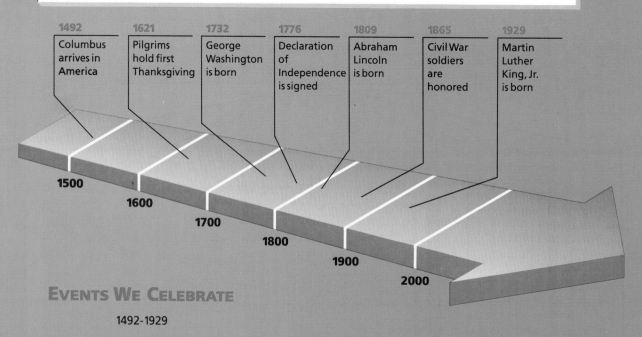

| 1492 | 1621 | 1732 | 1776 | 1809 | 1865 | 1929 |
|------|------|------|------|------|------|------|
| Columbus arrives in America | Pilgrims hold first Thanksgiving | George Washington is born | Declaration of Independence is signed | Abraham Lincoln is born | Civil War soldiers are honored | Martin Luther King, Jr. is born |

1500
1600
1700
1800
1900
2000

**EVENTS WE CELEBRATE**

1492-1929

190

## Columbus Day

**THINK ABOUT WHAT YOU KNOW**
What are your three favorite holidays?

**STUDY THE VOCABULARY**
**time line   explorer   navigation   cartography**

**FOCUS YOUR READING**
What kind of person was Columbus?

## A. Learning About Time Lines

Mrs. Allen's class has been studying American holidays. On these holidays we remember great people and events in the history of the United States.

Mrs. Allen's class made a huge **time line** showing some events we celebrate. A time line shows events in order. Often the events are from the past. A time line is divided into equal parts. Each part stands for the same amount of time, such as a year or 20 years. Look at the time line on the previous page. What amount of time does each part represent?

When the time line was finished and taped to the classroom wall, Mrs. Allen divided the class into six groups. Each group was assigned to give a short program on one American holiday.

Each group was to use the card catalog in the library to find books about the holiday. The card catalog lists books by author, subject, or title. You might find the card catalog in drawers or on a computer screen.

## B. Celebrating Columbus Day

Christopher Columbus

In October, Keisha's group prepared a report about Columbus Day. They wrote a TV interview. Keisha played the part of the TV host. Robert played Columbus, the **explorer**. An explorer travels to places that are unknown or not well known. Although there were many Native Americans in America, Europeans did not know America existed.

**TV HOST**: The second Monday in October is Columbus Day. Other countries in the Americas and parts of Italy and Spain celebrate Columbus Day.

And now, here is Columbus himself! Columbus, why do so many countries celebrate your journey from Europe to America in 1492?

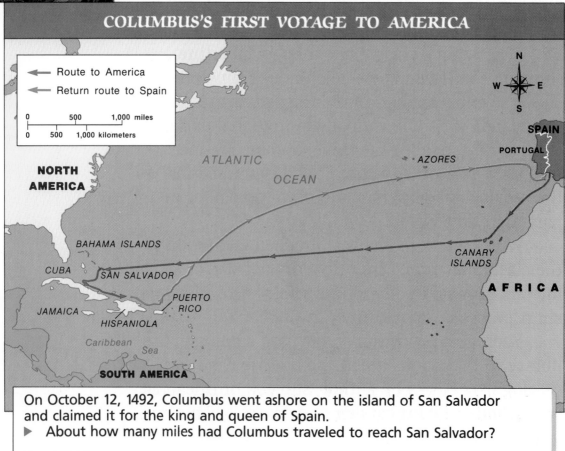

### COLUMBUS'S FIRST VOYAGE TO AMERICA

← Route to America
← Return route to Spain

0    500    1,000 miles
0   500  1,000 kilometers

N W E S

SPAIN
PORTUGAL

ATLANTIC OCEAN

AZORES

NORTH AMERICA

CANARY ISLANDS

AFRICA

BAHAMA ISLANDS

CUBA  SAN SALVADOR

PUERTO RICO

JAMAICA

HISPANIOLA

Caribbean Sea

SOUTH AMERICA

On October 12, 1492, Columbus went ashore on the island of San Salvador and claimed it for the king and queen of Spain.

▶ About how many miles had Columbus traveled to reach San Salvador?

**COLUMBUS**: H-m-m-. Frankly, I'm a little surprised at all the celebrating. After all, I did set out for the Indies. I wanted to find a shorter route to the Indies so I could bring back spices, gold, and precious stones. I really thought that I was in the Indies when I got to America! That's why I called the Native Americans Indians.

I guess they celebrate my day in America because after my trips there, many explorers and settlers left Europe for the Americas. They celebrate in Italy because that's where I was born and in Spain because the Queen and King of Spain gave me the money and ships for my trip.

Columbus looking for land

## C. Columbus's Life

**TV HOST**: But didn't you have a hard time convincing the king and queen to help you?

**COLUMBUS**: Yes, I did. It's lucky that I believed in what I was going to do, or I wouldn't have kept asking the king and queen for help.

**TV HOST**: Did you always want to be a sailor?

**COLUMBUS**: Oh, yes! My parents wanted me to become a weaver like other people in my family. But I wanted to see the world! At age 19, I went to sea. At 21, I saw the Atlantic Ocean for the first time. That did it! I decided to learn everything that I could about **navigation**, or steering a ship. I decided to learn **cartography** (kahr TAHG ruh fee), or mapmaking. If I was going to cross the Atlantic Ocean, I had to know a lot first!

**TV HOST**: So you studied hard. But in spite of your hard work, weren't some of your ideas about the Atlantic Ocean and the world still a little, well, wrong?

**COLUMBUS**: I was right about the most important thing, wasn't I? The world *is* round!

I do know now that the Atlantic Ocean is bigger than I thought it was. I also realize that if you sail west from Europe, the Americas are between Europe and the Indies. But the Americas weren't on maps before 1492. How could I know they were there?

Even people who study like I did and believe in what they are doing make mistakes! After all, they have to come up with their own ideas, and some of these ideas will be wrong. But people who dare to be wrong can do great and wonderful things!

**TV HOST**: Well, you do have a point, Columbus. Is that your advice for young people today?

**COLUMBUS**: Yes, of course. Study hard. Believe in yourself. Keep trying, and don't ever be afraid to be wrong now and then. There's no shame at all in that, no shame at all.

**TV HOST**: Thank you very much for your time, Mr. Columbus.

Keisha playing
TV host

LESSON **1** REVIEW

**THINK AND WRITE**

A. If you were planning a time line of your life, why would you have to know when things happened?

B. Why is Columbus Day celebrated in so many countries?

C. Why was it important for Columbus to believe in himself, study hard, and keep trying?

**SKILLS CHECK**

**WRITING SKILL**

What kinds of things do people learn from making mistakes? Write about a mistake you made. What did you learn from it?

194

## Thanksgiving Day

**THINK ABOUT WHAT YOU KNOW**

How do you celebrate Thanksgiving Day? What kinds of food do you eat?

**STUDY THE VOCABULARY**

**Pilgrim    tradition**

**FOCUS YOUR READING**

How was the first Thanksgiving like Thanksgiving today?

### A. The Pilgrims Come to America

In November, Ramón's group gave their report about Thanksgiving. With their teacher they also made corn bread, which they served to the class after the report. You can read the recipe for the corn bread on page 198.

**RAMÓN**: On the fourth Thursday in November, families and friends in the United States celebrate Thanksgiving Day together.

The first Thanksgiving lasted for three whole days. It was celebrated by the **Pilgrims** and their guests, the Indians.

**JOHN**: The Pilgrims came to America from England in 1620. They came to be free to worship God as they chose. They sailed in a boat named the *Mayflower*, which landed on the coast of what is

Pilgrims in America

now the state of Massachusetts. The Pilgrims began to build a community, which they called Plymouth.

The first winter in Plymouth was cold and snowy. There was not enough to eat, and half the people died. When spring came, the Indians helped the Pilgrims plant corn and other crops. Pilgrim families also planted kitchen gardens near their houses. There, they planted seeds they had brought from England.

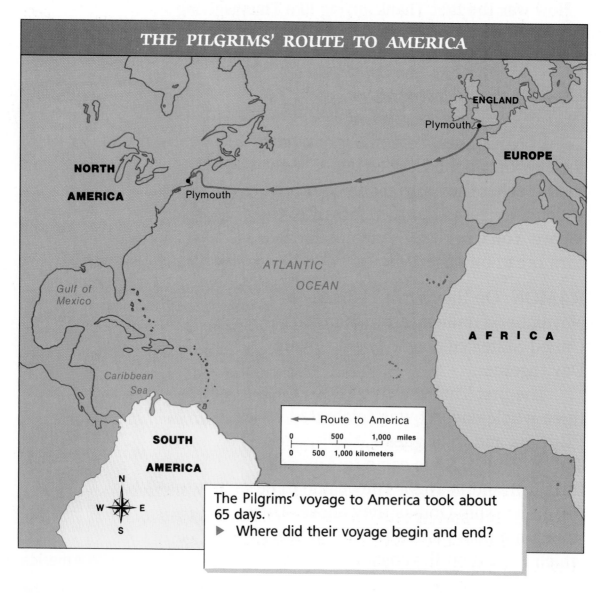

## THE PILGRIMS' ROUTE TO AMERICA

Route to America

0    500    1,000  miles
0   500  1,000 kilometers

The Pilgrims' voyage to America took about 65 days.
▶ Where did their voyage begin and end?

This painting shows the Pilgrims during the first winter in America.
▶ What made the winter so difficult for the Pilgrims?

## B. A Tradition Continues

**SARAH**: In the fall of 1621, there was a good harvest. There was enough food for everybody. The Pilgrims brought their **traditions** to America. Traditions are old beliefs and ways of doing things. One tradition was to celebrate the harvest.

Between September 21 and November 9, 1621, the Pilgrims held their first harvest celebration in America. They planned a feast, and Indians who had helped them were invited.

**RAMÓN**: To prepare for the feast, the Pilgrim men went fishing and hunting. The women made bread. The children picked wild berries and plums. The Indians went deer hunting.

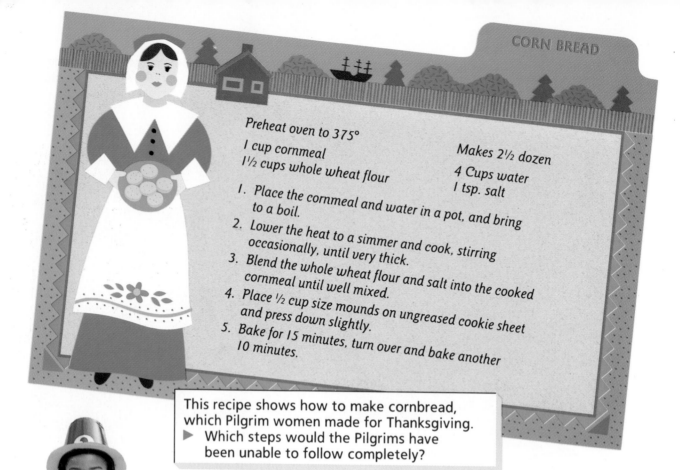

Preheat oven to 375°

1 cup cornmeal
1½ cups whole wheat flour

Makes 2½ dozen
4 Cups water
1 tsp. salt

1. Place the cornmeal and water in a pot, and bring to a boil.
2. Lower the heat to a simmer and cook, stirring occasionally, until very thick.
3. Blend the whole wheat flour and salt into the cooked cornmeal until well mixed.
4. Place ½ cup size mounds on ungreased cookie sheet and press down slightly.
5. Bake for 15 minutes, turn over and bake another 10 minutes.

This recipe shows how to make cornbread, which Pilgrim women made for Thanksgiving.
▶ Which steps would the Pilgrims have been unable to follow completely?

**SARAH**: We don't know everything that the Pilgrims and the Indians ate on the first Thanksgiving. But from two letters written at the time, we know that the Indians brought the meat of five deer. Wild turkey, fish, and bread were part of the feast. Probably there were vegetables, but no potatoes. Pumpkin might have been served, and perhaps some fruit tarts. There weren't many desserts though, because there was very little sugar.

**RAMÓN**: There were 140 people at the Thanksgiving feast. Ninety were Indian men, and fifty were Pilgrims. Only four of the Pilgrims were women. The other women had died during the hard winter.

All the food was put on the table at once, even the desserts. There were no table decorations because that was not part of the Pilgrims' tradition.

Ramón serving corn bread

People ate with spoons and knives, but there were no forks. A person would reach for food from a dish in the middle of the table. Fingers were often used for eating.

## C. A National Holiday

**JOHN**: Thanksgiving did not become a national holiday until many years after the Pilgrims' feast. In 1863, Sarah Josepha Hale, who wrote "Mary Had a Little Lamb" convinced President Lincoln to make Thanksgiving a national holiday.

**SARAH**: Today, people still enjoy a feast on Thanksgiving Day. Many of them eat roast turkey, cranberry sauce, mashed potatoes and sweet potatoes, peas or beans, and pumpkin pie. Most Americans give thanks to God for the good things they have received during the past year.

Thanksgiving feast today

*LESSON* **2** *REVIEW*

**THINK AND WRITE**

A. In your opinion, what would the Pilgrims have looked forward to during the winter of 1620?

B. How do you think the Pilgrims decided what food to serve at the feast?

C. Why, do you think, is Thanksgiving Day an important national holiday?

**SKILLS CHECK**

**WRITING SKILL**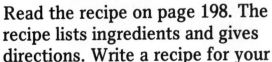

Read the recipe on page 198. The recipe lists ingredients and gives directions. Write a recipe for your favorite sandwich.

# Martin Luther King, Jr.'s Birthday

### THINK ABOUT WHAT YOU KNOW

What qualities does a great person have? How do these qualities help the person do great things?

### STUDY THE VOCABULARY

**civil rights**   **nonviolence**   **boycott**

### FOCUS YOUR READING

How did Dr. King use nonviolence to bring about change?

King's birthplace

MARTIN LUTHER KING, JR. WAS BORN IN THIS HOUSE JANUARY 15. 1929

## A. Dr. King's Early Experiences

In January, Pam and Mike gave their group's report about Martin Luther King. Pam began by telling the class that on the third Monday in January we celebrate the birth date of Dr. Martin Luther King, Jr. Mike added that Dr. King was an important leader for **civil rights,** which are the lawful rights of all Americans.

Martin Luther King was born on January 15, 1929, in Atlanta, Georgia. He was a bright child, who learned to read at a very young age. Like many other children, some of the first things he read were signs. When Martin saw signs that said "Whites Only" near water fountains, lunch counters, movies, and swimming pools, he asked what they meant. He soon discovered that

African Americans could not use the same places as white people. He could not understand this unfairness, and soon he began wanting to do something to change it.

## B. Using Nonviolence to Bring About Change

At the age of 15, Martin started college. He attended other schools, too. He began to learn about the ideas of Gandhi, a former leader in India. Gandhi taught people to use **nonviolence** to bring about change. When people use nonviolence, they do not hurt others. They find better ways to change things. They refuse to do things they know are wrong. Dr. King began to think that black people could use nonviolence to gain their civil rights.

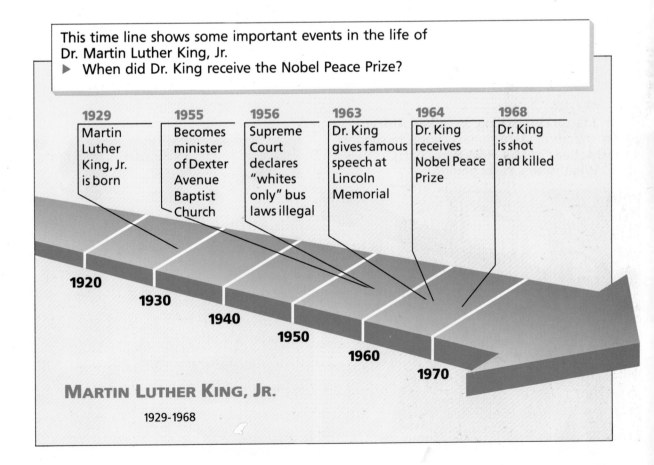

This time line shows some important events in the life of Dr. Martin Luther King, Jr.
▶ When did Dr. King receive the Nobel Peace Prize?

**1929** — Martin Luther King, Jr. is born

**1955** — Becomes minister of Dexter Avenue Baptist Church

**1956** — Supreme Court declares "whites only" bus laws illegal

**1963** — Dr. King gives famous speech at Lincoln Memorial

**1964** — Dr. King receives Nobel Peace Prize

**1968** — Dr. King is shot and killed

1920 1930 1940 1950 1960 1970

**MARTIN LUTHER KING, JR.**
1929-1968

After Dr. King finished school, he became the minister of the Dexter Avenue Baptist Church, in Montgomery, Alabama. Mrs. Rosa Parks lived in Montgomery, too. One night she took the bus home from work. She was very tired, and she sat down in a "whites only" seat. That was against the law. When the bus driver demanded that she give her seat to a white man, she refused. Mrs. Parks was arrested and taken to jail.

When the black people of Montgomery heard about Mrs. Parks, they were angry. Dr. King spoke to them. He said the "whites only" seats were wrong. Dr. King said the black people should not hate or do anything violent. Instead, they should **boycott**, or refuse to use, the buses. For almost a year, the black people of Montgomery did not ride the buses. Finally the United States Supreme Court said the "whites only" seats were illegal.

Dr. Martin Luther King, Jr., asked African Americans in Montgomery (right) to support the actions of Mrs. Rosa Parks (left).
▶ What is Mrs. Parks doing?

## C. Marches, Speeches, and the Nobel Prize

After Dr. King and the other black people in Montgomery won their rights on the buses, Dr. King led many marches to gain other rights. In some places he was laughed at, beaten, or thrown in jail. In August, 1963, Dr. King gave his most famous speech to more than 200,000 people. This speech included the words, "I have a dream." Dr. King's dream was of a United States where all people had equal rights and shared respect and love for one another.

In 1964, Dr. King received the Nobel Peace Prize, which is given to the person who has done the most for peace in the world. In 1968, Martin Luther King was shot and killed while he was trying to gain rights for poor people. But millions of people all over the world remember him today.

Dr. King accepting the Nobel Peace Prize

---

LESSON **3** REVIEW

### THINK AND WRITE

A. How did signs that said "Whites Only" take away the civil rights of black people?

B. In what way did Rosa Parks follow the ideas of Gandhi and King?

C. What was Dr. King's dream?

### SKILLS CHECK

**THINKING SKILL**

Dr. King had a dream about a better world. Draw a picture that shows something you would change to make the world a better place than it is today.

## Presidents' Day

THINK ABOUT WHAT YOU KNOW

Do you have a favorite President of the United States? What kind of person was that President?

STUDY THE VOCABULARY

**Emancipation Proclamation**  **plantation**
**slave**

FOCUS YOUR READING

How were President Washington and President Lincoln alike and different?

### A. What Is Presidents' Day?

Adam's group read poems for Presidents' Day, which is celebrated on the third Monday in February. This holiday honors two great men, George Washington and Abraham Lincoln. George Washington was the leader of the army that won our independence, or freedom, from Great Britain. People admired Washington for being a good leader. They asked him to become the first President of the United States.

Abraham Lincoln was our sixteenth President. He was born in a log cabin in Kentucky. He went to school for less than a year, but he read every book that he could get. When Lincoln became President, there were many **slaves** in the United States. Slaves belonged to other people and had to do what their owner's said. Lincoln wrote the **Emancipation Proclamation**, which led to freedom for slaves.

## B. Remembering Washington

**ADAM**: Our poem is "Washington," by Nancy Byrd Turner. When the poem begins, Washington is at his **plantation**, or large farm, called Mount Vernon. There is a word in the poem that you may not know. It is *whippoorwill*, which is a bird. When you listen to the poem, imagine that Washington is relaxing on his farm. Then he is asked to lead the soldiers in the war against Great Britain.

**ADAM, RAFAEL, AND JENNIFER**:

*Washington*

He played by the river when he was young,
He raced with rabbits along the hills,
He fished for minnows and climbed and swung,
And hooted back at the whippoorwills.
Strong and slender and tall he grew—
And then, one morning, the bugles blew.

Over the hills the summons came,
Over the river's shining rim.
He said that the bugles called his name,
He knew that his country needed him,
And he answered, "Coming!" and marched away
For many a night and many a day.

Perhaps when the marches were hot and long
He'd think of the river flowing by
Or, camping under the winter sky,
Would hear the whippoorwill's far-off song.
Working or playing, in peace or strife,
He loved America all his life!

Washington inspecting his troops

After Adam's group read their poem, they showed a picture of the Washington Monument, in Washington, D.C.. Many people honor our first President by visiting this monument.

When you think of George Washington, remember that he was a successful businessman and farmer. He could have led a comfortable life at Mount Vernon. But instead, he chose to serve his country in war and in peace.

As the leader of the American army against the British, Washington suffered with his troops. His soldiers loved him so much that they wanted to make him king of the United States. Instead, he became President and helped to create the kind of government we have today.

The Washington Monument (left) was built to honor George Washington (right).
► What do you think the artist wanted to show in his portrait of Washington?

**ADAM**: Our second poem is "Abraham Lincoln," by Mildred Plew Meigs. The poem tells what kind of person Lincoln was and why people loved him.

**CAM AND RANDY**:

### Abraham Lincoln

*Remember he was poor and country-bred;*
 *His face was lined; he walked with awkward gait.*
*Smart people laughed at him sometimes and said,*
 *"How can so very plain a man be great?"*

*Remember he was humble, used to toil.*
 *Strong arms he had to build a shack, a fence,*
*Long legs to tramp the woods, to plow the soil,*
 *A head chuck full of backwoods common sense.*

*Remember all he ever had he earned.*
 *He walked in time through stately White House*
  *doors;*
*But all he knew of men and life he learned*
 *In little backwoods cabins, country stores.*

*Remember that his eyes could light with fun;*
 *That wisdom, courage, set his name apart;*
*But when the rest is duly said and done,*
 *Remember that men loved him for his heart.*

Young Lincoln

**RANDY**: As President, Lincoln worked very hard. He wrote all his own speeches. He spent many hours each day talking with people, including widows who had lost their husbands in the war. At night, he often visited soldiers in the hospital. To relax, Lincoln sometimes went to the theater to see a play.

We can honor Abraham Lincoln (left) by visiting the Lincoln Memorial, in Washington, D.C.
► What thoughts about Lincoln might people have when they visit here?

**ADAM**: On April 14, 1865, Lincoln was shot as he watched a play at Ford's Theatre, in Washington, D.C. He died the next day.

A train carried Lincoln's body from Washington, D.C., to Springfield, Illinois, which was his home. People lined the tracks to say good-by to "Father Abraham" as the train passed. Today many people visit the Lincoln Memorial to honor this great President.

## LESSON 4 REVIEW

### THINK AND WRITE

A. How were George Washington and Abraham Lincoln alike?

B. In what ways did Washington show his love for his country?

C. What kind of person was Abraham Lincoln?

### SKILLS CHECK

**WRITING SKILL**

Write a poem about Washington or Lincoln. Tell what kind of person this President was.

## Memorial Day

**THINK ABOUT WHAT YOU KNOW**

Do you like watching a parade? What are some reasons people have parades?

**STUDY THE VOCABULARY**

**Civil War**   **veteran**

**FOCUS YOUR READING**

Why do people observe Memorial Day?

## A. The Civil War

In 1861, the **Civil War** in the United States began. This was a war between the northern and southern parts of our country. The North and the South did not agree about slavery. The South decided to break away from the North and form a country separate from the United States. The Civil War was fought by the North to keep the United States as one country.

The Civil War raged for four years. Finally the North defeated the South, and the war ended. Many soldiers had been hurt or killed. Often, soldiers who had lived through the war returned home to find that some of their friends or relatives were dead. Perhaps their houses had been burned to the ground.

General Lee, who led the soldiers fighting for the South, returned home when the war was over.
▶ What might he have been thinking about on his way home?

**209**

## B. Memorial Day Long Ago and Today

No one is exactly sure when Memorial Day got started. Right after the Civil War, some women in the South decorated both northern and southern soldiers' graves with flowers. **Veterans** of the northern army organized the first Memorial Day observance at the National Cemetery, near Washington, D.C. Veterans have served in the armed forces in defense of their country.

In 1966, the United States government said that Waterloo, New York, was officially the birthplace of Memorial Day. In 1866, a druggist in

This picture shows children on Memorial Day more than 100 years ago.
▶ What are the children doing to show that they remember the soldiers who died in war?

Waterloo had organized a celebration to honor veterans of the Civil War, both living and dead. There had been a parade to the cemetery, to salute the veterans from Waterloo. At the cemetery, flowers were placed on soldiers' graves.

Vietnam Veterans Memorial on Memorial Day

Memorial Day was once called Decoration Day. Today we still decorate the graves of soldiers who died in the Civil War and in other wars. The photograph at the right shows some of the flowers and flags brought to the Vietnam Veterans Memorial on a recent Memorial Day.

Many families place flowers at the graves of all their loved ones on Memorial Day. They use the day to remember these loved family members and friends.

In many states, Americans observe Memorial Day on the last Monday in May. Most southern states have their own day for honoring their dead. Although the date for celebrating Memorial Day varies from place to place, it is always in the spring. That is the season when flowers grow.

## LESSON 5 REVIEW

### THINK AND WRITE

A. What makes civil war so terrible?

B. In what ways do people honor the living and the dead on Memorial Day?

### SKILLS CHECK

**MAP SKILL**

Find Waterloo, New York, in your Gazetteer. Write three facts about Waterloo.

# Independence Day

THINK ABOUT WHAT YOU KNOW

How do you celebrate the Fourth of July? What is your favorite part of the celebration?

STUDY THE VOCABULARY

**delegate**    **colony**

FOCUS YOUR READING

What event do we celebrate on the Fourth of July?

## A. The Birthday of Our Country

During the last week of the school year, Nathan's group reported on Independence Day. Nathan explained why Independence Day is celebrated on July 4.

**NATHAN**: Independence Day is also called the Fourth of July. It is the birthday of our country, the United States of America.

The first Independence Day was celebrated on July 4, 1776. On that day, the Declaration of Independence was signed by people who had come to a meeting in Philadelphia, Pennsylvania. They were **delegates**, or representatives, from the American **colonies**. The Declaration said that the American colonies that belonged to Great Britain would become free and independent. A colony is a group of people who live in a place that is located a long way from the country that governs it.

Removing the symbol of Great Britain

On that first Independence Day, church bells were rung. Bonfires were lit. Cheering crowds filled the streets of cities and towns.

The United States has been an independent nation for more than 200 years. During all those years, the Fourth of July has been one of our biggest holidays.

**EMMA**: On the first Independence Day, bells rang out and bands played. Parades, picnics, and fireworks have been part of Fourth of July celebrations for a long time. At early celebrations, guns and cannons were fired. Sometimes people were hurt, and laws about the use of fireworks and firearms on the holiday were passed.

This picture shows people at an Independence Day celebration about 100 years ago.
▶ What are the people doing to celebrate the day?

## B. An Old-Fashioned Fourth of July

**ANN**: My great-grandmother told me how she celebrated Independence Day as a child. The cousins, aunts, uncles, and grandparents gathered at my great-grandmother's farm. Each family brought food—ham, beef, salads, stuffed eggs, apple sauce, bread, cakes, and pies.

My great-grandmother's grandpa told stories about coming to America. Someone played the fiddle or accordion. Everybody sang songs about heroes, hardships, or friendships.

Then there were games. They played tag, follow the leader, blindman's bluff, and marbles. Soon everyone went home to do their chores.

There were no fireworks, but just before bedtime, the children were allowed to bang and clang on anything they could find.

**NATHAN**: Celebrations of Independence Day have not changed very much. Many families today have a picnic. They watch a noisy fireworks display. The Fourth of July is still a birthday celebration for us all.

Fourth of July Picnic today

*LESSON* **6** *REVIEW*

### THINK AND WRITE

A. When was the first Independence Day?
B. How did the family in this lesson celebrate the Fourth of July?

### SKILLS CHECK

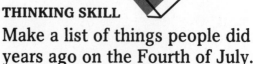

**THINKING SKILL**

Make a list of things people did years ago on the Fourth of July. Put a check by the things you might also do on the Fourth of July.

# CHAPTER 9 PUTTING IT ALL TOGETHER

## USING THE VOCABULARY

| | |
|---|---|
| explorer | Emancipation |
| cartography | Proclamation |
| Pilgrim | Civil War |
| traditions | veterans |
| civil rights | colony |
| nonviolence | delegate |

On a separate sheet of paper, write the word or words from above that best complete the sentences.

1. The lawful rights of all Americans are called _____.
2. A _____ is a representative from the American colonies.
3. An _____ travels to places that are unknown or not well known.
4. People who have fought in wars are called _____.
5. Mapmaking is called _____.
6. One way of bringing about change without hurting others is _____.
7. The _____ came to America from England in 1620.
8. A war between the northern and southern parts of our country was called the _____.
9. _____ are very old beliefs and ways of doing things.
10. Lincoln wrote the _____ which freed the slaves in the United States.

## REMEMBERING WHAT YOU READ

On a separate sheet of paper, answer the questions in complete sentences.

1. Why do we celebrate Columbus Day?
2. How did the families prepare for the Thanksgiving feast?
3. Who was Rosa Parks?
4. Who won the Civil War?
5. Why do we celebrate Independence Day?

## TYING LANGUAGE ARTS TO SOCIAL STUDIES

Invent a holiday of your own. What type of holiday would it be, and when would we celebrate it? Write a short description of your special day.

## A. WHY I NEED THIS SKILL

Like maps and graphs, time lines are tools for learning. They show when events happened, in the order they happened. Time lines usually show events from the past. For example, in Chapter 9 one time line shows some important dates in American history. Another time line shows important events in Dr. Martin Luther King, Jr.'s life.

## B. LEARNING THE SKILL

A time line is a scale drawing. Each segment, or part, of one time line represents the same amount of time as every other segment.

The time line below shows when members of Kelley's family were born. The time line begins with the year 1930 and ends with the year 2000. Each segment represents ten years.

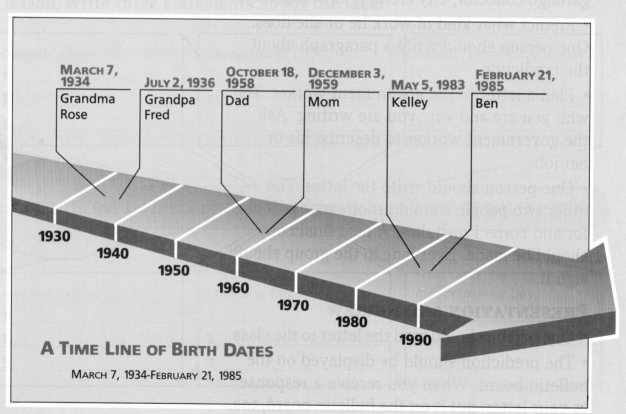

**MARCH 7, 1934** — Grandma Rose
**JULY 2, 1936** — Grandpa Fred
**OCTOBER 18, 1958** — Dad
**DECEMBER 3, 1959** — Mom
**MAY 5, 1983** — Kelley
**FEBRUARY 21, 1985** — Ben

1930  1940  1950  1960  1970  1980  1990

A TIME LINE OF BIRTH DATES
MARCH 7, 1934–FEBRUARY 21, 1985

The oldest person in Kelley's family is the first person on the time line. The youngest person is the last person on the time line.

Kelley's Uncle Paul was born on August 12, 1964. Where would his name go on the time line? Would Uncle Paul be shown before or after Dad and Mom?

## C. Practicing the Skill

You can make a time line of birth dates. You might want to make a time line of birth dates of United States Presidents or of movie stars, astronauts, or musicians. You could make a time line showing birth dates of your family members or friends.

First make a list of people and their birth dates. Write your list in order, from the oldest person to the youngest. Then decide what years your time line must include and how many years each segment will represent.

## D. Applying the Skill

A time line can help you remember everyday things as well as important events. You can make a time line for the school year. Have each segment stand for one month. Show the first day and last day of school. In between, write the events you want to remember. You might decorate the time line with a small picture for each event.

## A. WHY I NEED THIS SKILL

Did you ever read or hear something and wonder if it were true? Some things that people write or say are facts. Facts are statements that can be checked to see if they are true. Other things that people write or say are opinions. Opinions tell what someone feels or believes.

Knowing the difference between facts and opinions can help you become a careful reader and listener. You can become more skillful at deciding whether you agree with what you read or hear.

## B. LEARNING THE SKILL

Facts can be checked to see if they are true. For example, read this statement: *Tallahassee is the state capital of Florida.* You can check in several different books and on maps to see whether this statement is true.

Opinions are neither true nor false. They cannot be checked or proven to be true. For example, Jason had this opinion: *Oranges taste better than other fruit.* You might agree or disagree with this opinion. Jason's opinion is not right or wrong. It is just his opinion.

Sometimes people act as though their opinions were facts. What might happen when people forget the difference between opinions and facts?

## C. PRACTICING THE SKILL

Jennifer is running for class president. She made a speech to her third-grade class. Some of the things she said were facts, and some were opinions. Read her speech and decide whether each numbered statement is a fact or an opinion.

Number a sheet of paper from 1–12. Write *FACT* or *OPINION* after each number. Write *FACT* if the statement can be checked to see if it is true. Write *OPINION* if it expresses Jennifer's feelings or beliefs.

1. I am nine years old.
2. I am the best candidate.
3. I have gone to Oak Street School since kindergarten.
4. Our school playground has only two swing sets.
5. Our recess is too short.
6. Our school store is not very good.
7. Our school store does not sell colored markers.
8. I think we should have a party every Friday.
9. We have too much homework.
10. You should vote for me.

## D. APPLYING THE SKILL

Watch an ad on TV. Write the name of the product that is being advertised. Write some things from the ad that are facts. Write some things that are opinions. Then decide if you would like to buy that product.

Name of Product _____

| FACTS | OPINIONS |
|-------|----------|
|       |          |

Would I buy it?    **YES    NO**
Why, or why not? _____
_____

◄ Many tall buildings, both old and new, make up the skyline of New York City, the largest city in the United States. Towering above them all is the World Trade Center.

▶ In Mexico City, the capital of Mexico, brightly colored small boats crowd the waterways at Xochimilco. These canals were built by the Aztec Indians hundreds of years ago.

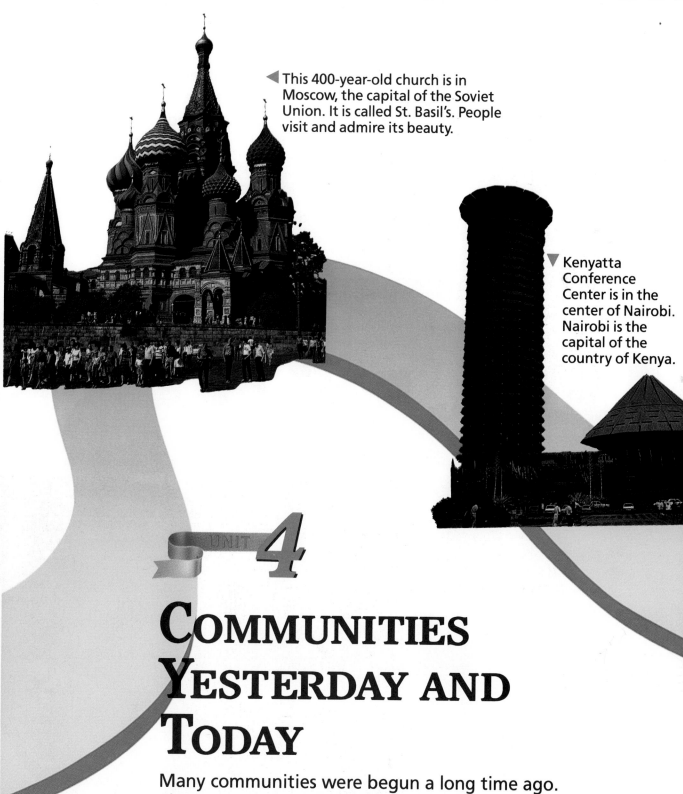

This 400-year-old church is in Moscow, the capital of the Soviet Union. It is called St. Basil's. People visit and admire its beauty.

Kenyatta Conference Center is in the center of Nairobi. Nairobi is the capital of the country of Kenya.

UNIT 4

# COMMUNITIES YESTERDAY AND TODAY

Many communities were begun a long time ago. The people who once lived in these places built the towns and cities that we see today. We learn from studying about the way these people lived.

# CHAPTER 10

# YESTERDAY AND TODAY IN NEW YORK CITY

In 1624, when the Dutch came to Manhattan, it was a quiet island. Today it is the busiest part of New York City, with many tall buildings and millions of people.

# New York City Begins

Have you ever traded something with another person? Why did you do this trading?

**trade**  **harbor**
**market**  **port**

How did New York City begin?

## A. Native Americans on Manhattan Island

This is the story of the beginning of New York City, the largest city in the United States today. Find New York City on a map in your Atlas. Today the busiest, most crowded part of New York City is on an island called Manhattan Island.

Long ago, Manhattan Island was a hilly woodland, with sparkling clean rivers and streams. For thousands of years, Native Americans, or Indians, lived in small villages on the island. The men hunted in the forests and fished in the waters. The women planted corn, beans, pumpkins, and melons. They made clothes from animal skins and the feathers of wild turkeys. The boys and girls helped their parents with the work.

## B. Dutch Traders and Settlers

In 1609, the first Dutch people sailed to Manhattan Island. They came across the Atlantic Ocean from the Netherlands, or Holland, in Europe. Find the Netherlands on a map in your Atlas. They came to **trade** with the Indians. To *trade* means to "exchange something that is valued for something else that is valued."

The Dutch traded beads, cloth, and other goods for Manhattan Island.
► What group traded the island for these things?

The Dutch people traded beads and cloth for furs from the Indians. When the early Dutch traders had obtained all the furs they wanted, they returned to the Netherlands, which was still their home.

In 1624, eight Dutch families came to settle on Manhattan Island. They built homes and made friends with the Native Americans. The Dutch families and the Indians did not live alone on the island. Many wild animals lived there, too. Mountain lions, bears, wolves, deer, beavers, and raccoons were just some of them.

After the Dutch bought Manhattan from the Indians, the Indians continued to live on the island. Some of them lived just outside the Dutch settlement, which they often visited. Trade continued between the two groups.

## C. New Amsterdam Grows

The little Dutch settlement was given the name New Amsterdam, after the city of Amsterdam in the Netherlands. As time went by, ships brought more people across the Atlantic Ocean to New Amsterdam. Cows, horses, pigs, and other farm animals came, too. The

In this picture, New Amsterdam looks like a town in the Netherlands.
▶ Describe the houses and the windmill in the picture.

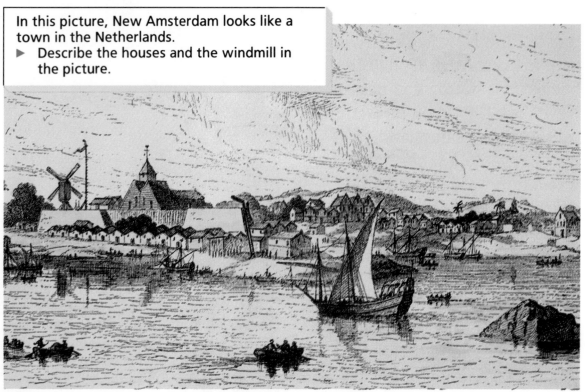

REDRAFT
of
THE CASTELLO PLAN
NEW AMSTERDAM
in
1660
JOHN WOLCOTT ADAMS
I.N. PHELPS STOKES
1916

This drawing shows a plan for New Amsterdam. Look hard, and you will see the wall that separates the settlement from the rest of Manhattan Island.

► What surrounded New Amsterdam on three sides?

animals came in ships that were just for cows, horses, or pigs and the people who took care of them.

Soon New Amsterdam began to look like a town in the Netherlands. Each house had a steep narrow roof and a porch in front. Bright red and yellow tulips bloomed in the gardens. Windmills, or buildings with a large wheel on top, pumped water and turned large stones that ground corn into grain.

## D. A Center of Trade

New Amsterdam was begun by traders. As you have learned, the first Dutch people came to trade with the Indians. As time went by, almost everybody in

New Amsterdam began to make things or grow things to be traded. Most people had one room in the front of their house where people could come and buy or trade things.

After a while every Saturday became market day. The **market** was held on the southern tip of the island, near the ocean shore. A market is an open place or a building where goods are sold. Dutch farmers brought eggs, butter, vegetables, and live chickens to the market. Indians brought animal skins and fish as well as brooms and baskets they had made. New Amsterdam housewives brought handmade cloth and lace.

There were not many coins or other kinds of money in New Amsterdam. At the Saturday market, both the Dutch and the Indians often used beads for money. The beads were called wampum (WAHM pum). A very valuable thing was sometimes traded for a beaver skin that could be made into a hat.

Near the New Amsterdam shore, sailing ships waited to load and unload goods.
▶ What do you think the artist wanted to show in this painting?

## E. An Important Port

While the grown-ups of New Amsterdam were trading things at the market, the children ran down to the **harbor** to see the big sailing ships. A harbor is a protected area of water where ships can safely stay near land. New Amsterdam had become an important **port**. A port is a place where ships come and go, dropping off and picking up things to be traded.

Ships from New Amsterdam carried furs, wood, and tobacco across the Atlantic Ocean to be traded in Europe. Boats from New Amsterdam carried cloth, furniture, tools, and guns up the Hudson River to be traded in northern settlements.

## F. A New Name

As the Dutch settlers of New Amsterdam went about their trading, the Dutch and the English were at war in Europe. In 1664 the English came by sea to capture New Amsterdam. They took over the settlement without firing a shot.

The English decided to give New Amsterdam a new name. They called it New York, after the city of York, in their home country of England.

---

LESSON *1* REVIEW

### THINK AND WRITE

A. How did the first people on Manhattan Island live?

B. Why did the first Dutch people come to Manhattan Island?

C. In what ways did New Amsterdam begin to look like a town in the Netherlands?

D. What did the Dutch and the Native Americans often use for money at the New Amsterdam market?

E. In your opinion, why did New Amsterdam become an important port?

F. Why did the English people give New Amsterdam a new name?

### SKILLS CHECK

**THINKING SKILL**

You have learned that trade is the exchange of one valued thing for another. What if there were no coins or paper money today? What could people use to trade for the things they wanted?

## Community Services in New Amsterdam

**THINK ABOUT WHAT YOU KNOW**

What are some services in your community? Who provides these services?

**STUDY THE VOCABULARY**

fort          inhabitant
watchman

**FOCUS YOUR READING**

What were some community services in New Amsterdam?

### A. A Story About a Leader

Hundreds of years ago, people in communities needed many of the same services that people in communities need today. In this lesson, you will learn about three services that were provided in the settlement of New Amsterdam.

One needed service was government. In 1647 a new Dutch leader came to town. His name was Peter Stuyvesant (STYE vuh sunt), and he was the new Director-General. The Director-General was somewhat like a mayor, but with more power than a mayor.

Peter Stuyvesant quickly became well known for his wooden leg and bossy ways. Many people thought he was stubborn and didn't listen to the people of the community. They called him "Hardheaded Pete."

One story that is told about Stuyvesant happened almost as soon as he came to town. At this time there were many farm animals in New Amsterdam, as well as cats and dogs. The

**230**

At the time shown in this painting, the animals of New Amsterdam still roamed the streets freely. However, things were about to change.

▶ What kind of announcement do you think the man is putting up on the tree?

livestock and pets were allowed to roam freely through the streets and gardens.

Peter Stuyvesant made up his mind to change things. He made laws to force people to control their animals and clean up their property. He built a wall across the northern end of New Amsterdam to keep out enemies and wild animals and to keep in the livestock and pets.

You can read part of a story about Peter Stuyvesant on the next page. Some things in the story have been changed to make it more interesting.

After a while, the merchants of New Amsterdam became tired of Peter Stuyvesant's telling them what to do. They soon demanded a council that would help govern the town. Reluctantly, Stuyvesant agreed.

# FROM: ON THE DAY PETER STUYVESANT SAILED INTO TOWN

**By: Arnold Lobel**
**Setting: New Amsterdam, 1647**

Arnold Lobel wrote about Peter Stuyvesant. He used imaginative details to make the story more interesting. Read the selection below to find some of these details.

*From Broadway to Wall Street old Stuyvesant stormed;*
*With a tap and a step he kept walking,*
*While some chickens and ducks made a nest in his hat*
*And some geese on the path made a squawking.*
*Yes, those geese on the path made a squawking.*

*Then a goat from behind, in a manner unkind,*
*Gave Peter a push on his seat.*
*A cow licked his nose and some pigs chewed his toes*
*As poor Stuyvesant sat in the street.*

*"This New World is a mess!"*
*Peter cried in distress.*
*"These animals need gates and*
*fences. Take these birds to a*
*cage!" Peter shouted in rage.*
*"Oh, good Dutchmen,*
*let's come to our senses!"*

## B. First Paid Police in America

Although the people of New Amsterdam did not enjoy being bossed around, they did want law and order. They especially wanted the community service of protection for themselves and their property.

There was a **fort**, or building with strong walls, guns, and soldiers, at the southern tip of town. The fort might give protection from enemies that came in ships. But there were no night **watchmen**, as there were in the Netherlands, to protect the people from criminals who might rob the residents of their property.

When the first night watchmen were hired in New Amsterdam, they became the first paid police force in America. At first the watchmen's only job was to walk the streets at night to see that everything was well. However, after a while the night watchmen did the job of police, firefighter, weather reporter, and news reporter, all in one. They also called out the time.

By the grace of God ... eleven o'clock and a cold, clear evening ...

This night watchman provided several needed services.
► What were some ways he helped the people of New Amsterdam?

233

The watchmen were often called the rattle watch. They carried wooden rattles that could be swung around to make noise. Every hour the watchman would swing his rattle and call out the time and a bit of news.

## C. The Schoolmaster

Education was a rather unusual service in New Amsterdam. Both boys and girls went to school. In most other places, girls stayed home and learned how to take care of the house. However, girls and boys were not exactly equal at the New Amsterdam school. For example, only boys were allowed to study arithmetic. Their parents had to pay for this teaching, which would prepare the boys to figure prices when they grew up to be traders.

When the first schoolmaster came to New Amsterdam, there were many parts to his job. Besides teaching the children, he visited sick people, directed the church choir, and delivered invitations to funerals.

This illustration shows a New Amsterdam schoolmaster listening to some students recite their lesson.
▶  How was the New Amsterdam school different from your school?

## D. Community Services Yesterday and Today

You have learned that the **inhabitants**, or people who live in a place, of New Amsterdam received some community services. The Director-General, the night watchmen, and the schoolmaster provided services that are still necessary in communities today.

In the next lesson you will study New York City today. In that city there is a mayor and a city council. There are many thousands of schoolteachers, police, and firefighters. As you might guess, New York City has many other kinds of service workers, too.

This boy goes to school in New York City today.
▶ What do you think the teacher is trying to do?

---

*LESSON* **2** *REVIEW*

### THINK AND WRITE

A. Do you think people would vote for a leader like Peter Stuyvesant today?
B. What were the night watchman's jobs?
C. How is a schoolteacher's job today different from the schoolmaster's job in New Amsterdam?
D. In your opinion, why are there so many schoolteachers, police, and firefighters in New York City today?

### SKILLS CHECK

**WRITING SKILL**

Think about the police in your community. Write a paragraph about police work today. Write another paragraph that compares police work today with the watchmen's work.

# New York City Today

Describe the largest community you have visited.

| | |
|---|---|
| public transportation | wants |
| subway | budget |
| salary | savings |
| needs | skyscraper |

How has New York City changed since it was known as New Amsterdam?

## A. Past and Present in New York City

Today, New York City is so big that it is divided into five large parts, called boroughs (BUR ohz). You can find the boroughs of Manhattan, Queens, the Bronx, Brooklyn, and Staten Island on the map on page 237. The borough of Manhattan is on Manhattan Island.

More than 7 million people live in New York City today. They come from every country in the world. The low buildings of New Amsterdam are gone now. About 100 years ago, they were destroyed in a big fire. But many place-names in New York City still show that New Amsterdam was here long ago. Amsterdam is the name of one street. Wall Street is named for the wall that Peter Stuyvesant built. The neighborhood and the river called Harlem got their names from the city of Haarlem, in the Netherlands.

In some ways, New York City has not changed since its New Amsterdam days. The city is still a busy place where trade goes on almost everywhere. But today trade goes on in huge

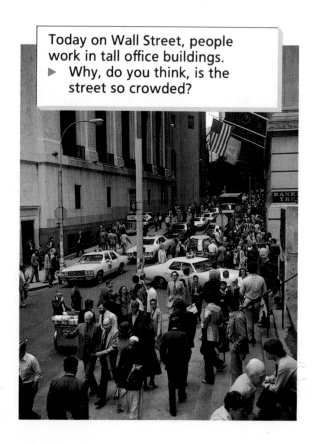

Today on Wall Street, people work in tall office buildings.
▶ Why, do you think, is the street so crowded?

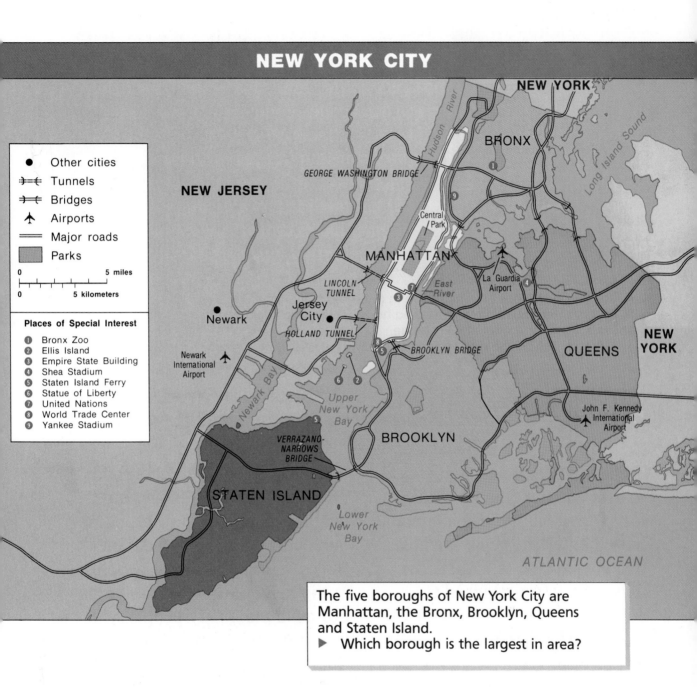

# NEW YORK CITY

NEW YORK

BRONX

NEW JERSEY

GEORGE WASHINGTON BRIDGE

Hudson River

Long Island Sound

Central Park

MANHATTAN

LINCOLN TUNNEL

Jersey City

Newark

HOLLAND TUNNEL

East River

La Guardia Airport

Newark International Airport

Newark Bay

Upper New York Bay

BROOKLYN BRIDGE

QUEENS

NEW YORK

VERRAZANO-NARROWS BRIDGE

STATEN ISLAND

Lower New York Bay

BROOKLYN

John F. Kennedy International Airport

ATLANTIC OCEAN

The five boroughs of New York City are Manhattan, the Bronx, Brooklyn, Queens and Staten Island.
▶ Which borough is the largest in area?

department stores and small shops, as well as in outdoor markets. Even on the sidewalks, some people lay out things to sell.

New York City is an important port, just as it was in its New Amsterdam days. Ships loaded with oil, cars, and many other products wait in the harbor to load and unload. Planes loaded with people and things constantly take off and land at the three big airports that serve the city and its suburbs.

A family in New York City might live in (pictured from left to right) a huge apartment building, an attached house, a walk-up apartment above a store, or a single-family home.

▶ What might be one good thing about living in each kind of home?

## B. Different Kinds of Homes

In New York City most of the land already has buildings on it. There is not enough land left for every family to live in a house with a big yard. Many families live in apartments. Others live in houses that are attached to neighboring houses on both sides. Fewer families in New York live in single-family houses.

Sarah and Dan live in an apartment. They live on the fourteenth floor of their building. There are four other apartments on their floor. When Sarah and Dan go outdoors, they take the elevator from their apartment to the ground floor.

## C. Many Neighborhoods

People who live in New York City live in neighborhoods. There are about 300 different neighborhoods in the city. Some neighborhoods are named for the country most of the people in the neighborhood came from. For example, many people who live in the neighborhood called Chinatown came to the United States from China. Many people who live in the neighborhood called Little Odessa are Jewish people who came from the Soviet Union. Odessa is a city in the Soviet Union.

Some other neighborhoods are named for their location in

the city. These neighborhoods have names such as Sheepshead Bay and Battery Park.

Sarah and Dan live in a neighborhood called the Upper West Side. Their family members walk to shops in the neighborhood to buy food and many other things they need.

When the family members leave the neighborhood, they take some kind of **public transportation**. Public transportation moves more than one person or family at one time. Buses and **subways** are two kinds of public transportation. A subway is a train that runs at least part of the way under the ground. Subways do not have to wait for traffic on busy streets.

On an ordinary day, Sarah and Dan might walk to school. Their father might take a bus to work. Their mother might take the subway to her job. If it is raining, their parents might call a taxi. A taxi is a car for hire.

This subway travels underwater between Manhattan and Brooklyn.
▶ In what other way does this subway travel?

## D. Providing for People's Wants and Needs

Millions of people work in New York City. They work to earn money. Sarah and Dan's parents each receive a **salary**, which is money paid regularly for work that has been done. Sarah and Dan's parents use their salary to provide for the **needs** and some of the **wants** of their family.

A need is something a person cannot live without, such as food, clothing, and shelter. A want is a good or service that a person would like to have but

| Monthly Expenses | | Income | |
|---|---|---|---|
| Food | 600 | marty | $1300 |
| Housing | 750 | Ruth | 1200 |
| Electricity | 300 | | |
| Oil | | | |
| Phone | | | |
| Transportation | 300 | | |
| Health | 150 | | |
| Other | 200 | | |
| Savings | 200 | | |
| Total Expenses | 2500 | | |

A family budget might look something like this one.
▶ How much does this family plan to save?

can live without. TV sets, vacations, and restaurant meals are wants.

Sarah and Dan's parents make a plan, called a **budget**, for using their money. Some money must be spent for the family's needs. When these needs are met, some of the leftover money can be used for things they want.

Other money is for **savings**, which is money kept for later use. Sometimes savings must be used for unexpected expenses or for hard times. Sarah and Dan's father could not work for two months. Family savings had to be used for some expenses.

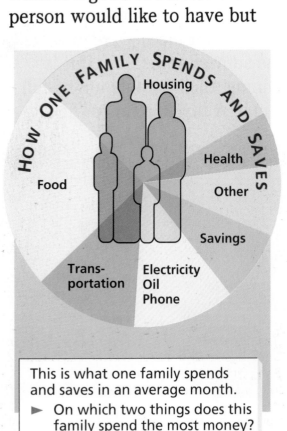

HOW ONE FAMILY SPENDS AND SAVES

Housing
Health
Other
Food
Savings
Transportation
Electricity Oil Phone

This is what one family spends and saves in an average month.
▶ On which two things does this family spend the most money?

240

Sarah and Dan know that their parents make choices about money. Last year their mom and dad had to decide between summer camp for the children and a family vacation. They did not have enough money for both.

Sometimes Sarah and Dan help to make choices. For example, this year they decided to take a cut in their allowances to help the family buy a new computer. The children want to use the computer for fun and for schoolwork.

## E. Interesting Places

Sarah has been studying New York City at school. She is in Mr. Smith's class. Today the class discussed some of their favorite places in the city.

"I like the Statue of Liberty best," said Ernestine. "It's fun to climb the stairs to look out from the statue's crown."

"My favorite place is the American Museum of Natural History," said Ralph. "I like to see the blue whale and the dinosaur bones best."

Many New Yorkers enjoy going to Central Park, in Manhattan, especially on weekends. There they might have a picnic, visit the zoo, and take a ride on the carousel shown in these pictures.
▶ Why, do you think, are parks important places in large cities?

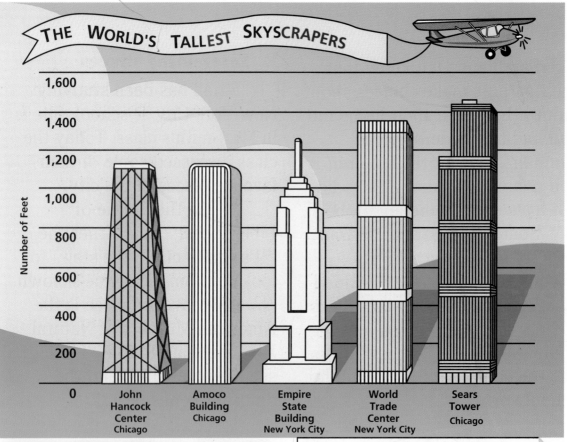

## THE WORLD'S TALLEST SKYSCRAPERS

Number of Feet

1,600
1,400
1,200
1,000
800
600
400
200
0

| John Hancock Center Chicago | Amoco Building Chicago | Empire State Building New York City | World Trade Center New York City | Sears Tower Chicago |

The world's tallest buildings are located in the United States.
▶ How many of the five tallest are in New York City?

Each year millions of people visit the Statue of Liberty.
▶ Why do so many people want to visit the statue?

Mr. Smith's class discussed their favorite New York City skyscrapers. A skyscraper is a very tall building.

"I like to ride the elevators to the observation deck on the 102nd floor of the Empire State Building," Sarah said. Then I can look out over the city. The cars in the streets below look like little toys. The boats in the harbor and on the rivers look like toys, too."

## F. City Service Workers

To end their study of New York City, Mr. Smith's class listed service workers in the city today. This is part of their list.

Sarah added *actor* and *ticket seller* to the list. Can you think of still other workers that could be added?

"Which service workers on our list were needed in New Amsterdam, too?" Mr. Smith asked the students. He asked them to remember that there were no televisions, radios, cars, computers, elevators, or subways long ago in New Amsterdam. How would you answer Mr. Smith's question?

Think about your own community. What service workers have always been needed there? What new kinds of service workers are there?

## LESSON 3 REVIEW

### THINK AND WRITE

A. In what ways has New York City stayed the same as it was in its New Amsterdam days?

B. Why do many people in New York City live in apartments?

C. In your opinion, why do people spend most of their time in their neighborhood?

D. How could a budget help a person to save money?

E. In your opinion, what place in New York City would be the most interesting to visit?

F. Why weren't there any subway engineers in New Amsterdam?

### SKILLS CHECK

**MAP SKILL**

Look at the map of New York City, on page 237. Find the borough with the most places in the index. Write the name of that borough. List three places you would like to visit and tell why.

## USING THE VOCABULARY

trade
market
port
fort
watchman
inhabitants

skyscrapers
public
    transportation
budget
savings

1. To _____ means "to exchange something that is valued for something else that is valued."
2. Very tall buildings are called _____.
3. A building with strong walls, guns, and soldiers is called a _____.
4. People who live in a place are called _____.
5. A _____ is a place where goods are sold.
6. One job of a _____ was to protect people and their property from criminals in the town.
7. A plan for using your money is called a _____.
8. A _____ is a place where ships can come and go, dropping off and picking up things to be traded.
9. _____ is money that is used at a later time.
10. _____ moves more than one person or family at one time.

## REMEMBERING WHAT YOU READ

On a separate sheet of paper, answer the questions in complete sentences.

1. What is the busiest, most crowded part of New York City?
2. Why was the little Dutch settlement named New Amsterdam?
3. Who was Peter Stuyvesant?
4. What are the five boroughs of New York City?
5. What is a budget?

## TYING MATH TO SOCIAL STUDIES

Look up the population of New York City in an encyclopedia or world almanac. Look up the population of the city that is closest to your community. Which city has the greater population, and by how many?

## THINKING CRITICALLY

On a separate sheet of paper, answer the following in complete sentences.

1. When might people today trade one thing for another?
2. Do you think the English made a good choice when they gave New Amsterdam the name *New York?*
3. Compare Peter Stuyvesant to the mayor in your community. List three ways they are alike. List three ways they are different.
4. New shoes can be a want or a need. When would new shoes be a want?
5. If the people of New Amsterdam could see New York City today, what do you think would surprise them most?

## SUMMARIZING THE CHAPTER

**Copy this graphic organizer on a separate sheet of paper. Under the main idea for each lesson, write three facts that support the main idea.**

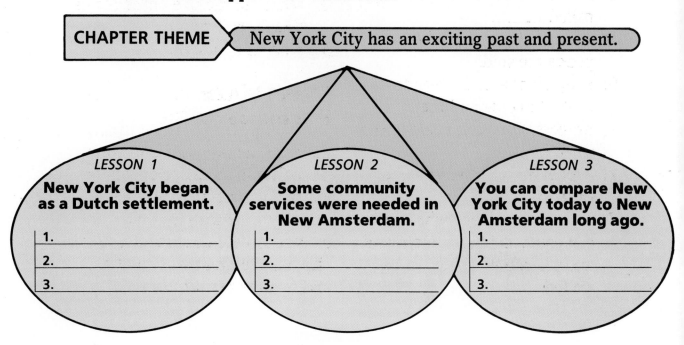

CHAPTER THEME — New York City has an exciting past and present.

LESSON 1
**New York City began as a Dutch settlement.**
1. _____
2. _____
3. _____

LESSON 2
**Some community services were needed in New Amsterdam.**
1. _____
2. _____
3. _____

LESSON 3
**You can compare New York City today to New Amsterdam long ago.**
1. _____
2. _____
3. _____

# CHAPTER 11

# YESTERDAY AND TODAY IN SAN FRANCISCO

*S*an Francisco was settled by Indians and then by the Spanish. In 1848, gold was found, and the city grew. Today cable cars travel up and down the many steep hills.

POWELL AND MARKET

HYDE and BEACH FISHERMANS WHARF

9

"I stop at the St. Francis"

# How San Francisco Began

## THINK ABOUT WHAT YOU KNOW

You have learned about the first people who lived on Manhattan Island. Predict who first lived where San Francisco is today.

## STUDY THE VOCABULARY

**expedition**   **presidio**
**mission**

## FOCUS YOUR READING

How did the San Francisco Bay area change after it was explored by Europeans?

## A. The Costanoan Indians

In Chapter 10 you learned about New York City. In this chapter you will learn about San Francisco. Both of these cities are located on important bays. Find New York City and San Francisco on a map in the Atlas. New York City is on the Atlantic coast. On which coast is San Francisco located?

You have learned that Indians were the first people to live where New York City is today. Indians were also the first people to live where San Francisco is today. The

Spaniards named these Indians Costanoans, from the word *costanos*, meaning "coast." However, today these Indians are called Ohlone.

Nature provided for all the basic needs of the Ohlones. For food, they caught fish in the bay, dug roots, and gathered wild seeds, nuts, and berries. For shelter, they built houses made of tree poles held together with mud. For clothes, they used deer and rabbit skins. On very cold mornings they covered their bodies with mud.

The Ohlones once lived where San Francisco is today. Their peaceful way of life was changed when Europeans came.
► What are the Ohlones doing?

In many ways the Ohlone children were like you. They played games like you do. They ran races, played with dolls, and threw balls. They also worked with their mothers and fathers. The children helped to build their family's house and to gather food. They learned many things from their families.

The Ohlone Indians had the same belief about the land as other American Indians. They believed that the land was part of nature, like the air was. They thought that a person could not own land any more than he or she could own the air.

## B. The Spanish Explorers

While the Ohlone Indians were living peacefully by the bay, ships from Europe sometimes sailed along the Pacific coast. The sailors could not see the bay. They did not find the narrow entrance through the hills from the ocean to the bay. This entrance was covered by a thick fog.

In 1769, people from the country of Spain discovered San Francisco Bay. But they didn't come by ship, and they discovered the bay by accident.

The government of Spain sent Gaspar de Portolá and his men on an **expedition** to Monterey (mahn tuh RAY) Bay. An expedition is a long journey to explore a region or take part in a battle. Portolá's group walked all the way from Mexico

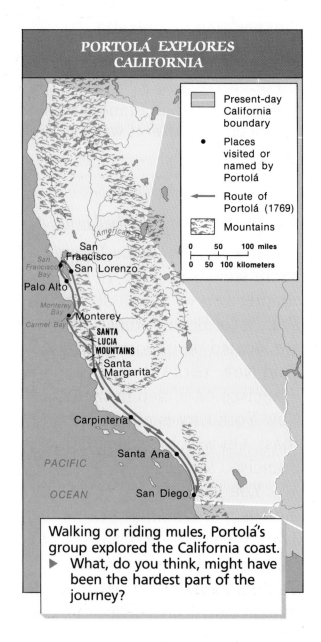

PORTOLÁ EXPLORES CALIFORNIA

Present-day California boundary

• Places visited or named by Portolá

← Route of Portolá (1769)

Mountains

0    50    100 miles
0  50  100 kilometers

San Francisco
San Lorenzo
Palo Alto
Monterey
SANTA LUCIA MOUNTAINS
Santa Margarita
Carpintería
Santa Ana
San Diego
PACIFIC OCEAN

Walking or riding mules, Portolá's group explored the California coast.
▶ What, do you think, might have been the hardest part of the journey?

Portolá and Father Serra, a priest, led their men from Mexico to San Diego. Portolá took a smaller group up the California coast.
▶ What event is shown in the picture?

to Monterey Bay, but they didn't recognize the bay when they saw it. Portolá sent a small group northward along the Pacific coast. This group discovered San Francisco Bay.

Imagine how these explorers felt when they came upon San Francisco Bay. They had been walking for hundreds of miles, over rough country, high hills, and hot deserts. They had seen giant trees, which Portolá named *palo colorado*, or "redwood." They were confused

because they had not found a bay that fit the description they had been given of Monterey Bay.

The explorers must have been amazed when they climbed to the top of a hill and saw the beautiful, flower-covered land below them. The clear blue waters of the bay that would later be called San Francisco Bay surrounded them on three sides.

Look at the map on page 248. You can follow the journey of Portolá's men from San Diego to San Francisco Bay.

## C. Spanish Settlement in the Bay Area

It was 1775, six years after Portolá had discovered San Francisco Bay. The king of Spain sent a young sea captain named Juan Manuel de Ayala (ah YAH lah) to explore the bay area. Captain Ayala guided his ship, the *San Carlos*, from the Atlantic Ocean into San Francisco Bay. The *San Carlos* was the first ship to sail into the bay.

In 1776 a group of soldiers, settlers, and priests from Mexico arrived in the bay area. They chose a spot to build a **mission**. A mission is a place where religious leaders, such as priests, live and work. The priests named the mission Mision San Francisco de Asis, after Saint Francis. Later the mission was called Mission Dolores, after a nearby lake.

The soldiers also built a **presidio**, or fort. Two little settlements grew up by the mission and the fort. Then a few people built houses on Yerba Buena Cove. All three settlements together became one settlement called *Yerba Buena*, which means "good herb," or "good grass." In 1846 the United States took control of Yerba

The Spanish people built a fort and a mission on the land where the Ohlones lived.
▶ How do you think the Ohlones felt about these changes on their land?

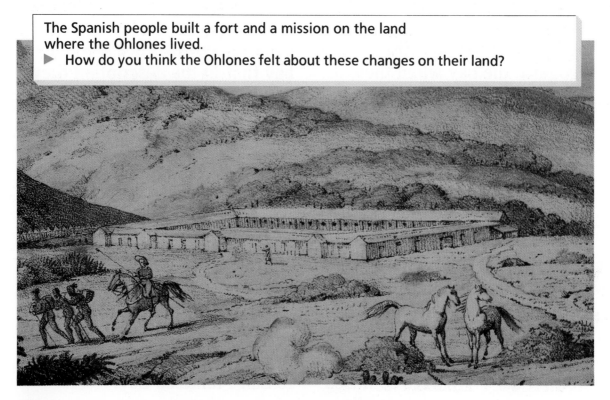

Buena from the Spanish. In 1847 the name *Yerba Buena* was changed to *San Francisco*.

The Costanoan Indians were very friendly. They helped the Spanish settlers grow crops and make things. The priests at the mission wanted the Indians to accept the Catholic religion, to live in or near the mission, and to work there.

Yerba Buena became San Francisco at the time this picture was made.
▶ How would you describe the town at this time?

Many Indians did live at the mission. In the meantime, Spanish settlers built big ranches on the land. They put up fences to claim the land as their own. There were many sad times for the Indians. Their way of life began to disappear.

## LESSON 1 REVIEW

### THINK AND WRITE

A. Why, do you think, did the Costanoan Indians have such a great respect for nature?
B. In your opinion, what was unusual about the discovery of San Francisco Bay?
C. San Francisco grew from what three early settlements?

### SKILLS CHECK

**MAP SKILL**

Find New York City and San Francisco on the map of North America in the Atlas. Using the scale on the map, find the distance between the two cities.

## San Francisco and the Gold Rush

**THINK ABOUT WHAT YOU KNOW**

How would you feel if thousands of new people moved into your town? What are some things that might happen?

**STUDY THE VOCABULARY**

gold rush     wagon train
prospector    profit
forty-niner

**FOCUS YOUR READING**

How did San Francisco change during the Gold Rush?

## A. News Comes to San Francisco

Until 1847, when Yerba Buena's name was changed to San Francisco, the settlement did not grow very much. In 1847, only 200 people lived there, and by 1848 the population had grown to only 450.

Then, on a peaceful spring day in 1848, something happened that would bring about great change. On this day, San Franciscans heard some big news. This news would lead to the **gold rush**, when thousands of people would come to California looking for gold.

Imagine that you are a child living in the little settlement of San Francisco. You see a man running down the street. He is shouting, "Gold, gold, gold from the American River!" He is showing people a bottle of yellow gold dust.

"Who is that man, Dad?"

"He's Mr. Sam Brannan," your dad answers quickly. "He publishes our newspaper, and he's just returned from Sutter's Mill, on the American River. The stories about gold in the river must be true!"

Miners used several methods to get gold from the ground.
▶ What were some tools the miners used?

returned to San Francisco to celebrate when they found gold.

Most of the prospectors were men who had left their families and their businesses to look for gold. Some of them came to California by ship. Often they were in such a hurry to find gold that they jumped from their ships before they reached land.

Many prospectors came to California across land, in prairie wagons pulled by oxen. Usually

## B. San Francisco Grows

In his newspaper, Sam Brannan wrote about finding gold in the American River. He sent copies of the newspaper to other places.

Thousands of **prospectors** began coming to California. Prospectors are people who are looking for valuable minerals, coal, or oil. So many prospectors came to California looking for gold in 1849 that they were called **forty-niners**. Many forty-niners came to San Francisco because it was the port closest to the gold fields. They also

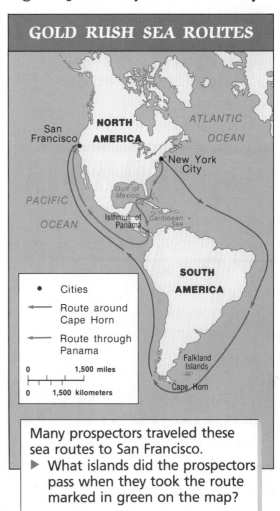

**GOLD RUSH SEA ROUTES**

- Cities
← Route around Cape Horn
← Route through Panama

0    1,500 miles
0    1,500 kilometers

Many prospectors traveled these sea routes to San Francisco.
▶ What islands did the prospectors pass when they took the route marked in green on the map?

they came in a **wagon train**, or a line of wagons. When they arrived in San Francisco, they were tired and hungry. They needed a place to stay.

There were not enough houses or hotels for the prospectors, so tents and shacks sprang up everywhere. When crews left their ships for the gold fields, other people made their homes in the ships. Many people just slept on the ground under blankets draped over poles.

By 1850, about 35,000 people lived in San Francisco. Many had come to find gold. Others had come to sell services and supplies to the miners. By 1853, it was said that any foreigner could find people in the city who spoke his or her language, and everybody knew the word *gold*.

## C. Not Enough Goods and Services

The California gold rush began in 1848 and lasted for only a few years. But during these years, San Francisco grew faster than any other city. What happens to a place when it grows this fast?

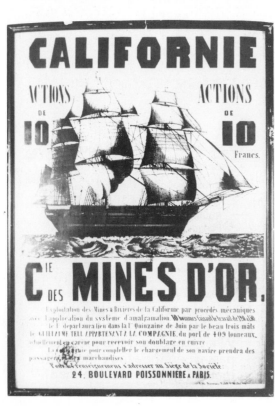

Trips to the gold fields were advertised throughout America and the world.
▶ What do you think the French ad says?

This picture shows San Francisco during the gold rush.
▶ Describe San Francisco at this time and compare it to
San Francisco in 1846–1847, as shown on page 251.

We've already seen that there weren't enough homes for all the newcomers. In fact, in 1849 there weren't enough goods of any kind. The prospectors needed supplies. They needed food, tin pans for washing the gold, and picks and shovels to dig through the rock to find gold.

Prices for the few goods that were available became very high. An egg cost one dollar. A sheet of paper could cost $150, and a bag of flour $400. When ships did begin to bring more goods, there weren't enough stores. Many goods were just piled up and sold outdoors. Or they were sold from a store set up in an abandoned ship.

There weren't enough services, either. There was no fire department, and huge fires often swept through the tents and wooden shacks. There weren't enough schools. Worst of all, there weren't enough police to keep law and order. While most of the people searching for gold were honest, there were bad characters, too. Some of them fought, drank, and stole things from other people.

### D. Solving the Problems

How did the people of San Francisco solve these problems? Many new merchants realized they could make big **profits** selling supplies and services to prospectors passing through town. Profit is the amount of money gained in a business deal after all expenses have been subtracted from the amount of money taken in.

255

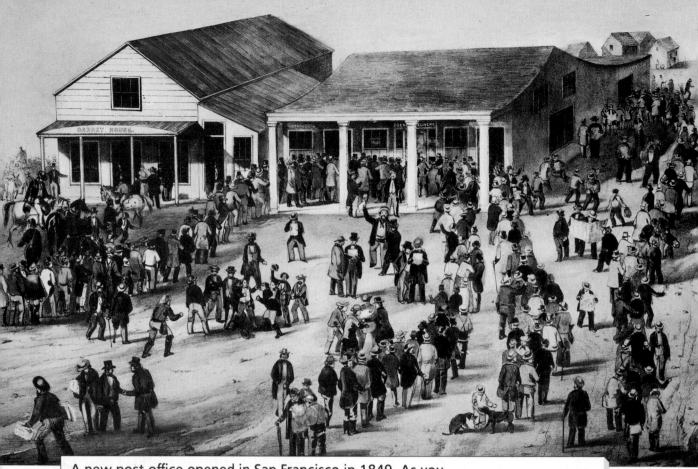

A new post office opened in San Francisco in 1849. As you can see, there were plenty of people waiting to use it.
▶ Why was mail so important to people at this time?

More houses were built. One interesting kind of house was brought from the eastern part of the United States. The parts were numbered and they could be put together in order like a child's building set. After there were so many fires, more houses were built of brick.

Community services were improved. Fire departments were started. Rich and poor people alike volunteered for these fire departments.

Churches, a post office, a school, a library, a theater, and even an opera house were built, so people would have good places to go. Sidewalks and roads were built, too.

A big problem remained. The sheriff and his men could not control the criminals in a town that was full of strangers and that was growing too fast. In 1851 a group of San Francisco citizens formed a committee to restore law and order. The committee members patrolled the streets. They arrested suspects and searched houses for stolen goods. They even hanged a few criminals. Many other criminals got scared and left town.

When the gold rush was over, in the mid-1850s, many merchants and prospectors returned to their homes far from San Francisco. But a great number of people from all over the world stayed in San Francisco and made it their new home. These people helped to make the San Francisco area one of the most interesting areas in the United States. Today, San Francisco is a center of business, culture, and agriculture. Each year over 2 million people come to San Francisco to enjoy the city.

In 1902, tall buildings lined Market Street, in San Francisco.
▶ What else had changed since the gold rush days?

LESSON 2 REVIEW

THINK AND WRITE

A. What was Sam Brannan's news?
B. How do you think the forty-niners felt when they arrived in San Francisco?
C. Why was there a shortage of goods and services during the early days of the gold rush?
D. What were some ways the people of San Francisco solved the problems caused by rapid growth?

SKILLS CHECK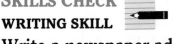
WRITING SKILL

Write a newspaper ad for a San Francisco store in 1849. Tell what you are selling, how much it costs, and why people should buy it.

## San Francisco Today

### THINK ABOUT WHAT YOU KNOW
Think of the things you know about cities. What kinds of transportation and buildings do many cities have?

### STUDY THE VOCABULARY
| | |
|---|---|
| cable car | wharf |
| conductor | pagoda |
| landmark | |

### FOCUS YOUR READING
What are some famous San Francisco landmarks?

## A. City of Bridges, Hills, and Cable Cars

The Zarzana family is visiting San Francisco for the first time. From the car window, Mike sees the Golden Gate Bridge. He looks in the guidebook to find out about the bridge.

"The Golden Gate Bridge spans the entrance to San Francisco Bay," Mike reads aloud. "The bridge connects San Francisco and northern California. The towers of the bridge are the first structures that sailors see when they come to San Francisco."

"There is another bridge just ahead of us," says Mr. Zarzana. "We will be driving on it to get to the city. This bridge is called the San Francisco-Oakland Bay Bridge. It is really

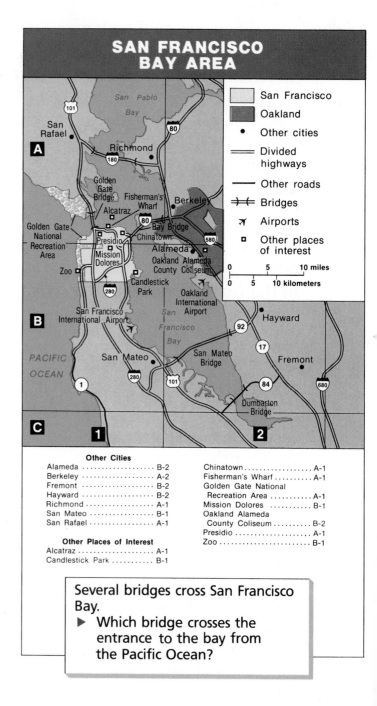

**SAN FRANCISCO BAY AREA**

Legend:
- San Francisco
- Oakland
- • Other cities
- ═ Divided highways
- ─ Other roads
- ╪ Bridges
- ✈ Airports
- ▫ Other places of interest

0 5 10 miles
0 5 10 kilometers

**Other Cities**
| | |
|---|---|
| Alameda | B-2 |
| Berkeley | A-2 |
| Fremont | B-2 |
| Hayward | B-2 |
| Richmond | A-1 |
| San Mateo | B-1 |
| San Rafael | A-1 |

**Other Places of Interest**
| | |
|---|---|
| Alcatraz | A-1 |
| Candlestick Park | B-1 |

| | |
|---|---|
| Chinatown | A-1 |
| Fisherman's Wharf | A-1 |
| Golden Gate National Recreation Area | A-1 |
| Mission Dolores | B-1 |
| Oakland Alameda County Coliseum | B-2 |
| Presidio | A-1 |
| Zoo | B-1 |

Several bridges cross San Francisco Bay.
▶ Which bridge crosses the entrance to the bay from the Pacific Ocean?

Cable cars and bridges are familiar sights in San Francisco today. The Golden Gate Bridge was completed in 1937.
▶ What is the longest bridge you have ever crossed?

several bridges that are connected for eight miles. The Bay Bridge, as it is usually called, connects the cities of San Francisco and Oakland."

In the city the Zarzana family drives up and down streets. "This is like a roller-coaster ride," Chris says. "The streets go up and down hills, and they are really steep. Our guide-book says one of the hilly streets is named Lombard Street. It has so many twists and turns that it is called the most crooked street in the world."

After they park the car, Chris, Mike, and their father take a ride on a **cable car**. A cable car is a streetcar that is pulled along a rail by an underground moving wire cable.

The **conductor**, or person in charge, tells them that the first cable car was invented in 1873 by Andrew S. Hallidie. He invented the San Francisco cable car because he felt sorry for the horses that had to pull buggies up and down the steep hills. The tired horses often fell and broke their legs.

**259**

## PHOTOGRAPH OF AN EARTHQUAKE

The people of San Francisco have rebuilt after earthquakes damaged their city. You may have seen photographs taken of the 1989 earthquake. This photograph shows San Francisco after an earthquake in 1906, when about 700 people were killed and 300,000 people lost their homes.

### Understanding Source Material

1. What does the old photograph show that words might not be able to tell?
2. What kinds of buildings were affected by the 1906 earthquake?

## B. Neighborhoods of San Francisco

Chris, Mike, and their father visited the neighborhoods of San Francisco. They learned that it is a city of more than 700,000 people. Many groups live there, including African Americans, Mexican Americans, and Asian Americans. San Francisco is like it was during the gold rush.

Like other cities, San Francisco has different kinds of neighborhoods. In the business district, many people work in skyscraper offices. In some residential (rez uh DEN shul) districts, where people live, there are row houses such as the ones pictured on this page.

Chinatown is a famous neighborhood that includes many businesses and places to live. More Chinese people live there than in any other place in the United States.

The Embarcadero is a neighborhood along the bay. Factories, warehouses, and piers, where ships dock, line the bay side of the Embarcadero.

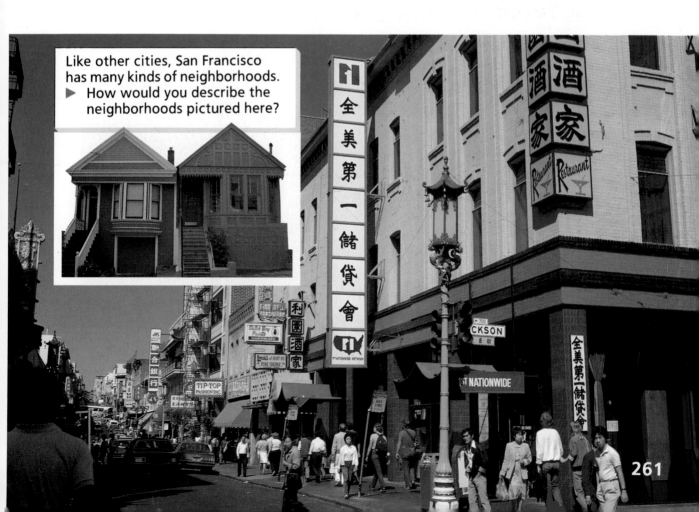

Like other cities, San Francisco has many kinds of neighborhoods.
▶ How would you describe the neighborhoods pictured here?

## C. Special Places in San Francisco

Chris and Mike discovered their favorite places in San Francisco. "I like the Transamerica building because on top it is shaped like a pyramid (PIHR uh mihd), with sloping sides that come together in a point at the top." Mike said.

The Transamerica building is a **landmark** in San Francisco. A landmark is something that is either natural or made by people, and that helps you find or recognize a place because it is easily seen. You can see the Transamerica building in the picture on page 319.

Fisherman's Wharf is another favorite place. A **wharf** is a structure that ships can lie alongside of while they load and unload people or goods. At Fisherman's Wharf some people were unloading fish from their boats. Others were repairing boats. Still others were selling the fish they had caught. The Zarzanas ate fish in a restaurant at Fisherman's Wharf.

The Zarzana family visited the San Francisco Zoo and had a picnic in Golden Gate Park. In

This pagoda can be seen in Golden Gate Park.
▶ How would you describe the pagoda?

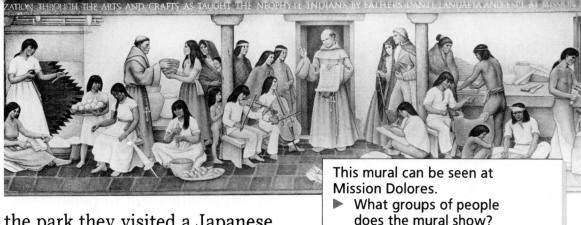

This mural can be seen at Mission Dolores.
► What groups of people does the mural show?

the park they visited a Japanese **pagoda** (puh GOH duh). A pagoda is a tower several stories high. Each story has an overhanging roof. Chris and Mike also went to the exploratorium and looked at the stars through a giant telescope.

The last night the family spent in San Francisco, they went to Candlestick Park to see the San Francisco Giants play the Chicago Cubs.

The Zarzana family also visited Mission Dolores and the Presidio. You will remember that the Presidio was once a Spanish fort. Today it is the headquarters of the Sixth Army.

One day the entire Presidio may be a park, but already many parts of it are open to visitors. The Zarzana family took a tour of the Presidio. They had a picnic and looked at the view of the Golden Gate Bridge. Chris especially liked visiting the Presidio Army museum, which was once an army hospital. He also liked seeing the six cannons from the old Spanish fort.

"One thing I really like about San Francisco," said Mike, "is the way you can see both the past and the present."

## LESSON 3 REVIEW

### THINK AND WRITE

A. Why did San Francisco need cable cars?
B. In your opinion, why does a large city have different kinds of neighborhoods?
C. What two places would you most like to visit in San Francisco?

### SKILLS CHECK

**THINKING SKILL**
What are the landmarks in your community? Write a paragraph about each landmark. Draw a picture of one of the landmarks.

## USING THE VOCABULARY

| | |
|---|---|
| expedition | forty-niner |
| mission | profit |
| presidio | pagoda |
| gold rush | conductor |
| prospector | wharf |

On a separate sheet of paper, write the word or words from above that best complete the sentences.

1. The person in charge of a cable car is called the _____.
2. An _____ is a long journey.
3. The _____ was the journey of thousands of people to California looking for gold.
4. A _____ is a place where religious leaders work.
5. At a _____, ships can load and unload.
6. A _____ is a fort.
7. _____ are people who are looking for valuable minerals.
8. Money gained after all expenses have been subtracted is _____.
9. The prospectors who came looking for gold were called the _____.
10. A _____ is a tall tower.

## REMEMBERING WHAT YOU READ

On a separate sheet of paper, answer the questions in complete sentences.

1. What was the name of the group of Indians who were the first to live where San Francisco is today?
2. Who discovered San Francisco Bay?
3. Why did many people come to San Francisco in 1848?
4. What are two landmarks of San Francisco today?
5. What groups of people live in San Francisco today?

## Tying Math to Social Studies

In 1847 200 people lived in San Francisco. By 1848 the population had grown to 450. How much did the population increase in this one-year time period? Why did the population continue to increase after 1848?

# THINKING CRITICALLY

On a separate sheet of paper, answer the following in complete sentences.

1. Compare and contrast the Ohlone children and the children of today.
2. Why, do you think, were there many sad times for the Indians after they helped the Spanish settlers grow their crops?
3. If the forty-niners could see San Francisco today, what might they think?
4. How do you think the Golden Gate Bridge got its name?
5. Today, how can a person see into the past of a city, such as San Francisco?

## SUMMARIZING THE CHAPTER

Copy this graphic organizer on a separate sheet of paper. Under the main idea for each lesson, write three facts that support the main idea.

**CHAPTER THEME**    San Francisco has an exciting past and present.

LESSON 1

**The Spanish first came to the San Francisco Bay area in 1769.**

1. _____
2. _____
3. _____

LESSON 2

**The gold rush changed San Francisco.**

1. _____
2. _____
3. _____

LESSON 3

**There are many things to do and see in San Francisco today.**

1. _____
2. _____
3. _____

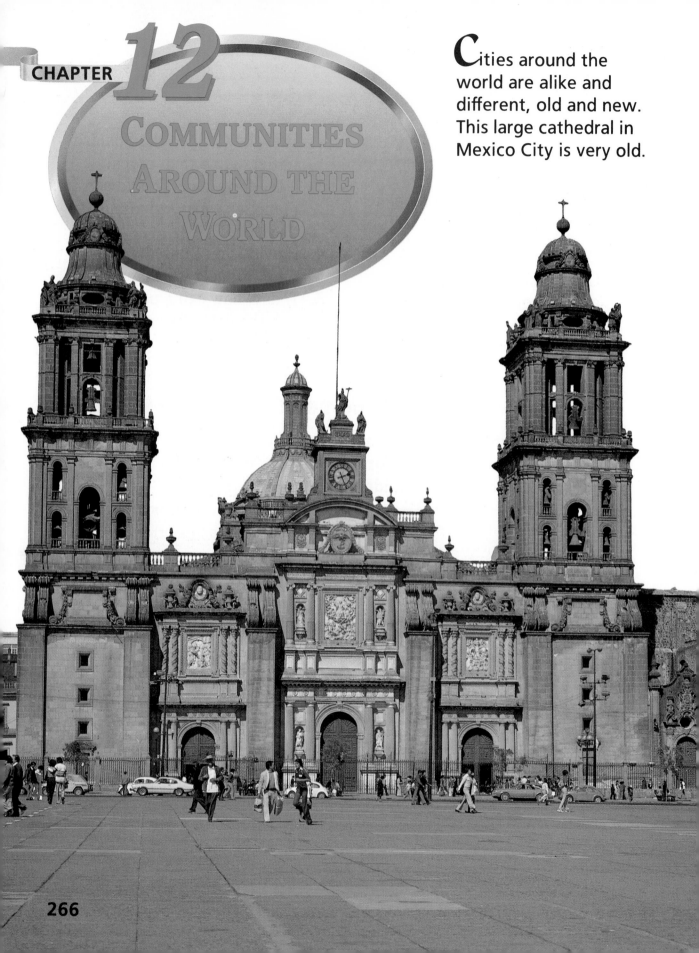

# CHAPTER 12

# COMMUNITIES AROUND THE WORLD

Cities around the world are alike and different, old and new. This large cathedral in Mexico City is very old.

## Learning About Latitude and Longitude

**THINK ABOUT WHAT YOU KNOW**

What are the four main directions? How do directions help us find places on a map?

**STUDY THE VOCABULARY**

| | |
|---|---|
| latitude | Prime Meridian |
| degree | Greenwich |
| longitude | coordinates |

**FOCUS YOUR READING**

How can latitude and longitude help us find places on the earth?

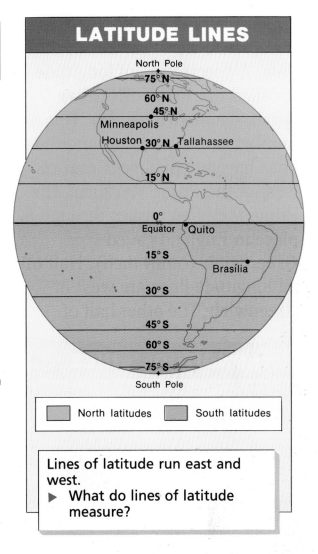

## LATITUDE LINES

North Pole
75° N
60° N
45° N
Minneapolis
Houston 30° N Tallahassee
15° N
0°
Equator Quito
15° S
Brasília
30° S
45° S
60° S
75° S
South Pole

North latitudes  South latitudes

Lines of latitude run east and west.
▶ What do lines of latitude measure?

## A. Latitude

To help us find places on maps, mapmakers use lines of **latitude** (LAT uh tood). One such line is called the Equator. The Equator is halfway between the North Pole and the South Pole. It is a very special line of latitude. It is numbered 0°. All other latitude lines measure distances north or south of the Equator. This distance is measured in **degrees**. The symbol for degrees is °.

Look at the map on this page. You will see that the city of Minneapolis, Minnesota, is located at 45 degrees north latitude. A short way to show 45 degrees north latitude is 45° N. Houston, Texas, is located at 30 degrees north latitude, or 30° N.

## B. Longitude

Lines of another kind are drawn on maps to help us find places. These are lines of **longitude** (LAHN juh tood). Look at the map on page 268.

Longitude lines are drawn from the North Pole to the South Pole. A special line of longitude is called the **Prime Meridian** (prym muh RIHD ee un). It is numbered 0°. All other longitude lines measure distances east or west of the Prime Meridian. The Prime Meridian passes through a place in England called **Greenwich** (GREN ihch). Half of all longitude lines are west of Greenwich. The other half of these lines are east of Greenwich. Let us find the city of Buenos Aires (BWAY nus ER eez), Argentina, on the map. Buenos Aires is in the Western Hemisphere. To make the city easier to find, you could tell someone that Buenos Aires is at 60° west longitude on the map.

Now find Leningrad, in the Soviet Union. Leningrad is east of the Prime Meridian. It is at 30° east longitude.

## C. Using Latitude and Longitude

The map on the next page shows a few cities. The map also has lines of latitude and longitude. These lines help us to find places, just as streets and avenues do. The lines of latitude and longitude are like the streets and avenues in that they too form a grid system.

If you wanted to tell someone where to find New York City, you could just say that it is in the United States. However, the United States is a large country, so you would have to give some more information. As you know, lines of latitude and longitude often help us find places on maps and globes.

**LONGITUDE LINES**

Lines of longitude run north and south.
▶ What do lines of longitude measure?

# USING LATITUDE AND LONGITUDE

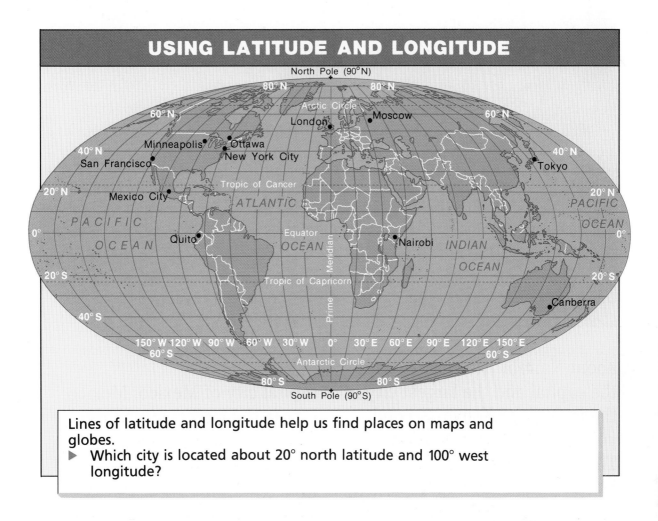

Lines of latitude and longitude help us find places on maps and globes.
▶ Which city is located about 20° north latitude and 100° west longitude?

You could say that New York City is located about 40° north latitude and 75° west longitude. Another way to show this would be to write 40°N/75°W. These would be the grid **coordinates** for New York City. Coordinates are a set of numbers used to find a place on a map or globe. If you know the latitude and longitude of a place, you can easily find it on a map. You do this by finding the place where the line of latitude and the line of longitude cross. To find New York City, put one finger on the line marked 40° north latitude. Put a finger on your other hand on the line marked 75° west longitude. Now move your fingers toward each other on these lines. The place where these two lines meet is the location of New York City.

In this chapter you will be learning about four cities that are located in different parts of the world. First, you will read

People have gathered for a parade in Mexico City.
▶ What is happening to the large Mexican flag?

about Nairobi. This city is both the capital and the largest city in the country of Kenya. Second, you will read about Moscow. This city is the capital of the Soviet Union, the largest country in the world. Next, you will read about Tokyo, one of the world's most populated cities. Tokyo is the capital of Japan. Last, you will read about Mexico City, the capital city of Mexico. Mexico City is the largest city in the world.

Look at the map on page 269. Nairobi, Moscow, Tokyo, and Mexico City are labeled on the map. Can you find each city? Which of these cities is at about 60° north latitude and about 30° east longitude?

LESSON *1* REVIEW

THINK AND WRITE

A. What do lines of latitude measure?
B. What do lines of longitude measure?
C. How are lines of latitude and longitude like streets and avenues on a map?

SKILLS CHECK

THINKING SKILL

How are the Equator and the Prime Meridian alike?

## Learning About Nairobi

### THINK ABOUT WHAT YOU KNOW

Imagine that you will visit an exciting place in Africa. What type of things may you see?

### STUDY THE VOCABULARY

| | |
|---|---|
| ancestor | tourist |
| wilderness | conservation |
| nomads | extinction |
| independence | |

### FOCUS YOUR READING

Why is Nairobi called the Conservation Capital of the World?

## A. Nairobi's Past

Jamal and Margaret's **ancestors** had lived in the city of Nairobi before they came to the United States. An ancestor is a person from whom one is descended—for example, a grandfather, grandmother or great-grandparent.

Nairobi is both the capital city and the largest city in the country of Kenya. This country is on the east coast of the continent of Africa.

Nairobi is sometimes called the City of Flowering Trees. This is because trees and shrubs line the wide streets of the city. Beautiful flowers and trees can also be seen in the city's parks.

Nairobi is a young city. Less than one hundred years ago, the land where the city is today was a **wilderness**. A wilderness is an area that is unsettled, or wild land.

Only a few people lived in the area before the city was there. These people were Africans whose families had lived nearby for hundreds of years. They planted crops and hunted the wild animals for food.

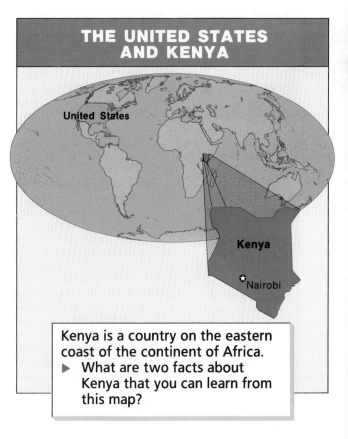

**THE UNITED STATES AND KENYA**

Kenya is a country on the eastern coast of the continent of Africa.
▶ What are two facts about Kenya that you can learn from this map?

Other Africans called **nomads** also lived in the area. These were people who moved from place to place to hunt wild animals and gather food.

The city of Nairobi began when the builders of the railroad camped in the area. They formed a community of workers. People also came to the area because of the farmland and the wild animals.

Many of Nairobi's early settlers were from Great Britain. Kenya became a colony of Great Britain, and these British people became the government leaders.

For many years the blacks in Nairobi suffered hardships and unjust treatment from their government leaders. After many years of unfairness, the people of Kenya won **independence**. This means they became free from the control of another country. They became a country of their own. Kenya became an independent nation on December 12, 1963.

The war for independence was led by Jomo Kenyatta (JOH moh ken YAHT uh). He was elected president of the new country, and Nairobi was named the capital.

Nairobi is a lovely city, with many parks and modern buildings.
▶ What kinds of plants grow in Nairobi?

# PEN PALS

This letter is from a student in Nairobi. The letter describes a special holiday. How is it like an American holiday?

Dear Roxanne,

It was great to get your letter! Since you asked about one of our special holidays, I want to tell you about Kenyatta Day.

Kenyatta Day is celebrated on October 20. The holiday honors Kenya's first president, Jomo Kenyatta, and other heroes who fought for Kenya's independence.

On this day, many of the children meet in Uhuru Park to sing with their school choirs. People dress in traditional Kenyan clothing and sing and dance. Each group of people uses its own language to express thanks.

During the day, the president of Kenya gives a speech. Later, the people gather for a great feast.

In the morning, it will be Kenyatta Day again. I am anxious for the day to come.

Please write soon and tell me about one of your special holidays.

Your pen pal,

Malik

## B. Many Groups of People

Nairobi's population is greater than one million. The people who now live in Nairobi came from many different African tribes. There are also people who came from England, Asia, and other parts of the world. President Kenyatta often used the word *harambee* when he worked with the different groups of people. The word means "let us all pull together." *Harambee* is a word from the Swahili language, the official language of Kenya. The people of Kenya pulled together after the war for independence to build new schools, churches, homes, and farm areas.

Nairobi has become a large city with tall buildings, wide streets, museums, and parks. The city has two large airports and an excellent highway system.

Tourism is an important business in Nairobi. Over 400,000 **tourists** visit Nairobi each year. A tourist is a person who takes a trip for pleasure or learning. One of the reasons people come to Nairobi is to see the beautiful parks. A variety of flowers, trees, and animals can be seen in these parks.

**274**

## C. The Conservation Capital of the World

One of Kenya's most important national parks is located just five miles from the center of Nairobi. The Nairobi National Park is different from the other parks in the city. This park was built to carefully protect the animals and plants from being destroyed. When plants and animals are protected in this way, it is called **conservation**. In addition to lions, the park has rhinoceroses, giraffes, zebras, antelopes, and many different kinds of monkeys.

Many people visit Nairobi National Park, where wild animals such as giraffes roam free.
► Why is this park important?

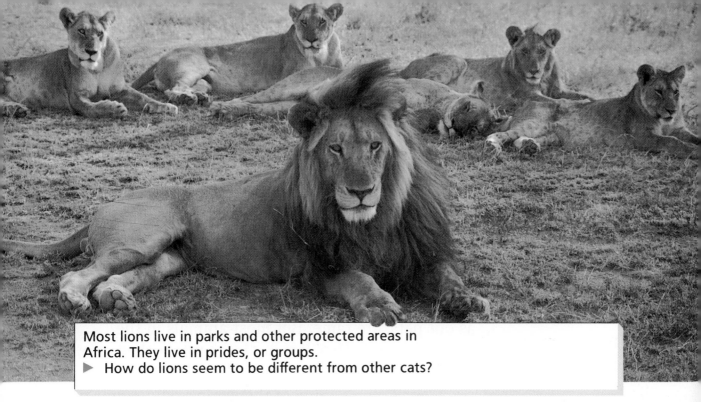

Most lions live in parks and other protected areas in Africa. They live in prides, or groups.
► How do lions seem to be different from other cats?

For years people have hunted the wild animals in Nairobi. When wild animals are hunted in this way they become in danger of **extinction**. This means that they would vanish forever.

The country of Kenya became concerned about saving the wildlife. This is one of the main reasons they developed a system of national parks. People can go through the Nairobi National Park and see many of the animals in their natural environment. Because of this concern and action by the people in Nairobi, the city is called the Conservation Capital of the World.

## LESSON 2 REVIEW

### THINK AND WRITE

A. Where is Nairobi located?
B. Compare the city of Nairobi to your community. List three ways your community is alike or different from Nairobi.
C. What are two ways we can protect the animals of our community?

### SKILLS CHECK

**THINKING SKILL**

Describe a place in Nairobi that you would like to visit. List three reasons why this spot was chosen.

## PROTECTING ENDANGERED ANIMALS

In the last lesson you learned how the people of Kenya are trying to protect wild animals. But the protection of wild animals is the duty of all of the world's people.

People share the earth with many kinds of animals—so many kinds, in fact, that they have never been counted. Some of these animals, such as our pets, are tame. But most animals in the world are wild. They live in places where there are few or no people.

Today, many kinds of the world's wild animals are endangered. This means that their numbers are small. They are in danger of becoming extinct, or of dying out.

Look at the animals on these pages. Do you recognize them? Most of these wild animals do not live in our country. They are only a few of the kinds of endangered animals that live in different parts of the world.

But we have many endangered animals in our own country. The Alaskan brown bear, spotted leopard, and whooping crane are but a few. Some of these animals have become endangered because of too much

Black rhinoceros

Spotted leopard

Brown pelican

hunting. Others are dying because of land development. As people clear the land for houses, the animals' food supply is destroyed. Still other animals are being poisoned by air and water pollution.

Today, Americans as well as people around the world are trying to protect these animals and help them survive. Hunting laws are being changed. Land is being set aside for the animals to live on. Pollution is being controlled. Some zoos are even trying to raise endangered animals. But there is still much to be done. It is the duty of all people to show that they care for the earth and all the living things on it.

## Thinking for Yourself

1. Do you know of a place in your community or state where animals are protected?
2. What are some things citizens can do to protect endangered animals?

Perigrine falcon

African elephant

## Learning About Moscow

**THINK ABOUT WHAT YOU KNOW**

The country of the Soviet Union covers parts of two continents. The two continents together are often called Eurasia. Can you name the two continents?

**STUDY THE VOCABULARY**

| | |
|---|---|
| fortress | communism |
| tsar | Kremlin |

**FOCUS YOUR READING**

How is communism different from the type of government present in the United States?

### THE UNITED STATES AND THE SOVIET UNION

The Soviet Union is the largest country in the world.
▶ Is Moscow located in the eastern or western part of the Soviet Union?

## A. Moscow's Past

Nicole and John's ancestors had lived in the city of Moscow in the Soviet Union before they came to the United States. This is Nicole and John's report.

The Soviet Union, which was called Russia long ago, is the largest country in the world. It covers a sixth of the earth's land area, more than twice the area of the United States. The Soviet Union is the world's third most populated country, with about 290 million people.

Moscow is the capital and most populated city in the Soviet Union. The metropolitan area of Moscow has a population of about 9 million people. A city's metropolitan area includes the city and the smaller towns and cities around the city. For hundreds of years, Moscow has been a center of business, industry, and entertainment. Find Moscow on the map on this page.

Moscow was founded by Yuri Dolgoruky in 1147. For protection Dolgoruky built a

278

wooden **fortress** on a hill overlooking the Moscow River. A fortress is a building with strong walls to defend against enemies. Moscow soon became the most important city in Russia.

Moscow remained the capital of Russia until a new capital was built by Peter the Great in St. Petersburg. This city is now called Leningrad.

Peter the Great was a well-known **tsar** who ruled in the 1600s and 1700s. The word *tsar* means "emperor." A tsar had complete power over the country and the people of that country. Peter the Great created an army and a navy for Russia and the country became one of the most powerful in the world.

Today Russia is known as the Soviet Union. Once again, Moscow is the capital of the country. Tsars do not rule the

Red Square is in the center of Moscow. At one end stands the famous St. Basil's Church, with its eight domes.
▶ What do these domes look like?

Soviet Union, which has a form of government called **communism**.

A communist government has much more control over the way people live than our government has. People under communism cannot say certain things. They cannot always live where they choose. They cannot own houses, land, or businesses. All those things belong to the government.

During the late 1980s the Soviet Union began to change. Mikhail Gorbachev and some other leaders worked to give more freedom to the people.

Children in the Soviet Union go to school six days a week. They study very hard.
▶ How is this school like yours?

## B. Everyday Life

The children in the Soviet Union begin school at the age of seven. They start school on the first day of September each year. Children in the Soviet Union attend school for six days each week. Sunday is the only day that they do not go to school. Students are required to attend school until the age of seventeen. Education is free. There are no private schools. There are schools for handicapped children and for gifted children.

Students stay with the same classmates from year to year. They usually finish high school with the same boys and girls that they met on the first day of the first grade.

The Moscow River runs along the Kremlin walls. Inside these walls are beautiful palaces and government buildings.
▶ Have you ever been in any government buildings?

All students in the Soviet Union follow the same course of study. They use books that are alike, and they also wear uniforms that are alike.

Many of the people in the Soviet Union live in apartment buildings. The people who live in Moscow must have permission from the government to live in this city.

Many people ride the subway to work. The subway is called the Metro. Moscow is the transportation center of the Soviet Union. Highways and railways extend in all directions from the city to all parts of the country. The city's leading industry is the manufacturing of autos, buses, and trucks.

People in Moscow shop for food and clothing in stores that are owned by the government. Things that we take for granted, such as TVs and autos, are limited in the Soviet Union.

One of the most famous landmarks in Moscow is an old fortress called the **Kremlin**. Look at the picture of the Kremlin on this page. Inside the fortress there are many buildings. One of these is called the Palace of Congresses. This is where the Russian parliament meets. A parliament is made up of people who make laws for the country. The main office of government is at the Kremlin. Many people who live in Moscow work for the Soviet government.

## C. Culture in Moscow

Moscow is known for its fine culture. People in Moscow like to go see the ballet. The Bolshoi Ballet of Moscow is one of the best in the world. These dancers perform their ballet in the Bolshoi Theater. It is one of the oldest theaters in the Soviet Union. Over 2,000 people can be seated in this theater. Moscow has some theaters that are especially for children. At these theaters, children can see puppet shows, plays, and ballets. The people of Moscow also like to visit museums, art galleries, and concert halls.

Many famous writers have lived in Moscow. The houses where famous writers lived have been preserved and have been made into museums.

The 1980 Summer Olympic Games were held in Moscow. Moscow was the first Soviet city to host the Olympics. Many sports facilities and hotels were built for the Olympics.

Ice skating is one of the most popular winter activities for people who live in Moscow. This is because it is very cold in the winter in the Soviet Union.

These dancers with the Bolshoi Ballet are performing *Carmen*.
▶ Have you ever seen a ballet?

Every year 7 million people go to Gorky Park. There are many things to do there.
▶ What are these people doing?

In the summer, people go to the parks. Moscow has three large parks and eleven smaller parks. There are lakes, ponds, and beautiful trees and flowers in the parks.

Gorky Park is the most famous park in Moscow. It has over 300 acres. In Gorky Park there is an area that has fun rides such as the ferris wheel and the merry-go-round. There is a big outdoor theater where concerts are held. As you can see, there are many forms of entertainment in Moscow.

## LESSON 3 REVIEW

### THINK AND WRITE

A. Why was a fortress built in Moscow?

B. What are two ways that the school systems of the United States and the Soviet Union are alike? What are two ways they are different?

C. Describe two activities that the people in Moscow and the people in your community enjoy.

### SKILLS CHECK

WRITING SKILL

If you were able to change the government of Moscow what would you do? Write a paragraph that describes your changes.

# Learning About Tokyo

What are some products that are made in Japan?

**emperor**     **calligraphy**
**technology**

How did the city of Tokyo become one of the world's most populated cities?

## A. Tokyo's Past

Miko and Richard were anxious to give their report about Tokyo. Miko and Richard lived in Tokyo before they came to the United States two years ago. Here is their report about Tokyo, the capital city of Japan.

Tokyo is one of the world's most populated cities. More than 8 million people live in Tokyo. Tokyo wasn't always a large city. Hundreds of years ago, Tokyo was just a small town. The town was built around a castle that stood where the Imperial Palace now stands. This is the home of Japan's **emperor**, or ruler.

In 1457 the town was named Edo. It was named after a powerful family who settled there. During most of its history, the town was called Edo. In 1868, Edo was renamed Tokyo. This is when Tokyo became the capital of Japan. *Tokyo* means "eastern capital."

The city of Tokyo was almost destroyed two times. In 1923 a terrible earthquake hit Tokyo and killed 59,000 people. In the 1940s much of the city was damaged during a war. The people worked for 20 years rebuilding the city.

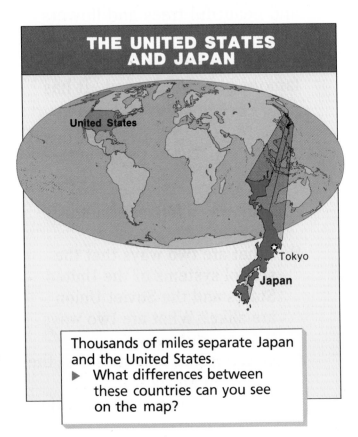

**THE UNITED STATES AND JAPAN**

United States

Tokyo

Japan

Thousands of miles separate Japan and the United States.
▶ What differences between these countries can you see on the map?

## B. Life in Tokyo

Tokyo is like an American city in many ways. It has tall buildings, overcrowded highways, and many people. Teenagers listen to tunes by American and European musicians. Many people go to restaurants. Some of these eating places have a variety of food, including hamburgers and other American dishes. People in Tokyo also enjoy baseball games, television shows, and movies.

Education is valued highly in Tokyo. Japanese children attend school Monday through Friday and half a day on Saturday. They go to school about 225 days per year. Children in the United States go to school about 180 days per year.

In Tokyo the schools attended by the younger children are called primary schools. Here the children learn to speak proper Japanese. They also learn history, math, science, music, arts and crafts, gym, and homemaking. By the end of primary school, the children have already learned **calligraphy**, which is the art of beautiful writing. It is an ancient art form from Asia. Calligraphy is done with a brush or pen.

Japanese children are required to know how to write Japanese and some Chinese. The Chinese language does not have an alphabet. It has thousands of characters that stand for words. Japanese has characters, too, but the characters represent either words or syllables.

Because education is so important in Japan, many children go to the Juku school. The Juku is an after-school program that helps the children prepare for tests. These tests show if the children should be moved to higher levels of study.

Japanese children work very hard to learn to write.
► Why might it be hard to learn to write Japanese?

Japanese factories make many different products. Cars built there are sent all over the world.
▶ Do you know any other countries that make cars?

There are many factories in Japan. Some are small with less than 20 workers. Others are large with as many as 20,000 workers. Automobiles, ships, machinery, iron, and steel are some leading products made in Japan.

Japan is one of the world's leaders in the making of VCR's, televisions, calculators, cameras, and computers. Japan is a leader in the field of **technology**. This is the use of science in solving problems in industry.

There are many fun things to do in Tokyo. For example, some people enjoy concerts, movies, and plays. Baseball is Tokyo's most popular sport. Many people enjoy watching the Tokyo Giants. The Japanese also enjoy bowling, golf, track and field contests, ice-skating, and tennis.

The National Diet Building and Tokyo Tower attract many visitors. Japan's Diet, or parliament, meets in the National Diet Building. The Tokyo Tower is the tallest tower in Tokyo.

The parks and gardens in Tokyo are beautiful places to visit. In the spring, cherry blossoms fill the parks and gardens. In the summer people enjoy the lotus blossoms. Veno Park is one of Tokyo's most popular parks. It includes Tokyo's largest concert hall, museums, a zoo, and a temple.

## C. Neighborhoods of Tokyo

Tokyo has many different neighborhoods. Let's discover more about Tokyo by reading about four of its famous neighborhoods.

Akihabara is filled with stores selling electronic goods. Televisions, compact disc players, and video cameras are just some of the things that can be found here.

The neighborhood of Shinjuko is the largest neighborhood in Tokyo. Its skyscrapers, theaters, restaurants, and shops attract people from other areas. One of the busiest train stations in the world is located here.

Ikebukuro is a busy neighborhood with several big department stores. While visiting one of these stores, a

Many Japanese people buy fresh fish at a fish market.
▶ Why, do you think, is fish so popular in Japan?

person may look at pets, toys, furniture, food, and clothes.

The neighborhood of Tsukiji has the city's largest fish market. Many restaurant and market owners come here to buy fish. Fish is one of the main foods of the people in Tokyo.

You can see from this report why Miko and Richard liked to live in Tokyo. There are so many places to go to have fun.

---

LESSON 4 REVIEW

### THINK AND WRITE

A. How was the city of Tokyo almost destroyed two times?
B. How is Tokyo like an American city?
C. Why would a person living in Tokyo visit the community of Akihabara?

### SKILLS CHECK

**THINKING SKILL**

Invent a product of your own. Describe what it will look like, how it will be used, how much it will cost, and what kinds of people may buy it?

# Learning About Mexico City

What things do you know about Mexico City?

| | |
|---|---|
| plaza | pollution |
| ruin | exhaust |

How is the history of Mexico City shown in the city today?

## A. Mexico City's Past

Robert and Marie asked Mrs. Peterson if they could give a report on Mexico City. Robert's grandparents had lived in Mexico City and had come to the United States many years ago. Robert and Marie were interested in finding out all they could about Mexico City. Let's see what they found out.

Mexico City is the largest city in the world. Over 9 million people live there. It is the capital city of Mexico. It is also the oldest city in the country.

Mexico City has an interesting history. It has been the capital city of different groups of people throughout history. The first people to settle in Mexico City were called the Aztecs (AZ teks). About 700 years ago the Aztecs built a capital city where Mexico City is located today. The city was called Tenochtitlán (te nawch tee TLAHN). It was a great city. The people who lived there built big pyramids. A *pyramid* is a carefully built stone structure with four triangular sides. These pyramids were burial places and places where people could go to worship. Some of these pyramids are still standing today.

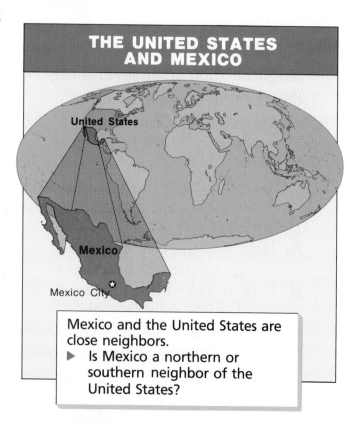

**THE UNITED STATES AND MEXICO**

United States

Mexico

Mexico City

Mexico and the United States are close neighbors.
► Is Mexico a northern or southern neighbor of the United States?

288

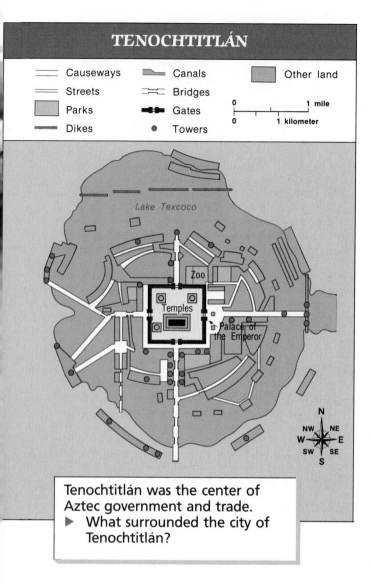

## TENOCHTITLÁN

| | | | |
|---|---|---|---|
| —— Causeways | ▬ Canals | ▨ Other land | |
| ═══ Streets | ⇥⇤ Bridges | | |
| ▨ Parks | ◼▬ Gates | 0 · · · 1 mile | |
| ⋯⋯ Dikes | ● Towers | 0 · · · 1 kilometer | |

Lake Texcoco

Zoo

Temples

Palace of the Emperor

N
NW · NE
W ✦ E
SW · SE
S

Tenochtitlán was the center of Aztec government and trade.
▶ What surrounded the city of Tenochtitlán?

In the 1500s, Spanish conquerors took over the land from the Aztecs. The Spanish were led by Hernando Cortés. Cortés and his army destroyed the capital city. In place of Tenochtitlán the Spanish built a new town called Mexico City. They used Mexico City as their capital. The Spanish people built palaces and churches that looked like buildings in Spain. Some of these buildings can be seen in Mexico City today.

The country of Mexico was ruled by the Spanish for almost 300 years. In 1810 the Mexican people revolted and set up their own government. In 1864 the ruler of France took over the government of Mexico. This government lasted three years. During this time many buildings were built that looked like buildings in France. In 1867, Mexico was once again governed by people in Mexico.

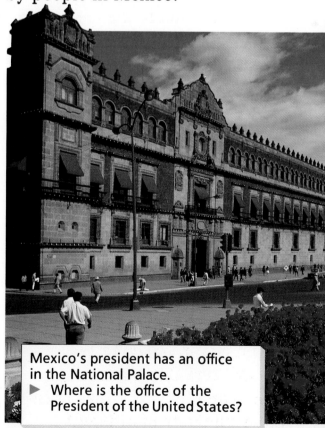

Mexico's president has an office in the National Palace.
▶ Where is the office of the President of the United States?

289

## B. Life in Mexico City

Some of the buildings from Mexico City's past have been carefully saved. The **Plaza** of Three Cultures is one of the interesting places to visit in the city. A plaza is a public square in a town or city. This plaza has **ruins** of ancient Aztec temples. A ruin is a thing from the past. The steps that lead up to the plaza were built by the Aztecs. One old church was built by the Spaniards in 1524. There are also new buildings that have been built by the people of modern-day Mexico City.

People can watch workers uncover Aztec ruins at the Plaza of Three Cultures.
▶ What ruins do you see here?

The Plaza of the Three Cultures combines ancient and modern Mexico. Many people visit it.
▶ What are some things that can be seen in this plaza?

Over half of the people in Mexico City are younger than 18 years old. Every week more people come to the city looking for work. There are not enough jobs for everyone.

On September 19, 1985, at 7 A.M., an earthquake hit Mexico. The greatest damage was to Mexico City. Many hotels, government buildings, hospitals, and apartment buildings were knocked down or badly damaged. Over 7,000 people died. Many countries, including the United States, helped Mexico City recover from the disaster.

## C. Mexico City Today

Mexico City is a huge, busy city. Since it is the capital of Mexico, many people who live there work for the government. There are also many factories located in Mexico City. Goods such as automobiles are manufactured there. Mexico City's major transportation system is called the Metro. The Metro is a subway known for its colorfully painted walls.

Air **pollution** is a serious problem in Mexico City. Pollution is the act of making the air, land, and water dirty. Sometimes cars and factories cause pollution. Pollution is caused by many things. The **exhaust** from all of the motor vehicles in the city damages the air. Exhaust is the smoke from a gasoline engine. The dust that comes from the unpaved streets also affects the city in a bad way. This dust escapes into the air and causes pollution. Industrial smoke also adds to the pollution in Mexico City.

Mexico City has a large number of industries. The government does not want new industries built in the city. They are trying to help some

The National University of Mexico is famous for its buildings and artwork.
▶ What is in this mural?

# PEN PALS

This letter is from a student in Mexico City. He tells about his life in that city. What are some activities that José enjoys?

Dear Students,

My name is José Antonio. I live in Mexico City. I am in the third grade. My brother and I go to an American school that is about 15 miles from our house. We ride the school bus. Our school buses are not yellow. They are a brick red color. Half of my classes are in English and half are in Spanish. My favorite subject is science. I like sports. We have an after-school sports program. I am learning football and tennis.

On Saturdays and Sundays my family and I like to visit different places in the city. We enjoy visiting the museums. I like the scientific experiments at the Technology Museum.

Sometimes we go downtown to the Zócalo. This is the old Spanish section of the city. On Sundays we are allowed a ride on a police department horse. The police talk to us and answer our questions.

Please write to me again.

In friendship,
José Antonio Poot Cassas

industries in Mexico City move out of the polluted areas.

Sports such as baseball, football, soccer, basketball, golf, horse racing, and tennis are familiar sports in Mexico City. Another game enjoyed by many is Jai Alai (hye uh LYE). This game is like handball. The players hit the ball against a wall with a basketlike racket.

One of the most famous city parks in the world is Chapultepac (chuh POOL tuh pek) Park. Many families go to the park on Sunday to relax. It is enjoyable for the people to visit the zoo, go on the amusement park rides, and watch the entertainers perform. Chapultepac Castle sits high on a hill in the park. This is where the rulers of Mexico City once lived. It is now the National Museum of History.

The dancers in the Ballet Folklorico wear bright costumes.
▶ What shows have you seen with beautiful costumes?

Tourists like to visit the Zona Rosa, or Pink Zone, of Mexico City. This downtown shopping area has theaters, hotels, stores, and restaurants. As you can see, there are many fun things to do and see in Mexico City.

---

LESSON 5 REVIEW

### THINK AND WRITE

A. Why does Mexico City have an interesting history?
B. Why do a great number of Mexicans come to live in Mexico City?
C. What are three ways communities can reduce air pollution?

### SKILLS CHECK

MAP SKILL

Look at the map on page 288. On which continent is Mexico located?

## USING THE VOCABULARY

| longitude | latitude |
|---|---|
| coordinates | nomads |
| ancestor | calligraphy |
| Kremlin | plaza |
| communism | tsar |

On a separate sheet of paper, write the word or words from above that best complete the sentences.

1. The Equator is a special line of _____.
2. A set of numbers used to find a place on a map or globe are called _____.
3. A person from whom one is descended is an _____.
4. _____ is an ancient art form in Asia; each drawing stands for a character in the alphabet.
5. _____ is a form of government that has control of the land and the people of the country.
6. The _____ is one of the most famous landmarks in Moscow.
7. The Prime Meridian is a special line of _____.
8. People who often move from place to place are _____.
9. A former ruler of Russia was called a _____.
10. A _____ is a public square in a town or city.

## REMEMBERING WHAT YOU READ

On a separate sheet of paper, answer the questions in complete sentences.

1. Where is the Equator located?
2. Where is Nairobi located?
3. Why did Dolgoruky build a fortress in Moscow?
4. Why was Tokyo once named Edo?
5. Who were the first people to settle in Mexico?

## TYING SCIENCE TO SOCIAL STUDIES

List three ways that conservation is practiced in your community. What is one way you can help.

## THINKING CRITICALLY

On a separate sheet of paper, answer the following in complete sentences.

1. Locate your town and state on a map. Find the degree of latitude.
2. Nairobi is sometimes called, "The City of Flowering Trees." If you could give your community a name, what would it be?
3. Compare the government of the Soviet Union to that of the United States. List three ways they are different.
4. Why do you think Tokyo is one of the world's most populated cities?
5. Why do you think Mexico City preserved many ruins?

## SUMMARIZING THE CHAPTER

Copy this graphic organizer on a separate sheet of paper. Under the main idea for each lesson, write three facts that support the main idea.

| CHAPTER THEME | It is exciting to learn about communities from around the world. |
| --- | --- |

**LESSON 1**

**Latitude and longitude help us locate places on a map.**

1. _____
2. _____
3. _____

**LESSON 2**

**Nairobi is a city in the country of Kenya.**

1. _____
2. _____
3. _____

**LESSON 3**

**Moscow is a city in the Soviet Union.**

1. _____
2. _____
3. _____

**LESSON 4**

**Tokyo is a city in the country of Japan.**

1. _____
2. _____
3. _____

**LESSON 5**

**Mexico City is a city in the country of Mexico.**

1. _____
2. _____
3. _____

# 13

## WORKING TOGETHER AROUND THE WORLD

*E*very day, people work together to make the world a better place. At the United Nations, people from many countries meet to try to solve world problems.

LESSON 1

## Where Does This Airplane Come From?

**THINK ABOUT WHAT YOU KNOW**

Have you ever visited an airport and watched the planes arriving and departing? How did you feel as you watched?

**STUDY THE VOCABULARY**

**interdependence  headquarters**

**FOCUS YOUR READING**

Why is cooperation important in building an airplane?

---

### A. How This Airplane Is Made

Mr. Toro's class has been studying different kinds of transportation. Today the students are especially excited. This is the day for their field trip to the Boeing aircraft factory. They have been learning about the Boeing 747. When they arrive at the factory, they are introduced to their tour guide, Mrs. Gregory. She explains that the final part of building the airplane is done here.

The Boeing Company is one of the largest airplane manufacturers in the United States. Boeing makes both small and large airplanes. Mrs. Gregory said that it takes one month to assemble, or put together, an airplane in this factory. Mrs. Gregory tells the class that over 600 people work on the assembly line. As you know, an assembly line is a group of workers who add parts to what is being made. For example, on an airplane assembly line, the frame of the airplane is rolled on its wheels to stations where a specific kind of work is done. At Boeing the airplane is moved

This is a factory where people build airplanes.
▶ What does this photograph show about the size of an airplane factory?

297

Airplanes are built in stages. Here the workers are attaching the wings.
▶ How do workers get to the high parts of the airplane?

from one station to another about every four days. The wings are attached to the center section of the body, and then the front and back sections are attached to the body. Later, all the parts inside of the plane, such as the seats, carpets, restrooms, and galleys, are installed. The galley is the area where the food is prepared.

## B. Many Communities Are Involved

Mrs. Gregory explains to the class that a lot of the parts needed to make the airplane are made in other factories. These factories are in different parts of the United States and the world. The parts that are made in other factories must be transported to the Boeing factory. Thousands of people work to build the airplane, but they don't all work at this factory.

Many different parts are needed to make an airplane. The outside of an airplane is usually made of aluminum or some other kind of metal. Boeing gets most of the aluminum that it needs from the state of Washington.

The students are curious about where the parts of the airplane are built. Mrs. Gregory uses the map of the world to locate the places. The nose section is put together in Kansas. The tail section is put together in Texas. These sections are then moved to Seattle on railroad cars. Many small parts are put together into bigger parts before the final assembly takes place at this factory. Some engines are made by a company in Connecticut. Other engines are made in England. Companies in nearly every state of the United States and in many other countries supply parts to help build the Boeing 747.

Portland, Oregon, is the site of another Boeing factory. This factory uses raw materials to make parts of the airplane. They make such things as the wings and the fuselage. The fuselage is the body of the aircraft.

Mrs. Gregory asks one of the students to come to the map and point to where the factory they are visiting is located. John raises his hand and goes to the map. He tells Mrs. Gregory that the factory is near Seattle, Washington. Mrs. Gregory explains that the large airplanes are made in a building just north of Seattle.

At the Boeing factory in Seattle, several airplanes can be built at the same time.
▶ How is building a plane different from building some other machines?

## C. Transportation and Interdependence

It would be almost impossible to put an airplane together without good means of transportation. Boeing chose Seattle as the place to build its plant because this city can be reached by land, sea, and air.

Boeing has even built special trains to transport large pieces of airplanes to Seattle. Also, some materials are now shipped by airplane. These different means of transportation make it possible for states and countries to depend on each other. This is called **interdependence**.

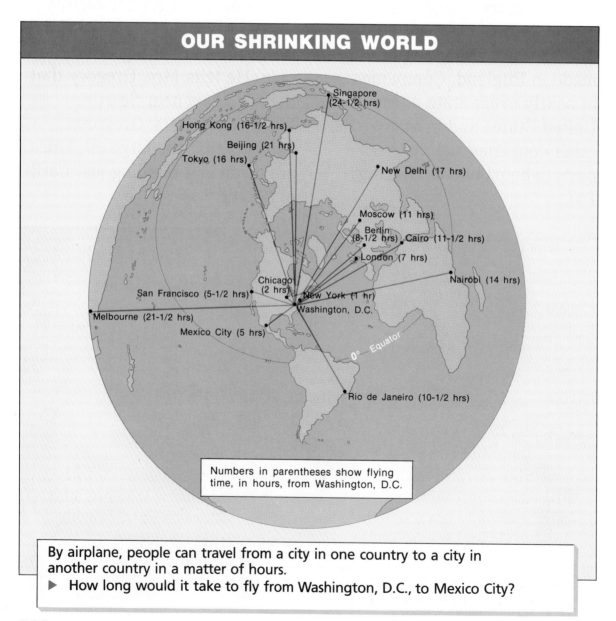

## OUR SHRINKING WORLD

Singapore (24-1/2 hrs)
Hong Kong (16-1/2 hrs)
Beijing (21 hrs)
Tokyo (16 hrs)
New Delhi (17 hrs)
Moscow (11 hrs)
Berlin (8-1/2 hrs)  Cairo (11-1/2 hrs)
London (7 hrs)
Nairobi (14 hrs)
Chicago (2 hrs)
San Francisco (5-1/2 hrs)
New York (1 hr)
Washington, D.C.
Melbourne (21-1/2 hrs)
Mexico City (5 hrs)
0° Equator
Rio de Janeiro (10-1/2 hrs)

Numbers in parentheses show flying time, in hours, from Washington, D.C.

By airplane, people can travel from a city in one country to a city in another country in a matter of hours.
▶ How long would it take to fly from Washington, D.C., to Mexico City?

Boeing airplanes are bought by many different airline companies. They are used to travel all over the world.
▶ What are some places you've flown to?

You have learned that many people in different places work to build an airplane. The planes are sold to companies all over the world. The planes then fly back and forth to all parts of the world. Seattle is the **headquarters**, or business center, of the Boeing Company. But the making, selling, and use of a Boeing airplane are excellent examples of interdependence.

LESSON *1* REVIEW

THINK AND WRITE
A. How long does it take to assemble an airplane in the Boeing aircraft factory?
B. Why are many communities involved in making the airplane?
C. How do communities all over the world depend on each other through transportation?

SKILLS CHECK
WRITING SKILL
Write a short paragraph on where the parts of an airplane are built. Draw a picture to go with your paragraph. You might draw an airplane and label some of the important parts.

# Working in Another Country

## THINK ABOUT WHAT YOU KNOW

People in the United States need to speak to people in countries all over the world. How are we able to do this?

## STUDY THE VOCABULARY

**teleconference   communication
fax machine        satellite**

## FOCUS YOUR READING

Why is it important that the United States talk to other countries?

After a long flight it feels good to arrive.
▶ Where do you think these people have landed?

## A. Traveling to Japan

Airplanes enable some people who live in one country to do part of their work in other countries. Anna's mother works for a bank. The bank has offices in Japan, Germany, and Brazil. Find these countries in an Atlas. Sometimes Anna's mother, Mrs. Stevens, visits one of these offices. This week Mrs. Stevens will travel to Japan. She has invited Anna to go with her. They will fly from Los Angeles to Tokyo, Japan. Anna's mother helped Anna make a list. Anna packed her things for the trip.

The trip from Los Angeles to Tokyo is 5,470 miles. Over 11 hours after they leave Los Angeles, Anna and her mother arrive in Tokyo. Anna and her mother take a taxi ride to their hotel. Anna suddenly realizes that she is very tired. She looks at her watch and discovers that it is 9:00 P.M. at her home in the United States. Anna looks out the window of the taxi and sees that the sun is shining very brightly. She asks her mother to tell her the time in Tokyo. Her mother reminds her of the 17-hour time difference between

| MONEY AROUND THE WORLD | | |
|---|---|---|
| Country | Unit of Money | Equals |
| U.S.A | 1 dollar | 100 cents |
| Mexico | 1 peso | 100 centavos |
| Kenya | 1 shilling | 100 cents |
| U.S.S.R. | 1 ruble | 100 kopecks |
| Japan | 1 yen | 100 sen |

This table shows some units of money in different countries.
▶ How are these units of money alike?

clerk a five-dollar bill. The clerk exchanges her money for Japanese money.

It is almost dinner time, so Anna and her mother go to dinner at a restaurant near the hotel. A man who works at her mother's bank in Japan joins them for dinner. His name is Jara Kurisaka. Anna's mother introduces Anna. He bows toward Anna, and Anna bows politely to him. He then explains to Anna that in Japan a person bows when he or she is introduced to someone. This is a very old custom. The bow shows respect for the other person.

Los Angeles and Tokyo. When it is 9:00 P.M. in Los Angeles, it is 2:00 P.M. the next day in Tokyo.

When they arrive at their hotel, Anna's mother takes out her purse to pay the taxicab driver. Anna notices that the money looks different from American money. After they get inside the hotel, Anna's mother explains that the American money must be exchanged for Japanese money. Then, Anna and her mother walk to a bank. Anna decides to exchange her money also. She gives the bank

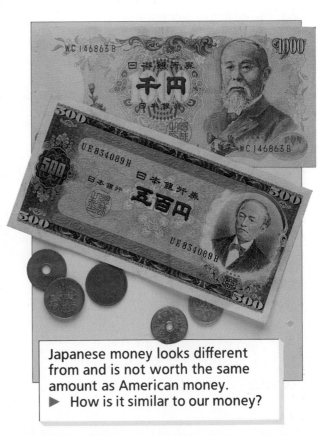

Japanese money looks different from and is not worth the same amount as American money.
▶ How is it similar to our money?

Anna's new friend helps her read the menu. He tells her that in Japan the most important food is rice. It is served at all meals. Vegetables such as water chestnuts, bamboo shoots, and bean sprouts are also part of the Japanese diet. Anna decides that she wants rice and vegetables. When her food arrives, it is beautifully arranged. Chopsticks are used instead of knives and forks. Anna is delighted with her meal. Anna and her mother return to their hotel. It has been a good day.

## B. Workers at the Bank

The next morning, Anna wakes up excited about going with her mother to do business at the bank. Before they leave the hotel, Anna's mother uses the telephone to talk to workers at the bank in Los Angeles. Anna discovers that one of the most important inventions and ways of talking with other people is the telephone. We can use the telephone to talk with someone in our own community or with someone in another country.

Tokyo, Japan's capital, is a very busy city. People from all over the world travel there for business and pleasure.
▶ How would you describe this scene in Tokyo?

Nowadays it is easy to keep in touch with people all over the world with the help of communications equipment.
▶ What are some ways you can communicate with people in foreign countries?

When Anna and her mother arrive at the bank, her mother goes to a meeting. Anna sits quietly in the meeting room. Once again, Anna is surprised that all the people speak English. As Anna sits quietly listening, her mother is using a computer to get some information. Computers offer people ways to both give and receive information.

Early in the afternoon Mrs. Stevens and some of the other people are together for a **teleconference**. They use a telephone system that allows each person to hear and to talk with some of the people at the bank in the United States. This way the people in Japan are able to conduct business with the people in Los Angeles without making a special trip.

After the teleconference, Anna's mother writes a report. The workers in Los Angeles need the report the same day. Anna wonders how her mother will get the report to them that fast. Then Anna remembers that telegrams can be sent all over the world. She asks her mother if she is going to send a telegram.

Anna's mother tells her that there is now a machine that is faster than the telegraph machine. It is called a **fax machine**. Her mother takes the report to the fax machine, dials a number, and places the report in the machine. The report is instantly received in Los Angeles.

## C. Mass Communication Around the World

Anna decides that being involved in business in another part of the world is interesting and exciting. She is surprised that

| Form of Communication | Top Three Countries | Total Number |
|---|---|---|
| Television | U.S.A. | 185 million |
| | U.S.S.R. | 140 million |
| | Japan | 66 million |
| Radio | U.S.A. | 479 million |
| | U.S.S.R. | 136 million |
| | Japan | 85 million |
| Telephone | U.S.A. | 183 million |
| | Japan | 61 million |
| | W.Germany | 35 million |

**TELEVISION, RADIOS AND TELEPHONES: WHO HAS THE MOST?**

This table shows several ways people can communicate
▶ Which form of communication do you think people use most?

she learned so much about **communication** by traveling with her mother. *Communication* means "the giving and receiving of information." Communication helps us learn about our community, our country, and our world. Anna thought it was interesting to see people using different forms of communication in their work.

You have probably realized that communication is one way of bringing people together. By communicating we learn more about other people. Think about Anna's trip. Anna saw some of the ways that people and ideas are brought together by communication. Speaking, listening, reading, and writing are all forms of communication. These forms of communication occur through various means, such as newspapers, television, and letters. Can you recall some of the means of communication that Anna saw people use? Did you name telephone, computer, report, and fax machine?

Can you think of some other ways of communicating? Did you think of magazines, books, radio, and **satellites**? A satellite is an object that circles the earth, carrying special communication equipment. Giant rockets have lifted the satellites thousands of miles into space. On the ground, special stations send signals to a satellite. From out in space, the satellite sends the signals back to stations in another country. Satellites are used to communicate with people in other countries.

In the future we may be able to communicate in ways that we have not yet thought of today. What kinds of changes in communication do you think will take place in the future?

People can communicate around the world today. They may begin to understand each other's problems and work to solve them.

This weather satellite circles the earth, sending signals.
▶ What kinds of information might we get from a weather satellite?

## LESSON 2 REVIEW

### THINK AND WRITE

A. In Japan when a person is introduced to someone, it is polite to bow toward that person. What type of greeting do we use when we meet someone in the United States?

B. Why are fax machines important?

C. What are three ways that people in the United States communicate with people in other countries?

### SKILLS CHECK

**THINKING SKILL**

Make a chart listing ways to communicate. Make two columns labeled PRESENT and FUTURE. Place an x next to each means of communication that is used today. Place an x next to each that you think will be used in the future. For example:

WAYS TO COMMUNICATE

| | Present | Future |
|---|---|---|
| Telephone | x | x |

## People Helping People

### THINK ABOUT WHAT YOU KNOW
Remember a time when you helped someone who needed help. How did that make you feel?

### STUDY THE VOCABULARY
**Eskimo**  **conflict**
**culture**

### FOCUS YOUR READING
Why is it important that people cooperate with each other?

## A. Working Together to Save Animals

It was freezing weather in Alaska during the month of October 1988. Look at the world map in the Atlas and locate Alaska. Winter had come early that year. During the first three weeks of October, temperatures had dropped to below zero. The sea water froze quickly in zero-degree weather. In three hours a layer of ice had formed on the water. In the ocean, not too far from Point Barrow, Alaska, three young California gray whales had been trapped in the ice and could not swim to a warmer place, where the water was not frozen. The whales had survived for more than a week by breathing through two jagged holes in the ice. They were about 7 miles from warmer open water.

People from all over the world found out about the situation of these three whales. It was reported in every newspaper. Millions of people in different countries also got the

information from television. Immediately, people became concerned and wanted to help rescue the whales.

To help save the three whales, a trail had to be opened through the ice so that they could swim to warmer waters. For such a trail to be made, the ice had to be broken. A 5-ton ball was carried by helicopter and dropped on the ice to crack it. Then big chain saws were used to cut through the ice.

Finally, an icebreaker from the Soviet Union finished the job of clearing a path through the ice to open water.

Alaskan natives, called Inuits or **Eskimos**, helped in the rescue effort. The National Guard of Alaska, the government of Alaska, and the United States government all helped in the rescue. Marine biologists came to help. These are people who study the ocean and the plants and animals in the ocean. They

People from all over helped each other save the whales in Alaska. Television stations carried the story everywhere.
▶ Have you ever worked in a group to accomplish something important?

are experts. Some marine biologists came from as far away as the Soviet Union. They gave the whales names—Bonnet, Crossbeak, and Bone. Two of the three whales were able to follow the water trail through the ice and survive.

People from all over the world had helped in the rescue effort. When people from different countries and different **cultures**, or ways of life, come together and cooperate, many good things can happen.

Being a Peace Corps volunteer is a very satisfying job.
▶ What are some ways you'd like to help people in poorer areas?

## B. Helping Others Around the World

People helping people is the main idea behind the Peace Corps. What is the Peace Corps? How did it get started? When John F. Kennedy was running for President of the United States, he was late for a speech he was to give at the University of Michigan. It was after midnight when he arrived at the university, but there were thousands of students still waiting to hear him speak. He talked to them about how they could help other people in the world. He told them they should use their skills and talents by going to countries that needed help for their people. People in those countries were often poor and hungry. Many could not read or write, and there weren't enough doctors or nurses to help them when they got sick.

After the students heard Mr. Kennedy, they were excited and said that they would like to do something to help. It was then that Mr. Kennedy suggested a program called the Peace Corps. People of all ages could volunteer to spend two years helping poor people solve their own problems. Volunteers would be sent to countries that asked for help.

On March 1, 1961, less than three months after John F. Kennedy became President, the Peace Corps was started. By August 30, 1961, the first group of 50 Peace Corps volunteers went to a country named Ghana.

What do Peace Corps members do? Let's read a story about one of these volunteers. His name is Ken Hill. He went to a country named Turkey as a member of the Peace Corps.

"I was 23 years old when I joined the Peace Corps. I had graduated from college and was a junior high history teacher. It was an exciting moment when I applied to the Peace Corps. I later got my appointment to go to Turkey. I had never been there. I read all I could to find out about that country. I spent the first few months attending a training school. There I was taught the Turkish language. I learned about the history, culture, and customs of Turkey. When I arrived in Turkey, I was given a small hut to live in. I lived in the village with the people I was to help. I got to know all the people in the village. I worked every day

These people are about to join the Peace Corps. They are with President Kennedy.
► How do you think they feel?

helping them. We built houses and schools. I also helped them to build an irrigation system, which would give them more water to help grow more food. Most of these people did not have enough food. One of the most exciting things I got to do was to teach children how to read and write. Those were the best two years of my life. Helping other people made me feel very good."

The Peace Corps today is still one of the best ways United States citizens can serve their country and the world.

## C. Working Together for a Better World

It was recess time for Mrs. Allen's third-grade class. The most popular activity during recess was to play tether ball. Since there were only two tether ball poles, the students were

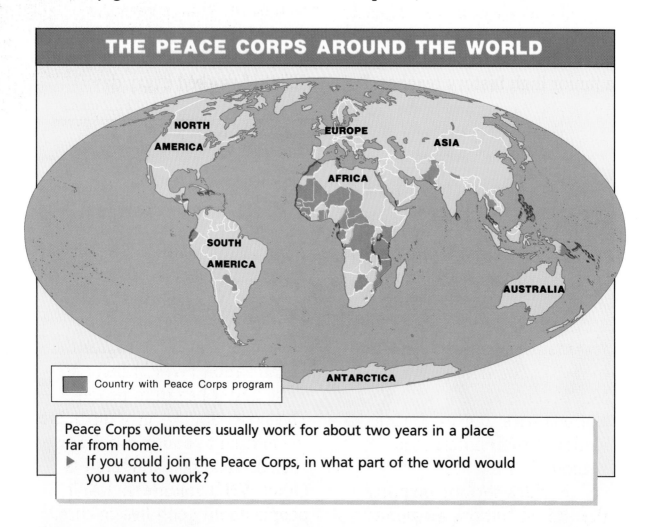

**THE PEACE CORPS AROUND THE WORLD**

NORTH AMERICA

EUROPE

ASIA

AFRICA

SOUTH AMERICA

AUSTRALIA

ANTARCTICA

Country with Peace Corps program

Peace Corps volunteers usually work for about two years in a place far from home.
▶ If you could join the Peace Corps, in what part of the world would you want to work?

supposed to take turns. John and Mark thought it was their turn. But Suzi and Megan disagreed. They thought it was their turn. All of them began to argue and shout and push each other. This was against the rules. Someone had to settle the quarrel. Mrs. Allen's class was lucky. The class had agreed that each week a team of students would have responsibility for settling all the arguments on the playground. These students were to manage any **conflicts**. A conflict is a disagreement. The team had been taught how to settle quarrels. Very quickly the team got John and Mark and Suzi and Megan to calm down and agree on whose turn it was.

Here is where the General Assembly of the United Nations (UN) meets to discuss world peace.
▶ Why is the UN important?

When countries argue among themselves, whose job is it to settle their arguments? The United Nations was created in 1945 to assist the countries of our world in settling their arguments. That job is just like the job of conflict managers in Mrs. Allen's class. The United Nations tries to get countries to work out their differences without fighting.

Besides settling disputes, the United Nations does many other things to help countries throughout the world. The United Nations Children's Fund, commonly called UNICEF, works to help children get the food, medicine, and clothing they need. The World Health Organization (WHO) helps to bring better health to people. The WHO doctors give medicine to children to stamp out diseases such as smallpox and tetanus. Other WHO volunteers teach people about good health care.

School children can do many things to help people in the United States and other countries. These youngsters are working on a project together.
▶ What has your school done to help others?

The people learn what foods are healthful to eat and how to find clean water to drink.

There are many other world organizations that help people cooperate with each other and solve their problems. The Lions Club International works to help prevent blindness. The World Association of Girl Scouts works with young girls to teach them about camping, health, and cleanliness. The National Audubon Society works to protect all the different kinds of birds in the world. The world is truly a better place when we try to cooperate and help each other.

LESSON 3 REVIEW

THINK AND WRITE
A. What people helped to rescue the whales trapped in Alaska?
B. What is the purpose of the Peace Corps?
C. What is the United Nations?

SKILLS CHECK
MAP SKILL
Refer to the map on page 312. Find three countries that you think the Peace Corps may provide help to.

314

## USING THE VOCABULARY

headquarters
interdependence
teleconference
fax machine
communication

satellite
Eskimos
culture
conflict

On a separate sheet of paper, write the word or words from above that best complete the sentences.

1. The Alaskan natives are called the _____.
2. When states and countries depend on each other, they are showing _____.
3. _____ is the giving and receiving of information and ideas.
4. The business center can also be called the _____.
5. A _____ is a way of life.
6. _____ is a telephone system that allows each person to hear and talk with someone in another place.
7. A disagreement is a _____.
8. A _____ relays messages instantly.
9. An object that circles the earth, carrying special communication equipment is a _____.

## REMEMBERING WHAT YOU READ

On a separate sheet of paper, answer the questions in complete sentences.

1. What product does the Boeing Company make?
2. What is the fuselage?
3. Why is the teleconference system used?
4. Why is the satellite system of communication used?
5. Why was the United Nations created?

## TYING ART TO SOCIAL STUDIES

Plan a project in your classroom that will help other people around the world. Design a poster that will show others what can be done to solve a problem or improve a condition.

315

## THINKING CRITICALLY

On a separate sheet of paper, answer the following in complete sentences.

1. What are the names of the five states that help in making the airplane?
2. How are interdependence and building an airplane alike?
3. What are two things that change when traveling to a foreign country? Explain your answer in detail.
4. What are five ways that we communicate every day?
5. Describe one community service in your area that is similar to the Peace Corps.

## SUMMARIZING THE CHAPTER

Copy this graphic organizer on a separate sheet of paper. Under the main idea for each lesson, write three facts that support the main idea.

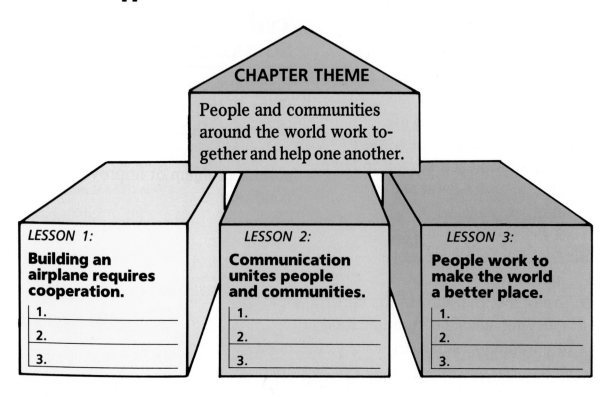

CHAPTER THEME

People and communities around the world work together and help one another.

LESSON 1:

**Building an airplane requires cooperation.**

1.
2.
3.

LESSON 2:

**Communication unites people and communities.**

1.
2.
3.

LESSON 3:

**People work to make the world a better place.**

1.
2.
3.

## COOPERATIVE LEARNING

In this unit you learned about the past and present in several cities. In this activity you will work with four other classmates to make an exciting board game about the past and present in your own community. The object of the game will be to reach the square marked FUTURE by answering questions correctly.

**REMEMBER TO:**
- Give your ideas.
- Listen to others' ideas.
- Plan your work with the group.
- Present your project.
- Discuss how your group worked.

### PROJECT

• With your group, choose a name for the board game.

• Two people should make question-and-answer cards about the past and present in your community. One side of an index card should have a question. The other side should have an answer. Below the answer, write *1*, *2*, or *3* for the number of moves around the game board a correct answer is worth.

• Two people should make a game board of heavy posterboard or cardboard with colored squares drawn around the board. They should label the squares with names of special places in your community.

• One person should make game pieces that can be moved along the game board.

### PRESENTATION AND REVIEW

• One person will explain your game.

• Each group will take a turn playing another group's game.

• Discuss your game with your group. How well does it teach about your community?

317

Using
**SKILLBUILDER**
Line Graphs

## A. WHY I NEED THIS SKILL

A line graph shows change that takes place over time. You can see whether there has been change by noticing whether the line on the graph goes up or down.

## B. LEARNING THE SKILL

The line graphs below show average monthly temperatures in New York City and San Francisco. The months of the year are shown at the bottom of each graph. Degrees Fahrenheit are shown at the left side of each graph.

On the graph for New York City, find the dot for the February temperature. On the graph for San Francisco, find the dot for the February temperature. Which city has the lower temperature in February?

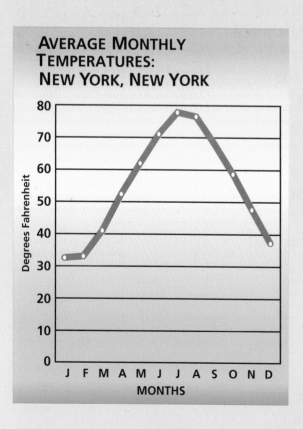

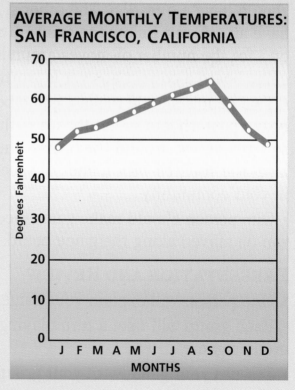

## C. PRACTICING THE SKILL

Answer these questions about the graphs.

1. What is the title of each graph?
2. Which city has the most changeable temperature?
3. Which city is colder in winter?
4. Which months are the warmest in San Francisco?
5. In August, San Francisco is about how many degrees cooler than New York City?

## D. APPLYING THE SKILL

You can make a line graph that shows temperatures in your area. Plan your graph to show temperatures for seven days. Write the days of the week at the bottom of the graph. Write the numbers and marks for degrees Fahrenheit along the left side of the graph.

Record the temperature for each of the seven days. Then place a dot for each day's temperature on the graph. If you need help, look at the graphs for New York City and San Francisco.

**319**

# SKILLBUILDER

*and Categorizing*

## A. WHY I NEED THIS SKILL

There are many ideas in your social studies book. Classifying these ideas may help you understand and remember them. To *classify* means "to put things that are alike in some way into categories, or groups."

## B. LEARNING THE SKILL

In Chapter 10 you learned about different kinds of service workers in New York City. These workers could be classified on a word map. The word map below classifies three groups of service workers.

SERVICE WORKERS

| Transportation Workers | Health Workers | City Workers |
|---|---|---|
| taxi driver<br>subway engineer<br>bus driver<br>sailor | dentist<br>nurse<br>doctor | mayor<br>teacher<br>fire fighter<br>police officer |

## C. PRACTICING THE SKILL

On a sheet of paper, copy the word map below. Classify the items listed at right by placing them on your word map. You may wish to add other places in New York City to your word map, too.

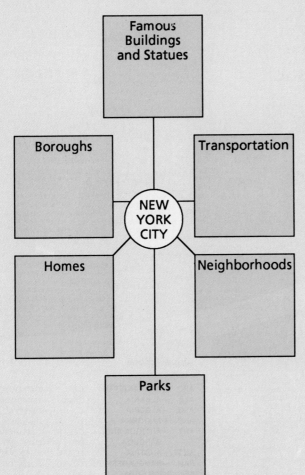

Empire State Building
single-family house
Upper West Side
Manhattan
subway
Statue of Liberty
bus
Queens
Sheepshead Bay
Central Park
Little Odessa
Staten Island
Chinatown
apartment
Bronx
taxi
Brooklyn
row house
Harlem
Museum of Natural History

## D. APPLYING THE SKILL

Choose another city that you learned about in Unit 4 and make a word map for it. You might want to classify information about San Francisco, Nairobi, Moscow, Tokyo, or Mexico City.

# Atlas

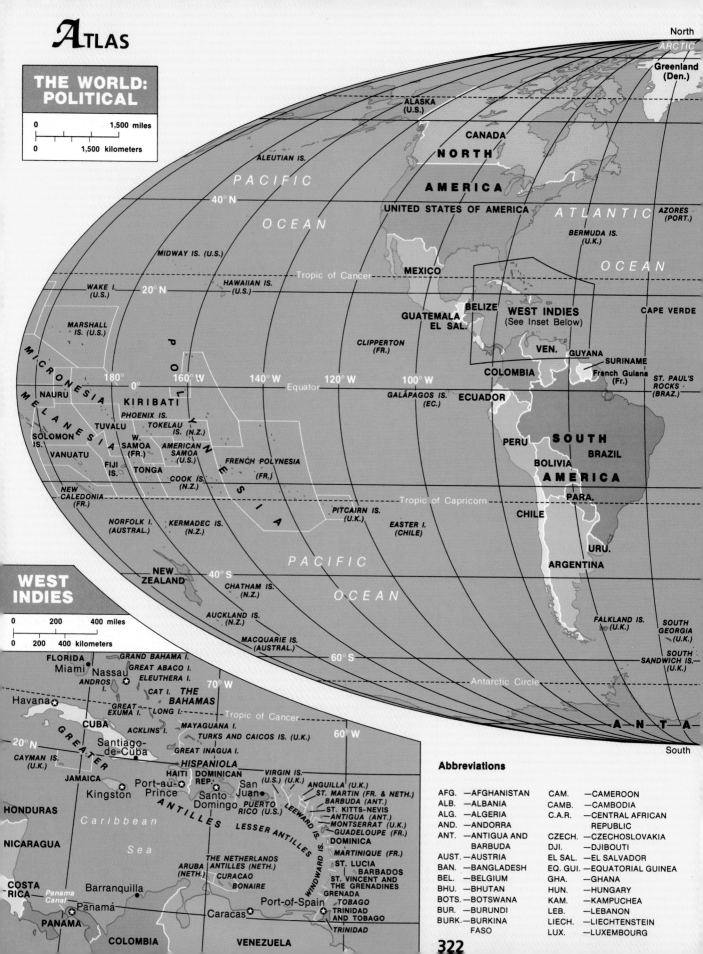

## THE WORLD: POLITICAL

0      1,500 miles

0      1,500 kilometers

North

ARCTIC

**Greenland (Den.)**

ALASKA (U.S.)

**CANADA**

**NORTH AMERICA**

ALEUTIAN IS.

40° N

**UNITED STATES OF AMERICA**

ATLANTIC

AZORES (PORT.)

MIDWAY IS. (U.S.)

BERMUDA IS. (U.K.)

OCEAN

PACIFIC

Tropic of Cancer

**MEXICO**

WAKE I. (U.S.)

20° N

HAWAIIAN IS. (U.S.)

**BELIZE**

**WEST INDIES** (See Inset Below)

CAPE VERDE

MARSHALL IS. (U.S.)

**GUATEMALA EL SAL.**

OCEAN

**VEN.**

**GUYANA**

CLIPPERTON (FR.)

**SURINAME**

French Guiana (Fr.)

**COLOMBIA**

ST. PAUL'S ROCKS (BRAZ.)

MICRONESIA

MELANESIA

NAURU

180°

160° W

0°

140° W

120° W

100° W

Equator

**ECUADOR**

GALÁPAGOS IS. (EC.)

KIRIBATI

PHOENIX IS.

**PERU**

**SOUTH AMERICA**

**BRAZIL**

POLYNESIA

TUVALU

TOKELAU IS. (N.Z.)

SOLOMON IS.

W. SAMOA (FR.)

AMERICAN SAMOA (U.S.)

**BOLIVIA**

VANUATU

FIJI IS.

TONGA

FRENCH POLYNESIA (FR.)

COOK IS. (N.Z.)

**PARA.**

NEW CALEDONIA (FR.)

Tropic of Capricorn

**CHILE**

NORFOLK I. (AUSTRAL.)

KERMADEC IS. (N.Z.)

PITCAIRN IS. (U.K.)

EASTER I. (CHILE)

**URU.**

**ARGENTINA**

40° S

**NEW ZEALAND**

CHATHAM IS. (N.Z.)

PACIFIC

AUCKLAND IS. (N.Z.)

FALKLAND IS. (U.K.)

SOUTH GEORGIA (U.K.)

MACQUARIE IS. (AUSTRAL.)

OCEAN

60° S

SOUTH SANDWICH IS. (U.K.)

Antarctic Circle

A N T A

South

## WEST INDIES

0   200   400 miles

0   200   400 kilometers

70° W

GRAND BAHAMA I.

**FLORIDA**

Miami

Nassau

GREAT ABACO I.

ELEUTHERA I.

ANDROS I.

CAT I.

**THE BAHAMAS**

Havana

**CUBA**

GREAT EXUMA I.

LONG I.

Tropic of Cancer

60° W

ACKLINS I.

MAYAGUANA I.

20° N

Santiago-de-Cuba

TURKS AND CAICOS IS. (U.K.)

CAYMAN IS. (U.K.)

GREAT INAGUA I.

**HISPANIOLA**

VIRGIN IS. U.S. (U.K.)

ANGUILLA (U.K.)

**JAMAICA**

**HAITI**

**DOMINICAN REP.**

San Juan

ST. MARTIN (FR. & NETH.)

Kingston

Port-au-Prince

Santo Domingo

PUERTO RICO (U.S.)

BARBUDA (ANT.)

ST. KITTS-NEVIS

ANTIGUA (ANT.)

MONTSERRAT (U.K.)

GUADELOUPE (FR.)

**HONDURAS**

ANTILLES

LESSER ANTILLES

DOMINICA

MARTINIQUE (FR.)

Caribbean

**NICARAGUA**

THE NETHERLANDS ANTILLES (NETH.)

ST. LUCIA

BARBADOS

Sea

ARUBA (NETH.)

CURAÇAO

BONAIRE

ST. VINCENT AND THE GRENADINES

GRENADA

**COSTA RICA**

Barranquilla

Panama Canal

Panamá

WINDWARD IS.

TOBAGO

TRINIDAD AND TOBAGO

**PANAMA**

Caracas

Port-of-Spain

TRINIDAD

**COLOMBIA**

**VENEZUELA**

## Abbreviations

| | | | |
|---|---|---|---|
| AFG. | —AFGHANISTAN | CAM. | —CAMEROON |
| ALB. | —ALBANIA | CAMB. | —CAMBODIA |
| ALG. | —ALGERIA | C.A.R. | —CENTRAL AFRICAN |
| AND. | —ANDORRA | | REPUBLIC |
| ANT. | —ANTIGUA AND | CZECH. | —CZECHOSLOVAKIA |
| | BARBUDA | DJI. | —DJIBOUTI |
| AUST. | —AUSTRIA | EL SAL. | —EL SALVADOR |
| BAN. | —BANGLADESH | EQ. GUI. | —EQUATORIAL GUINEA |
| BEL. | —BELGIUM | GHA. | —GHANA |
| BHU. | —BHUTAN | HUN. | —HUNGARY |
| BOTS. | —BOTSWANA | KAM. | —KAMPUCHEA |
| BUR. | —BURUNDI | LEB. | —LEBANON |
| BURK. | —BURKINA | LIECH. | —LIECHTENSTEIN |
| | FASO | LUX. | —LUXEMBOURG |

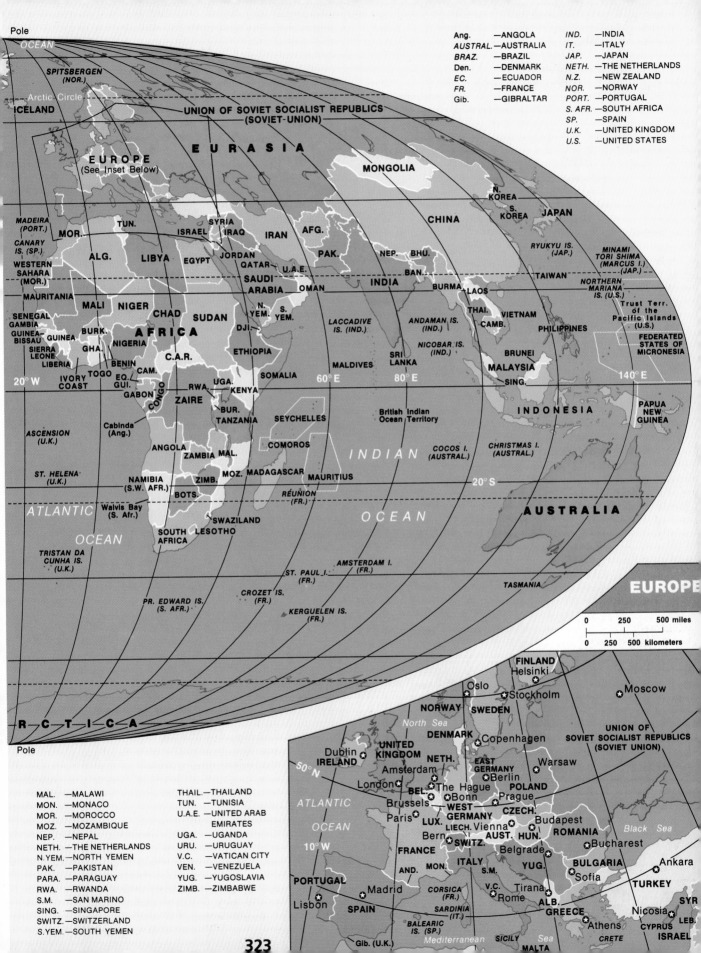

Pole
OCEAN
*SPITSBERGEN*
(NOR.)
Arctic Circle
ICELAND
UNION OF SOVIET SOCIALIST REPUBLICS
(SOVIET-UNION)

EUROPE
(See Inset Below)

E U R A S I A

MONGOLIA

*MADEIRA*
(PORT.)
MOR.
TUN.
SYRIA
IRAQ
ISRAEL
IRAN
AFG.
N. KOREA
S. KOREA
JAPAN
CHINA
*CANARY IS. (SP.)*
ALG.
LIBYA
EGYPT
JORDAN
QATAR
U.A.E.
PAK.
NEP. BHU.
BAN.
*RYUKYU IS. (JAP.)*
*MINAMI TORI SHIMA (MARCUS I.) (JAP.)*
WESTERN SAHARA (MOR.)
SAUDI ARABIA
OMAN
INDIA
BURMA
LAOS
TAIWAN
*NORTHERN MARIANA IS. (U.S.)*
MAURITANIA
MALI
NIGER
CHAD
SUDAN
N. YEM.
S. YEM.
DJI.
THAI.
CAMB.
VIETNAM
Trust Terr. of the Pacific Islands (U.S.)
SENEGAL
GAMBIA
GUINEA-BISSAU
GUINEA
BURK.
NIGERIA
ETHIOPIA
*LACCADIVE IS. (IND.)*
*ANDAMAN IS. (IND.)*
PHILIPPINES
FEDERATED STATES OF MICRONESIA
SIERRA LEONE
LIBERIA
GHA.
BENIN
A F R I C A
C.A.R.
MALDIVES
*NICOBAR IS. (IND.)*
SRI LANKA
BRUNEI
20° W
IVORY COAST
TOGO
EQ. GUI.
CAM.
SOMALIA
60° E
80° E
MALAYSIA
SING.
140° E
GABON
CONGO
ZAIRE
RWA.
UGA.
KENYA
GUINEA
BUR.
TANZANIA
SEYCHELLES
I N D O N E S I A
PAPUA NEW GUINEA
*ASCENSION (U.K.)*
Cabinda (Ang.)
ANGOLA
ZAMBIA
MAL.
COMOROS
British Indian Ocean Territory
I N D I A N
*COCOS I. (AUSTRAL.)*
*CHRISTMAS I. (AUSTRAL.)*
*ST. HELENA (U.K.)*
NAMIBIA (S.W. AFR.)
ZIMB.
MOZ.
MADAGASCAR
MAURITIUS
20° S
BOTS.
*RÉUNION (FR.)*
O C E A N
A U S T R A L I A
ATLANTIC
Walvis Bay (S. Afr.)
SWAZILAND
OCEAN
SOUTH AFRICA
LESOTHO
*TRISTAN DA CUNHA IS. (U.K.)*
*AMSTERDAM I. (FR.)*
*ST. PAUL I. (FR.)*
TASMANIA
*PR. EDWARD IS. (S. AFR.)*
*CROZET IS. (FR.)*
*KERGUELEN IS. (FR.)*

A R C T I C A
Pole

EUROPE

0    250    500 miles
0    250    500 kilometers

FINLAND
Helsinki
Oslo
Stockholm
Moscow
NORWAY
SWEDEN
North Sea
DENMARK
Copenhagen
UNION OF SOVIET SOCIALIST REPUBLICS (SOVIET UNION)
Dublin
IRELAND
UNITED KINGDOM
NETH.
Amsterdam
EAST GERMANY
Warsaw
50° N
London
The Hague
Berlin
POLAND
ATLANTIC
BEL.
Brussels
Bonn
Prague
Paris
WEST GERMANY
CZECH.
OCEAN
LUX.
LIECH.
Vienna
Budapest
Black Sea
10° W
Bern
AUST.
HUN.
ROMANIA
FRANCE
SWITZ.
Belgrade
Bucharest
Ankara
AND.
MON.
ITALY
YUG.
BULGARIA
S.M.
Sofia
TURKEY
PORTUGAL
Madrid
*CORSICA (FR.)*
V.C.
Rome
Tirana
ALB.
Nicosia
SYR.
Lisbon
SPAIN
*SARDINIA (IT.)*
GREECE
CYPRUS
LEB.
*BALEARIC IS. (SP.)*
Athens
ISRAEL
Gib. (U.K.)
Mediterranean
*SICILY*
Sea
CRETE
MALTA

323

CANADA

MINNESOTA
Duluth

MICHIGAN

Minneapolis
St. Paul — Green Bay
WISCONSIN

Madison
Milwaukee
Cedar
Rapids
Rockford
Chicago
Gary

IOWA
Des
Moines
Davenport
ILLINOIS

INDIANA
Indianapolis
Springfield

Kansas City
Kansas
City
St. Louis
Jefferson City
MISSOURI

MICHIGAN

Lansing
Grand
Rapids
Detroit

Toledo
Akron
Fort Wayne
OHIO
Columbus
Cincinnati
Wheeling
Huntington
Frankfort
Louisville
Lexington
KENTUCKY

WEST
VIRGINIA
Charleston

Cleveland

PENNSYLVANIA
Harrisburg
Pittsburgh

MAINE
Augusta
Montpelier
Lewiston
Burlington
Portland
VERMONT
Rutland
Concord
NEW HAMPSHIRE
Manchester
Nashua
Albany
Worcester
Boston
MASSACHUSETTS
Waterloo
Springfield
Pawtucket
Rochester
Hartford
Providence
NEW YORK
New Haven
Warwick
Buffalo
Bridgeport
RHODE ISLAND
Jersey City
CONNECTICUT
Newark
New York
Trenton
NEW JERSEY
Philadelphia
Wilmington
Newark
Baltimore
Dover
Rockville
DELAWARE
Washington,
Annapolis
D.C.
MARYLAND

Richmond

Raleigh

Greensboro
NORTH CAROLINA
Charlotte

Norfolk
Virginia Beach

ATLANTIC

OCEAN

40° N

35° N

75° W

70° W

ARKANSAS
North
Little Rock
Fort
Smith
Little Rock

Memphis

Nashville
Knoxville
TENNESSEE
Charlotte

Columbia
SOUTH CAROLINA
North Charleston
Charleston

THE UNITED STATES
OF AMERICA

Birmingham
Atlanta

MISSISSIPPI
ALABAMA
GEORGIA
Meridian
Columbus
Montgomery
Shreveport
Jackson

LOUISIANA
Mobile
Biloxi
Baton Rouge
New Orleans

Savannah

Jacksonville

Tallahassee

30° N

~ Rivers
✪ National capital
✱ State capitals
● Other cities

0        100      200 miles
0    100    200 kilometers

FLORIDA
Tampa
St. Petersburg

25° N

Gulf   of   Mexico

Miami

Tropic of Cancer

325

90° W

85° W

80° W

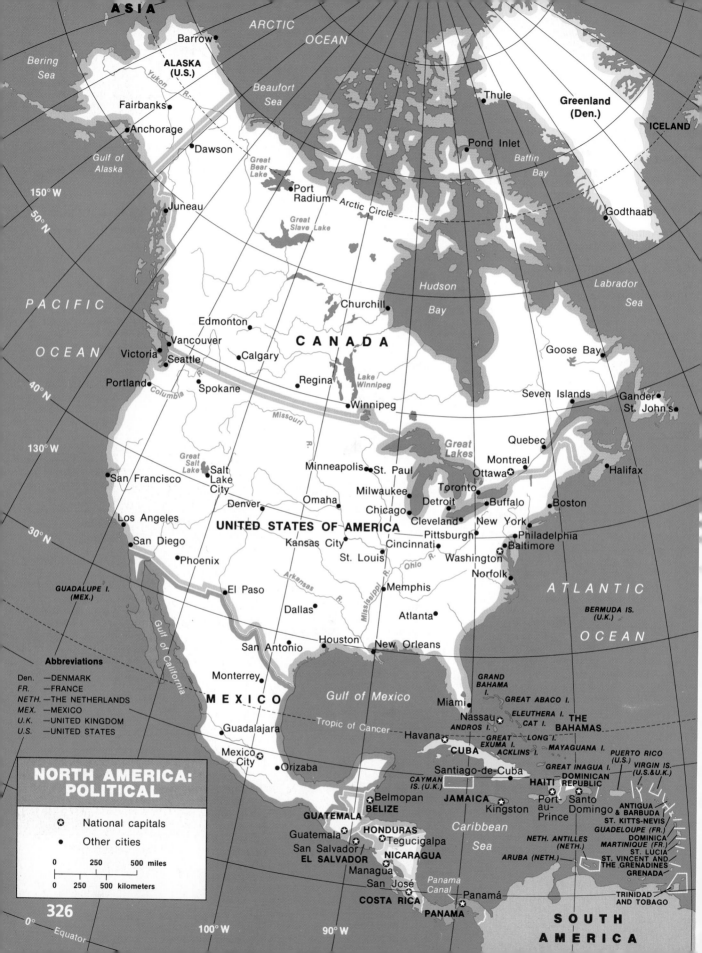

# NORTH AMERICA: POLITICAL

ASIA

ARCTIC OCEAN

Barrow

**ALASKA (U.S.)**

Fairbanks

Anchorage

*Bering Sea*

*Gulf of Alaska*

Dawson

*Yukon R.*

Juneau

150° W

50° N

*Beaufort Sea*

Thule

**Greenland (Den.)**

ICELAND

Pond Inlet

*Baffin Bay*

*Great Bear Lake*

Port Radium

Arctic Circle

*Great Slave Lake*

Godthaab

*PACIFIC OCEAN*

Edmonton

Vancouver

Victoria

Seattle

Portland

*Columbia*

Spokane

Calgary

**C A N A D A**

Regina

*Lake Winnipeg*

Winnipeg

Churchill

*Hudson Bay*

Goose Bay

*Labrador Sea*

Seven Islands

Gander

St. John's

40° N

130° W

*Missouri R.*

Quebec

Montreal

Ottawa

Halifax

San Francisco

*Great Salt Lake*

Salt Lake City

Minneapolis

St. Paul

*Great Lakes*

Denver

Omaha

Milwaukee

Chicago

Toronto

Detroit

Buffalo

Boston

Los Angeles

**UNITED STATES OF AMERICA**

Kansas City

St. Louis

Cleveland

Cincinnati

*Ohio R.*

Pittsburgh

New York

Philadelphia

Baltimore

Washington

San Diego

Phoenix

*Arkansas R.*

*Mississippi R.*

Memphis

Norfolk

*ATLANTIC OCEAN*

30° N

**GUADALUPE I. (MEX.)**

El Paso

Dallas

Atlanta

*BERMUDA IS. (U.K.)*

*Gulf of California*

San Antonio

Houston

New Orleans

Monterrey

**M E X I C O**

*Gulf of Mexico*

Miami

*GRAND BAHAMA I.*

*GREAT ABACO I.*

Guadalajara

Tropic of Cancer

Nassau

*ELEUTHERA I.*

*CAT I.*

**THE BAHAMAS**

*ANDROS I.*

Havana

*GREAT EXUMA I.*

*LONG I.*

Mexico City

Orizaba

**CUBA**

*ACKLINS I.*

*MAYAGUANA I.*

**PUERTO RICO (U.S.)**

*VIRGIN IS. (U.S.&U.K.)*

Santiago-de-Cuba

*GREAT INAGUA I.*

**DOMINICAN REPUBLIC**

*CAYMAN IS. (U.K.)*

**HAITI**

Belmopan

**BELIZE**

**JAMAICA**

Kingston

Port-au-Prince

Santo Domingo

*ANTIGUA & BARBUDA*

*ST. KITTS-NEVIS*

**GUATEMALA**

**HONDURAS**

Tegucigalpa

*Caribbean Sea*

*GUADELOUPE (FR.)*

*DOMINICA*

*MARTINIQUE (FR.)*

Guatemala

San Salvador

**EL SALVADOR**

**NICARAGUA**

Managua

*NETH. ANTILLES (NETH.)*

*ARUBA (NETH.)*

*ST. LUCIA*

*ST. VINCENT AND THE GRENADINES*

**GRENADA**

San José

*Panama Canal*

Panamá

**COSTA RICA**

**PANAMA**

*TRINIDAD AND TOBAGO*

**SOUTH AMERICA**

0°

Equator

100° W

90° W

## Abbreviations

Den. —DENMARK
FR. —FRANCE
NETH. —THE NETHERLANDS
MEX. —MEXICO
U.K. —UNITED KINGDOM
U.S. —UNITED STATES

## NORTH AMERICA: POLITICAL

✪ National capitals

• Other cities

0    250    500 miles

0    250    500 kilometers

Barranquilla
Cartagena
Valencia
Maracaibo
Caracas
Barquisimeto
Cúcuta
San Cristóbal
Medellín
Bucaramanga
Bogotá
Cali
COLOMBIA
MALPELO I.
(COL.)

VENEZUELA
GUYANA
Georgetown
Paramaribo
Cayenne
SURINAME
French
Guiana
(Fr.)

Abbreviations
COL. —COLOMBIA
Fr. —FRANCE
U.K. —UNITED KINGDOM

10° N

River

Orinoco

Quito
0°
ECUADOR
Guayaquil
Iquitos

Equator

Belém
São Luis
Manaus

Amazon
River

Fortaleza

PERU

Trujillo

Callao
Lima
Cuzco
Lake Titicaca
Arequipa
BOLIVIA
La Paz
Sucre

10° S

Recife
Maceió

BRAZIL

Salvador

Brasília
(Federal District)

Belo Horizonte

20° S

PACIFIC

OCEAN

Chuquicamata
Antofagasta

PARAGUAY
Asunción

Rio de Janeiro
São Paulo
Niterói
Santos
Curitiba

Tropic of Capricorn

ATLANTIC

SAN FELIX I.  SAN AMBROSIO I.
(CHILE)      (CHILE)

CHILE

Tucumán

River
Paraná

Pôrto Alegre

30° S

Valparaiso
Santiago
JUAN FERNÁNDEZ IS.
(CHILE)
Concepción

Córdoba
Santa
Fe
Paraná
Rosario
Buenos Aires
La Plata

ARGENTINA

Bahía Blanca

URUGUAY
Montevideo

Río de la Plata

Mar del Plata

OCEAN

40° S

50° S

FALKLAND IS. (U.K.)
(MALVINAS IS.)

Punta Arenas

Strait of
Magellan

327

SOUTH AMERICA:
POLITICAL

✪  National capitals
•  Other cities

0        500 miles
0        500 kilometers

90° W    80° W    70° W    60° W    50° W    40° W    30° W

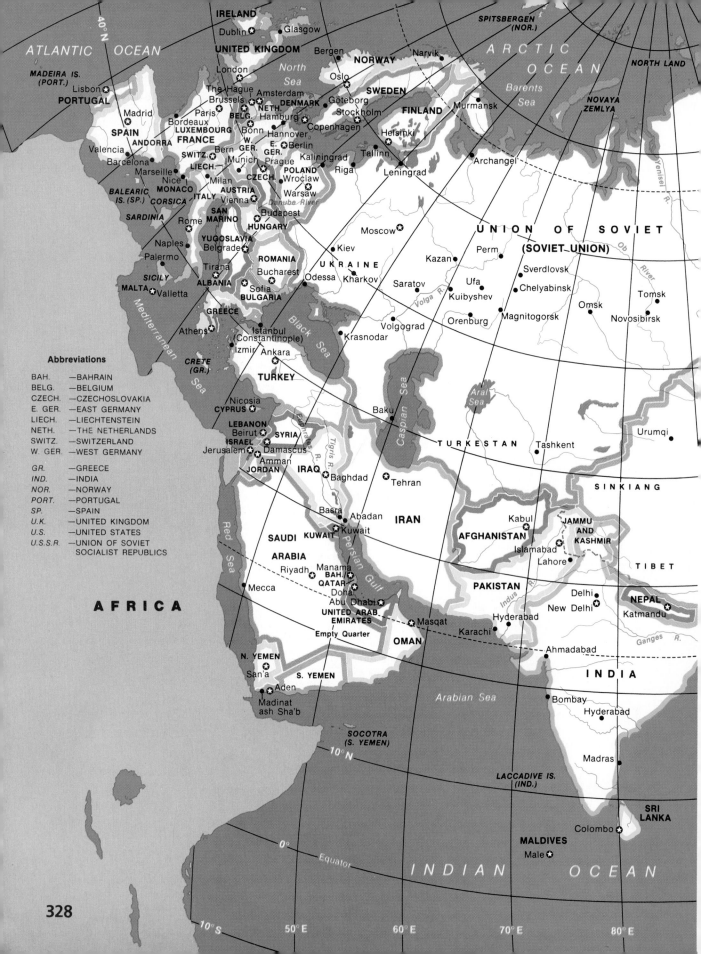

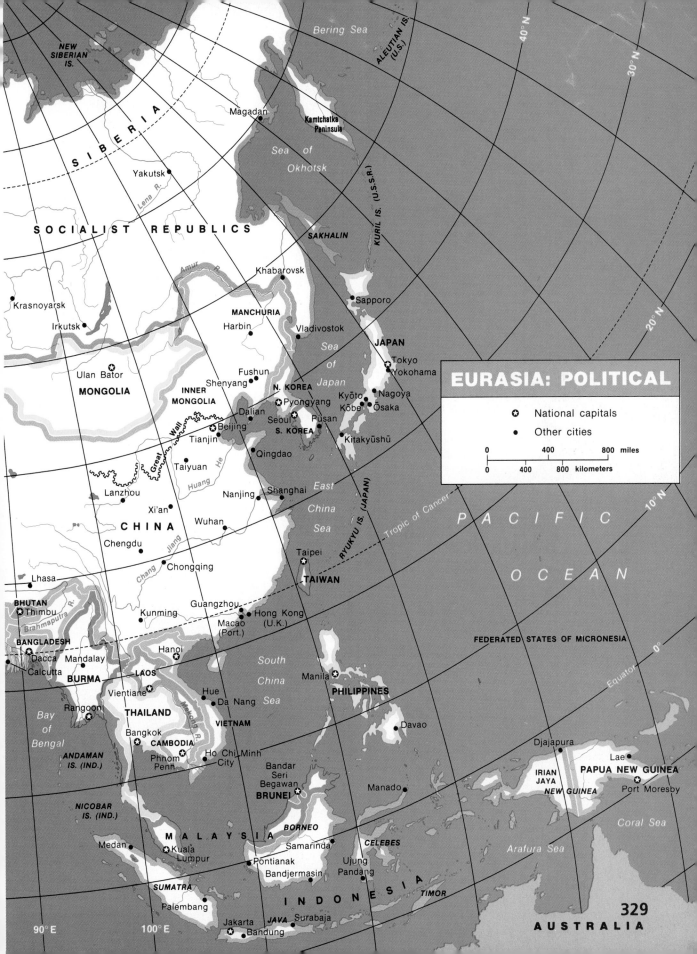

# EUROPE: POLITICAL

☆ National capitals
• Other cities

miles
600      400      200      0
600      400      200      0
kilometers

**Abbreviations**

DEN. —DENMARK
FR. —FRANCE
GR. —GREECE
IT. —ITALY
SP. —SPAIN
SWITZ. —SWITZERLAND
U.K. —UNITED KINGDOM

ASIA
ASIA
ASIA

Caspian Sea

Baku
Tbilisi
Yerevan

Perm
Izhevsk
Kuibyshev

Ufa

Kazan

Perm

Yaroslavl
Gorki

Saratov

Moscow
Tula

Voronezh

Volgograd

Volga River

Krasnodar

Don River

**UNION OF SOVIET SOCIALIST REPUBLICS
(SOVIET UNION)**

Rostov

Dnepropetrovsk
Donetsk
Krivoi Rog

Kharkov

Zaporozhye

Kiev

Odessa

River

Dnieper

Crimea

Black Sea

Barents Sea

FINLAND

Tampere

Helsinki

Tallinn

Leningrad

Riga

Minsk

Vilnius

Warsaw

Lvov

Dniester

RHODES
(GR.)

CYPRUS

Nicosia
Limassol

CRETE
(GR.)

Aegean Sea

Athens

GREECE

Salonika

Plovdiv

Sofia

**BULGARIA**

Bucharest

**ROMANIA**

Cluj

Timisoara

Skopje

**ALBANIA**

Durrës
Tirana

Miskolc

Budapest

Vienna

**HUNGARY**

Belgrade

Sarajevo

**YUGOSLAVIA**

Zagreb

Danube

Graz

**AUSTRIA**

Adriatic Sea

**SWEDEN**

Trondheim

Stockholm

Göteborg

Oslo

Bergen

**NORWAY**

Gulf of Bothnia

Baltic Sea

Gdańsk

Copenhagen

Århus

**DENMARK**

**POLAND**

Poznań

Łódź
Wrocław

Kraków

Ostrava

**CZECHOSLOVAKIA**

Prague

Dresden

Leipzig

Berlin

Oder R.

Vistula R.

**EAST GERMANY**

Bremen

Hannover

Hamburg

Elbe R.

Bonn

Cologne

Düsseldorf

Duisburg
Essen
Dortmund

Frankfurt

**WEST GERMANY**

Stuttgart

Munich

**LIECHTENSTEIN**

Zurich

**SWITZ.**

Bern

Milan

Turin

Genoa

**MONACO**

Nice

Marseille

**SAN MARINO**

**VATICAN CITY**

Rome

Florence

Po R.

**ITALY**

Naples

**CORSICA
(FR.)**

**SARDINIA
(IT.)**

**SICILY
(IT.)**

Palermo

**MALTA**

Valletta

Mediterranean Sea

**AMSTERDAM**

The Hague

Rotterdam

**THE NETHERLANDS**

Antwerp

Ghent
Brussels

**BELGIUM**

**LUXEMBOURG**

Luxembourg

**FRANCE**

Paris

Lyons

Toulouse

Bordeaux (?)

Bay of Biscay

Rhine R.

Rhône R.

North Sea

FAEROE IS.
(DEN.)

SHETLAND IS.
(U.K.)

ORKNEY IS.
(U.K.)

OUTER HEBRIDES
(U.K.)

Glasgow

Belfast

**IRELAND**

Dublin

Cork

**UNITED KINGDOM**

Leeds
Manchester
Liverpool
Sheffield
Birmingham

London

English Channel

**ICELAND**

Reykjavik
Kopavogur

ARCTIC OCEAN

Arctic Circle

70° N

10° E

0°

10° W

20° W

50° N

20° E

ATLANTIC OCEAN

**ANDORRA**

Barcelona

Saragossa

Madrid

Valencia

**SPAIN**

Seville

Oporto

Lisbon

**PORTUGAL**

Gibraltar
(U.K.)

**A F R I C A**

Balearic Is.
(SP.)

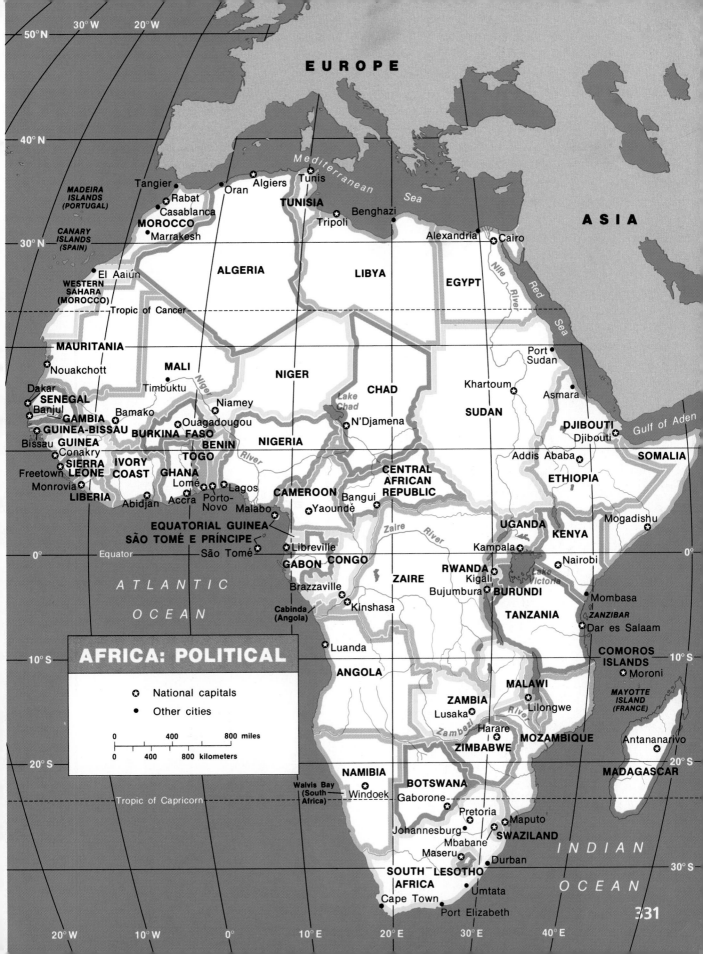

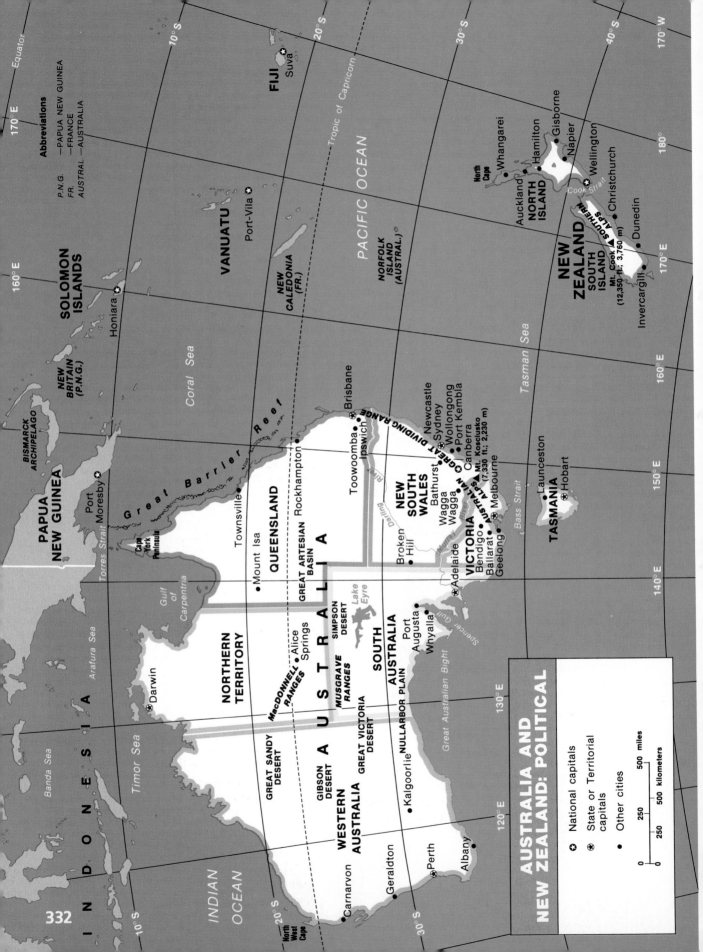

INDONESIA

Banda Sea

Timor Sea

Arafura Sea

BISMARCK
ARCHIPELAGO

NEW
BRITAIN
(P.N.G.)

PAPUA
NEW GUINEA

Port
Moresby ✪

Torres Strait

Cape
York
Peninsula

Gulf
of
Carpentria

INDIAN
OCEAN

North
West
Cape

Carnarvon

Geraldton

Perth ✪

Albany

GREAT SANDY
DESERT

GIBSON
DESERT

WESTERN
AUSTRALIA

GREAT VICTORIA
DESERT

Kalgoorlie

NULLARBOR PLAIN

Darwin ✪

NORTHERN
TERRITORY

MacDONNELL
RANGES

Alice
Springs

MUSGRAVE
RANGES

SIMPSON
DESERT

A U S T R A L I A

Lake
Eyre

SOUTH
AUSTRALIA

Great Australian Bight

Spencer Gulf

Port
Augusta

Whyalla

Adelaide ✪

Mount Isa

QUEENSLAND

GREAT ARTESIAN
BASIN

Townsville

Great Barrier Reef

Coral Sea

SOLOMON
ISLANDS

Honiara ✪

VANUATU

Port-Vila ✪

NEW
CALEDONIA
(FR.)

FIJI

Suva

PACIFIC OCEAN

Tropic of Capricorn

NORFOLK
ISLAND
(AUSTRAL.)

Rockhampton

Brisbane ✪
Toowoomba
Ipswich

River

Darling

Broken
Hill

NEW
SOUTH
WALES

Bathurst

Wagga
Wagga

Newcastle
Sydney ✪
Wollongong
Port Kembla

Canberra ✪

GREAT DIVIDING RANGE

Mt. Kosciusko
(7,330 ft.; 2,230 m)

Murray

VICTORIA

Bendigo
Ballarat
Geelong

Melbourne ✪

AUSTRALIAN ALPS

Tasman Sea

Launceston

TASMANIA

Hobart ✪

Bass Strait

NEW
ZEALAND

North
Cape

Whangarei

Auckland ✪

NORTH
ISLAND

Hamilton

Gisborne

Napier

Wellington ✪

Cook Strait

Christchurch

SOUTHERN ALPS

Mt. Cook
(12,350 ft.; 3,760 m)

SOUTH
ISLAND

Dunedin

Invercargill

Equator

10° S

20° S

30° S

170° E
160° E
170° E
160° E
150° E
140° E
130° E
120° E
180°
170° E
170° W
40° S

**AUSTRALIA AND
NEW ZEALAND: POLITICAL**

✪ National capitals

✪ State or Territorial
capitals

• Other cities

0   250   500 miles

0   250   500 kilometers

Some words in this book may be new to you or difficult to pronounce. Those words have been spelled phonetically in parentheses. The syllable that receives stress in a word is shown in small capital letters.

For example: **Chicago** (shuh KAH goh)

Most phonetic spellings are easy to read. In the following Pronunciation Key, you can see how letters are used to show different sounds.

---
**PRONUNCIATION KEY**

| a | after | (AF tur) | | oh | flow | (floh) | | ch | chicken | (CHIHK un) |
|---|---|---|---|---|---|---|---|---|---|---|
| ah | father | (FAH thur) | | oi | boy | (boi) | | g | game | (gaym) |
| ai | care | (kair) | | oo | rule | (rool) | | ing | coming | (KUM ing) |
| aw | dog | (dawg) | | or | horse | (hors) | | j | job | (jahb) |
| ay | paper | (PAY pur) | | ou | cow | (kou) | | k | came | (kaym) |
| | | | | | | | | ng | long | (lawng) |
| e | letter | (LET ur) | | yoo | few | (fyoo) | | s | city | (SIH tee) |
| ee | eat | (eet) | | u | taken | (TAY kun) | | sh | ship | (shihp) |
| | | | | | matter | (MAT ur) | | th | thin | (thihn) |
| ih | trip | (trihp) | | uh | ago | (uh GOH) | | thh | feather | (FETHH ur) |
| eye | idea | (eye DEE uh) | | | | | | y | yard | (yahrd) |
| y | hide | (hyd) | | | | | | z | size | (syz) |
| ye | lie | (lye) | | | | | | zh | division | (duh VIHZH un) |

---

**GAZETTEER**

The Gazetteer is a geographical dictionary. It shows latitude and longitude for cities and certain other places. Latitude and longitude are shown in the form: 36°N/84°W. This means "36 degrees north latitude and 84 degrees west longitude." The page reference tells where each entry may be found on a map.

## A

***Africa*** (AF rih kuh). The earth's second largest continent. p. 36.

***Albany*** (AWL buh nee). **1.** A city in Oregon that is known for its lumbering industry. (45°N/123°W). p. 65. **2.** The capital of New York State. (42°N/73°W). pp. 324–325.

***American River*** (uh MER ih kun RIHV ur). A river that flows southwest into the Sacramento River, in California. p. 248.

***Amsterdam*** (AM stur dam). The capital of the Netherlands and a major trading center. (52°N/4°E). p. 330.

***Antarctica*** (ant AHRK tih kuh). The earth's third smallest continent. p. 36.

***Appalachian Mountains*** (ap uh LAY chun MOUNT unz). A mountain range in eastern North America. Extends from Canada to Alabama. p. 54.

***Arctic Ocean*** (AHRK tihk OH shun). The large body of salt water north of the Arctic Circle. p. 54.

***Arkansas River*** (AHR kun saw RIHV ur). A river that runs across the central part of the state of Arkansas. p. 88.

***Asia*** (AY zhuh). The earth's largest continent. p. 36.

**Atlanta** (at LAN tuh). The capital of and most populated city in Georgia. (34°N/84°W). pp. 324–325.

**Atlantic Ocean** (at LAN tihk OH shun). The large body of salt water separating North America and South America from Europe and Africa. p. 54.

**Australia** (aw STRAYL yuh). The smallest continent on the earth. p. 36.

**B**

**Baltimore** (BAWL tuh mor). A city in Maryland, located on the Patapsco River at the upper end of the Chesapeake Bay. (39°N/77°W). pp. 324–325.

**Baton Rouge** (BAT un roozh). The capital of Louisiana. Located on the Mississippi River. (30°N/91°W). p. 31

**Buenos Aires** (BWAY nus ER eez). The capital of Argentina. (35°S/58°W). p. 268.

**C**

**Calabash** (KAL uh bash). A small fishing community in North Carolina, located near the border of North Carolina and South Carolina. (34°N/79°W). p. 68.

**Central America** (SEN trul uh MER ih kuh). The narrow strip of land on the southern end of North America. Made up of seven countries. p. 35.

**Chicago** (shuh KAH goh). The third largest city in the United States. Located in Illinois, on the southern tip of Lake Michigan. (42°N/88°W). p. 101.

**Copenhagen** (koh pun HAY gun). The capital of Denmark and an important seaport. (56°N/13°E). p. 330.

**D**

**Detroit** (dih TROIT) A major manufacturing center and most populated city in Michigan. (42°N/83°W). p. 113.

**Detroit River** (dih TROIT RIHV ur). A river that separates Detroit, Michigan, from Windsor, a city in Canada. p. 113.

**E**

**Eastern Hemisphere** (EES turn HEM ih sfihr). The half of the earth east of the Prime Meridian. p. 37.

**Equator** (ee KWAYT ur). 0° line of latitude. The map line that circles the earth halfway between the North Pole and the South Pole. p. 37.

**G**

**Great Lakes** (grayt layks). The largest group of freshwater lakes in the world. They are in North America and consist of Lakes Superior, Michigan, Huron, Erie, and Ontario. p. 54.

**Great Plains** (grayt playnz). A very large plain located in the western and central parts of the United States. p. 54.

**Greenwich** (GREN ihch). A place in London, England. Located at 0° longitude. p. 268.

**Gulf of Mexico** (gulf uv MEKS ih koh).

A body of salt water bordered by the United States, Mexico, and Cuba. p. 32.

## H

**Halstead** (HAWL sted). A farming community in Kansas located on a branch of the Arkansas River. (38°N/98°W). p. 88.

**Houston** (HYOOS tun). A city in Texas, south of the Missouri River. (30°N/95°W). p. 101.

**Hudson River** (HUD sun    RIHV ur). A river in the state of New York that ends at New York City. Forms border between New York and New Jersey. p. 237.

## I

**Indian Ocean** (IHN dee un OH shun). The large body of salt water between Africa and Australia. p. 36.

## L

**Leningrad** (LEN un grad). The second most populated city in the Soviet Union. (60°N/30°E). p. 268.

**Long Beach** (lawng    beech). A city located in southern California, on the Pacific coast. (34°N/118°W). pp. 324–325.

**Los Angeles** (laws    AN juh lus). Second largest city in the United States. Located in southern California, on the Pacific coast. (34°N/118°W). p. 101.

## M

**Manhattan Island** (man HAT un EYE lund). The busiest, most crowded part of New York City. p. 237.

**Mexico City** (MEKS ih koh    SIHT ee). The capital of Mexico. The most populated city in the world. (19°N/99°W). p. 269.

**Minneapolis** (mihn ee AP ul ihs). The largest city in Minnesota. Located on the Mississippi River, at the Falls of St. Anthony. (45°N/93°W). p. 267.

**Mississippi River** (mihs uh SIHP ee RIHV ur). One of the longest rivers in the United States. It rises in northern Minnesota and flows into the Gulf of Mexico near New Orleans, Louisiana. p. 31.

**Missouri River** (mih ZOOR ee    RIHV ur). One of the longest rivers in the United States; it joins Mississippi River near St. Louis, Missouri. p. 54.

**Mojave Desert** (moh HAV vee DEZ urt). A desert located in southern California. p. 54.

**Monterey Bay** (mahnt uh RAY    bay). An inlet of the Pacific Ocean, located in western California. p. 248.

**Montgomery** (munt GUM ur ee). The capital of Alabama. (32°N/86°W). pp. 324–325.

**Moscow** (MAHS koh). The capital and largest city of the Soviet Union. (56°N/38°E). p. 269.

**Moscow River** (MAHS koh    RIHV ur). A river in the Soviet Union that flows east through Moscow.

## N

**Nairobi** (nye ROH bee). The largest city

and capital of Kenya, located on the east coast of the continent of Africa. (1°S/37°E). p. 269.

**New Amsterdam** (noo AM stur dam). The name of the settlement that was renamed New York in 1664. p. 227.

**New York City** (noo york SIHT ee). The most populated city in the United States. (41°N/74°W). p. 101.

**North America** (north uh MER ih kuh). A continent in the Western Hemisphere. p. 35.

**Northern Hemisphere** (NOR thurn HEM ih sfihr). The half of the earth that is north of the Equator. p. 37.

**North Pole** (north pohl). The most northern place on the earth. p. 24.

## O

**Oakland** (OHK lund). A city in California, on the eastern side of San Francisco Bay. (38°N/122°W). p. 258.

## P

**Pacific Ocean** (puh SIHF ihk OH shun). The large body of salt water off the western coast of the United States. The earth's largest ocean. p. 54.

**Pensacola** (pen suh KOH luh). A city in Florida, located on the Gulf of Mexico. (30°N/87°W). p. 141.

**Philadelphia** (fihl uh DEL fee uh). The most populated city in Pennsylvania. The city where the Declaration of Independence was signed and the Constitution was adopted. (40°N/75°W) p. 101.

**Phoenix** (FEE nihks) The largest city in Arizona. It is located in southwestern part of the state. (33°N/112°W). p. 101.

**Plymouth** (PLIHM uth). **1.** The Pilgrim community in Massachusetts. (41°N/70°W). **2.** The community in England from which they sailed to America. (50°N/4°W). p. 196.

**Point Barrow** (point BAR oh). The most northern point of Alaska. (71°N/157°W). pp. 324–325.

**Portland** (PORT lund). The most populated city in Oregon, located on the Willamette River. (46°N/123°W). pp. 324–325.

## Q

**Quito** (KEE toh). A city in Equador. It lies almost on the Equator. (0° lat./79°W). p. 267.

## R

**Rocky Mountains** (RAHK ee MOUNT unz). A mountain range located in the western part of the United States. p. 54.

**Roswell** (RAHZ wel). A city located in southeastern New Mexico. It is the capital of Chavez County. (33°N/105°W). p. 135.

## S

**St. Augustine** (saynt AW gus teen). A city in Florida. The oldest permanent existing settlement on the continent of North America. (24°S/44°E). p. 141.

**San Antonio** (san un TOH nee oh). A city in south central part of Texas.

The third largest city in the state. (29°N/98°W). p. 101.

**San Diego** (san dee AY goh). A seaport in California, near the border of Mexico. (33°N/117°W). p. 101.

**San Francisco** (san frun SIHS koh). A seaport of more than 700,000 people in northern California. (37°N/122°W). p. 253.

**San Francisco Bay** (san frun SIHS koh bay). An inlet of the Pacific Ocean, in west California. p. 248.

**Seattle** (see AT ul). The largest city in Washington. A seaport and center of airplane manufacturing. (48°N/122°W). pp. 324–325.

**Sierra Nevada** (see ER uh nuh VAD uh). A group of mountains located in eastern California. p. 54.

**South America** (south uh MER ih kuh). The earth's fourth largest continent. p. 36.

**South Pole** (south pohl). The most southern place on the earth. p. 24.

**Southern Hemisphere** (SUTH urn HEM ih sfihr). The half of the earth that is south of the Equator. p. 37.

**Springfield** (SPRING feeld). The capital city of Illinois. It is located in the central part of the state. (39°N/89°W). pp. 324–325.

**T**

**Tallahassee** (tal uh HAS ee). The capital of Florida. Located in the panhandle of Florida. (30°N/84°W). p. 141.

**Tenochtitlán** (te nawch tee TLAHN). The Aztec city located where Mexico City now stands. (19°N/99°W). p. 289.

**Tokyo** (TOH kee oh). The capital of Japan. One of the world's most populated cities. (36°N/140°E). p. 269.

**Tulsa** (TUL suh). A city in northeastern Oklahoma. A center for the oil industry. (36°N/96°W). p. 63.

**W**

**Washington, D.C.** (WAWSH ing tun dee see). The capital of the United States. Located on the Potomac River. (39°N/77°W). p. 159.

**Waterloo** (WAWT ur loo). A town in the west central part of the state of New York. (42°N/76°W). pp. 324–325.

**Western Hemisphere** (WES turn HEM ih sfihr). The half of the earth west of the Prime Meridian. North America and South America are located in this hemisphere. p. 37.

**West Indies** (west IHN deez). A group of islands that stretch about 2,500 miles from near Florida to near Venezuela. Located in the northern and eastern parts of the Caribbean Sea. p. 35.

**Wichita** (WIHCH uh taw). The largest city in Kansas. (38°N/97°W). p. 88.

**Williamson** (WIHL yumz sun). A mining community in West Virginia. (38°N/82°W). p. 59.

**Windsor** (WIHN zur). An industrial city in Canada. (42°N/83°W). p. 113.

# STATE CHARTS

## ALABAMA

Montgomery

Birmingham
Mobile
Montgomery

## ALASKA
Largest Cities

Juneau

Anchorage
Fairbanks
Juneau

## ARIZONA
Largest Cities

Phoenix

Phoenix
Tucson
Mesa

## ARKANSAS
Largest Cities

Little Rock

Little Rock
Fort Smith
North
Little Rock

## CALIFORNIA
Largest Cities

Sacramento

Los Angeles
San Diego
San Jose

## COLORADO
Largest Cities

Denver

Denver
Colorado
Springs
Aurora

## CONNECTICUT
Largest Cities

Hartford

Bridgeport
Hartford
New Haven

## DELAWARE
Largest Cities

Dover

Wilmington
Newark
Dover

## FLORIDA
Largest Cities

Tallahassee

Jacksonville
Miami
Tampa

## GEORGIA
Largest Cities

Atlanta

Atlanta
Columbus
Savannah

## HAWAII

**Largest Cities**

Honolulu
Pearl City
Kailua

## KANSAS

**Largest Cities**

Wichita
Kansas City
Topeka

## IDAHO

**Largest Cities**

Boise
Pocatello
Idaho Falls

## KENTUCKY

**Largest Cities**

Louisville
Lexington–
Fayette,
Owensboro

## ILLINOIS

**Largest Cities**

Chicago
Rockford
Peoria

## LOUISIANA

**Largest Cities**

New Orleans
Baton Rouge
Shreveport

## INDIANA

**Largest Cities**

Indianapolis
Fort Wayne
Gary

## MAINE

**Largest Cities**

Portland
Lewiston
Bangor

## IOWA

**Largest Cities**

Des Moines
Cedar Rapids
Davenport

## MARYLAND

**Largest Cities**

Baltimore
Rockville
Hagerstown

## MASSACHUSETTS — Largest Cities

Boston

Boston
Worcester
Springfield

## MICHIGAN — Largest Cities

Lansing

Detroit
Grand Rapids
Warren

## MINNESOTA — Largest Cities

St. Paul

Minneapolis
St. Paul
Duluth

## MISSISSIPPI — Largest Cities

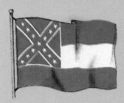

Jackson

Jackson
Biloxi
Meridian

## MISSOURI — Largest Cities

Jefferson City

Kansas City
St. Louis
Springfield

## MONTANA — Largest Cities

Helena

Billings
Great Falls
Butte–
Silver Bow

## NEBRASKA — Largest Cities

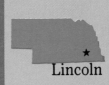

Lincoln

Omaha
Lincoln
Grand
Island

## NEVADA — Largest Cities

Carson City

Las Vegas
Reno
North
Las Vegas

## NEW HAMPSHIRE — Largest Cities

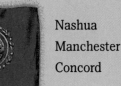

Concord

Nashua
Manchester
Concord

## NEW JERSEY — Largest Cities

Trenton

Newark
Jersey City
Paterson

## NEW MEXICO — Largest Cities

Santa Fe

Albuquerque
Santa Fe
Las Cruces

## OKLAHOMA — Largest Cities

Oklahoma City

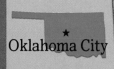

Oklahoma City
Tulsa
Lawton

## NEW YORK — Largest Cities

Albany

New York
Buffalo
Rochester

## OREGON — Largest Cities

Salem

Portland
Eugene
Salem

## NORTH CAROLINA — Largest Cities

Raleigh

Charlotte
Raleigh
Greensboro

## PENNSYLVANIA — Largest Cities

Harrisburg

Philadelphia
Pittsburgh
Erie

## NORTH DAKOTA — Largest Cities

Bismarck

Fargo
Bismarck
Grand Forks

## RHODE ISLAND — Largest Cities

Providence

Providence
Warwick
Pawtucket

## OHIO — Largest Cities

Columbus

Columbus
Cleveland
Cincinnati

## SOUTH CAROLINA — Largest Cities

Columbia

Columbia
Charleston
North Charleston

# STATE CHARTS

## SOUTH DAKOTA — Largest Cities

Pierre ★

Sioux Falls
Rapid City
Aberdeen

## VIRGINIA — Largest Cities

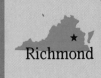

Richmond ★

Virginia
Beach
Norfolk
Richmond

## TENNESSEE — Largest Cities

Nashville ★

Memphis
Nashville–
Davidson
Knoxville

## WASHINGTON — Largest Cities

Olympia ★

Seattle
Spokane
Tacoma

## TEXAS — Largest Cities

Austin ★

Houston
Dallas
San Antonio

## WEST VIRGINIA — Largest Cities

Charleston ★

Huntington
Charleston
Wheeling

## UTAH — Largest Cities

Salt Lake City ★

Salt Lake City
West Valley
Provo

## WISCONSIN — Largest Cities

Madison ★

Milwaukee
Madison
Green Bay

## VERMONT — Largest Cities

Montpelier ★

Burlington
Rutland
Bennington

## WYOMING — Largest Cities

Cheyenne ★

Cheyenne
Casper
Laramie

# The United States: 50 Largest Cities

| City | Rank | Population | City | Rank | Population |
|------|------|-----------|------|------|-----------|
| New York, NY | 1 | 7,352,700 | Nashville-Davidson, TN | 26 | 481,400 |
| Los Angeles, CA | 2 | 3,352,710 | Austin, TX | 27 | 464,690 |
| Chicago, IL | 3 | 2,977,520 | Kansas City, MO | 28 | 438,950 |
| Houston, TX | 4 | 1,698,090 | Oklahoma City, OK | 29 | 434,380 |
| Philadelphia, PA | 5 | 1,647,000 | Fort Worth, TX | 30 | 426,610 |
| San Diego, CA | 6 | 1,070,310 | Atlanta, GA | 31 | 420,220 |
| Detroit, MI | 7 | 1,035,920 | Portland, OR | 32 | 418,470 |
| Dallas, TX | 8 | 987,360 | Long Beach, CA | 33 | 415,040 |
| San Antonio, TX | 9 | 941,150 | St. Louis, MO | 34 | 403,700 |
| Phoenix, AZ | 10 | 923,750 | Tucson, AZ | 35 | 385,720 |
| Baltimore, MD | 11 | 751,400 | Albuquerque, NM | 36 | 378,480 |
| San Jose, CA | 12 | 738,420 | Honolulu, HI | 37 | 376,110 |
| San Francisco, CA | 13 | 731,600 | Pittsburgh, PA | 38 | 375,230 |
| Indianapolis, IN | 14 | 727,130 | Miami, FL | 39 | 371,100 |
| Memphis, TN | 15 | 645,190 | Cincinnati, OH | 40 | 370,480 |
| Jacksonville, FL | 16 | 635,430 | Tulsa, OK | 41 | 368,330 |
| Washington, DC | 17 | 617,000 | Charlotte, NC | 42 | 367,860 |
| Milwaukee, WI | 18 | 599,380 | Virginia Beach, VA | 43 | 365,300 |
| Boston, MA | 19 | 577,830 | Oakland, CA | 44 | 356,860 |
| Columbus, OH | 20 | 569,570 | Omaha, NE | 45 | 353,170 |
| New Orleans, LA | 21 | 531,700 | Minneapolis, MN | 46 | 344,670 |
| Cleveland, OH | 22 | 521,370 | Toledo, OH | 47 | 340,760 |
| El Paso, TX | 23 | 510,970 | Sacramento, CA | 48 | 338,220 |
| Seattle, WA | 24 | 502,200 | Newark, NJ | 49 | 313,800 |
| Denver, CO | 25 | 492,200 | Buffalo, NY | 50 | 313,570 |

## A

**ancestor** (AN ses tur). A person from whom one is descended. p. 271.

**assembly line** (uh SEM blee lyn). A row of people gathered together in a line to make something. p. 105.

## B

**ballot** (BAL ut). A list of all the people who want to be leaders. p. 147.

**bar graph** (bahr graf). A kind of graph that shows information in bars. p. 75.

**Bill of Rights** (bihl uv ryts). The first ten additions to the Constitution. p. 181.

**border** (BOR dur). To touch another area. Also, the line between two countries, states, or other places. p. 31.

**boycott** (BOI kaht). Refusing to do something until a law is changed. p. 202.

**budget** (BUJ iht). A plan for using money. p. 240.

## C

**cable car** (KAY bul kahr). A streetcar that is pulled along a rail by an underground cable. p. 259.

**calligraphy** (kuh LIHG ruh fee). The art of beautiful writing. p. 285.

**candidate** (KAN duh dayt). A person trying to be elected to office. p. 148.

**capital** (KAP ut ul). A city where laws and plans for a state or a nation are made. p. 138.

**capitol** (KAP ut ul). A building where a legislature meets to make laws for a state or a nation. p. 138.

**cartography** (kahr TAHG ruh fee). The art of making maps. p. 193.

**chamber of commerce** (CHAYM bur uv KAHM urs). A group of business people who help their community. p. 112.

**citizen** (SIHT uh zun). A person who is a member of a nation. p. 149.

**citizenship** (SIHT uh zun shihp). How a person carries out the responsibilities of being a citizen. p. 172.

**city** (SIHT ee). The largest kind of community. p. 9.

**civil rights** (SIHV ul ryts). The rights that all Americans are entitled to under the law. p. 200.

**Civil War** (SIHV ul wor). The war between the North and the South. It began in the United States in 1861 over the issues of independence for the South and slavery. p. 209.

**climate** (KLYE mut). The kind of weather a place has over a long period. p. 76.

**coal** (kohl). A black or brown rock that can be burned to give off heat. p. 56.

**coast** (kohst). The land that borders the ocean. p. 52.

**colony** (KAHL uh nee). A place that is located at a distance from the country that governs it. p. 212.

**combine** (KAHM byn). A machine used to cut grain. p. 85.

**communication** (kuh myoo nih KAY shun). The giving and receiving of information. p. 306

**communism** (KAHM yoo nihz um). A type of government that strictly controls the way people of a country live and work. p. 279.

**community** (kuh MYOO nuh tee). A place where people live, work, and play. p. 5.

**commuter** (kuh MYOOT ur). A person

who travels regularly to work from one location to another.  p. 114.

*compass rose* (KUM pus rohz). A drawing that shows where north, south, east, and west are on a map.  p. 24.

*conductor* (kun DUK tur). A person who is in charge of a cable car.  p. 259.

*conflict* (KAHN flihkt) noun. (kun FLIHKT) verb. A disagreement. (noun). To disagree (verb).  p. 313.

*Congress* (KAHNG grus). The group of people who are elected to make laws for the United States.  p. 154.

*conservation* (kahn sur VAY shun). The care of natural resources so they will not be spoiled and wasted but used wisely.  p. 91.

*Constitution* (kahn stuh TOO shun). The set of laws by which the United States is governed.  p. 181.

*consumer* (kun SOOM ur). A person who buys goods and services.  p. 106.

*continent* (KAHN tuh nunt). A large body of land on the earth. The continents are North America, South America, Asia, Africa, Europe, Australia, and Antarctica.  p. 34.

*coordinates* (koh OR duh nihts). A set of numbers used to find a place on a map or globe.  p. 269.

*council* (KOUN sul). A group of men and women who make laws and plans for a community.  p. 132.

*county* (KOUNT ee). A political division of a state.  p. 59.

*crop* (krahp). A plant that is grown in large amounts for food and other uses. p. 73.

*culture* (KUL chur). A way of life.  p. 310.

*custom* (KUS tum). A way of doing things.  p. 116.

## D

*debate* (dee BAYT). A discussion of a certain topic between people.  p. 150.

*Declaration of Independence* (dek luh RAY shun uv ihn dee PEN duns). The paper that declared the American colonies to be free of British control. It stated the reasons for their wish for such freedom. On July 4, 1776, this paper was signed by the leaders of the colonies. p. 181.

*degree* (dih GREE). A unit for measuring latitude and longitude.  p. 267.

*delegate* (DEL uh gut). A person who represents a number of other people and speaks for them at a meeting or in a legislature.  p. 212.

*desert* (DEZ urt). A region with very little rainfall and few plants.  p. 51.

*designer* (dih ZYN ur). A person who plans new products.  p. 107.

*direction* (duh REK shun). The point toward which something faces or the line along which something moves or lies. Example: Directions on the earth are north, south, east, and west.  p. 24.

*drill* (drihl). A machine that makes a long trench, or ditch, and puts seeds deep in the ground.  p. 84.

## E

*elect* (ee LEKT). Leaders who are chosen to make decisions for everyone. p. 132.

*election* (ee LEK shun). The method of choosing leaders by voting.  p. 147.

## Emancipation Proclamation • gristmill

**Emancipation Proclamation** (ee man suh PAY shun prahk luh MAY shun). A document that freed the slaves in the United States.  p. 204.

**emperor** (EM pur ur). A ruler.  p. 284.

**Equator** (ee KWAYT ur). An imaginary line drawn around the earth on maps and globes. It is halfway between the North Pole and the South Pole. The equator divides the earth into the Northern Hemisphere and the Southern Hemisphere.  p. 36.

**Eskimo** (ES kuh moh). An Alaskan native, also called Inuit.  p. 309.

**exhaust** (eg ZAWST). The smoke from a gasoline engine.  p. 291.

**expedition** (eks puh DIHSH un). A long journey made to explore a region or to take part in battle.  p. 248.

**explorer** (ek SPLOR ur). A person who travels to places that are unknown or not well known.  p. 192.

**extinction** (ek STINGK shun). The destruction of a kind of animal, so that those animals disappear from the earth forever.  p. 275.

### F

**fax machine** (faks muh SHEEN). A machine that is able to send and receive messages in an instant.  p. 306.

**flowchart** (FLOH chahrt). A drawing that can show how something is done or how it works.  p. 103.

**fort** (fort). A building with strong walls, guns, and soldiers.  p. 233.

**fortress** (FOR trihs). A building with strong walls to defend against enemies.  p. 279.

**forty-niners** (FORT ee NYN urz). The prospectors who came to California looking for gold.  p. 253.

**freighter** (FRAYT ur). A large ship that is used for carrying goods.  p. 114.

**fuel** (FYOO ul). Anything that is burned to make heat or to make power for running machines.  p. 56.

### G

**geography** (jee AHG ruh fee). The study of the earth and the ways people use it.  p. 49.

**gold rush** (gohld rush). The time when thousands of prospectors came to California looking for gold.  p. 252.

**globe** (glohb). A ball shaped object that shows how the earth looks from space.  p. 23.

**goods** (goodz). Things that are made and offered for sale.  p. 100.

**government** (GUV urn munt). Group of people who make laws and provide services.  p. 131.

**governor** (GUV ur nur). The leader of the state's government who works with the state legislature to make laws for the state.  p. 138.

**grain** (grayn). The seeds of certain grasses, such as wheat, rye, oats, and corn.  p. 80.

**grain elevator** (grayn EL uh vayt ur). A large building for storing grain.  p. 86.

**Greenwich** (GREN ihch). A place in England through which the Prime Meridian passes.  p. 268.

**gristmill** (GRIHST mihl). A building where water power once turned huge wheels to grind grains into flour.  p. 15.

## H

**harbor** (HAHR bur). A protected area of water where ships can safely stay near land. p. 229.

**harvest** (HAHR vihst). A gathering in of ripe crops from the land of which they grew. p. 85.

**headquarters** (HED kwort urz). A business center. p. 301.

**hemisphere** (HEM ih sfihr). A half of the earth. p. 36.

**history** (HIHS tuh ree). A story of the past. p. 13.

## I

**immigrant** (IHM uh grunt). A person from another country who comes to live in a new country. p. 12.

**independence** (ihn dee PEN duns). To be free from the control of another country. p. 272.

**inhabitant** (ihn HAB ih tunt). A person who lives in a place. p. 235.

**interdependence** (ihn tur dee PEN duns). States and countries that depend on one another. p. 300.

**inventor** (ihn VEN tur). A person who makes something that has never been made before. p. 120.

**island** (EYE lund). A body of land with water all around it. p. 52.

## K

**Kremlin** (KREM lihn). A large fortress in the center of Moscow, where the government offices of the Soviet Union are. p. 281.

## L

**lake** (layk). A body of water with land all around it. p. 51.

**landmark** (LAND mahrk). An object, either natural or made by people, that helps you find or recognize a place. p. 262.

**latitude** (LAT uh tood). A distance, measured in degrees, north and south of the Equator. p. 267.

**law** (law). A rule that people must obey. p. 131.

**line graph** (lyn graf). A kind of graph that shows information by using lines. p. 83.

**livestock** (LYV stahk). Farm animals, such as cows, horses, and pigs. p. 73.

**longitude** (LAHN juh tood). A distance, measured in degrees, east and west of the Prime Meridian. p. 267.

**lumbering** (LUM bur ing). Cutting trees and preparing the logs for sale. p. 64.

**lumberjack** (LUM bur jak). A person who is a logger. p. 64.

## M

**manufacture** (man yoo FAK chur). The making of goods by hand or machine. p. 99.

**map** (map). A drawing that shows what the earth looks like from above. p. 26.

**map key** (map kee). A special part of a map that explains the symbols on a map. p. 26.

**market** (MAHR kiht). An open place or a building where goods are sold. p. 228.

**mayor** (MAY ur). A community leader who helps to make laws and sees that the laws are carried out. p. 132.

## mineral ● Pilgrim

**mineral** (MIHN ur ul). A substance found in the earth, such as coal, oil, iron, and gold. p. 56.

**mining** (MYN ing). The way minerals are taken from the earth. p. 58.

**mission** (MIHSH un). A place where religious leaders, such as priests, live and work. p. 250.

**monument** (MAHN yoo munt). A building or stone that is set up to help people remember a special person or event. p. 162.

**mountain range** (MOUNT un raynj). A group of mountains. p. 50.

**mural** (MYOOR ul). A large painting. p. 117.

**museum** (myoo ZEE um). A place where old things, such as paintings, clothing, and tools, are found. p. 13.

### N

**national anthem** (NASH uh nul AN thum). The official song of a country. p. 183.

**Native American** (NAYT ihv uh MER ih kun). An American Indian. p. 13.

**natural resource** (NACH ur ul REE sors). Something in nature that is useful to people. p. 6.

**naturalized citizen** (NACH ur ul yzd SIHT uh zun). A person from another country who must do many things that are required by United States laws in order to become a citizen. p. 176.

**navigation** (nav uh GAY shun). The act of steering a ship. p. 193.

**needs** (needz). Things that a person can not live without, such as food, clothing, or shelter. p. 240.

**nomads** (NOH madz). People who move from place to place to hunt wild animals and to gather food. p. 272.

**nonviolence** (nahn VYE uh luns). To bring about change without hurting others. p. 201.

**North Pole** (north pohl). The most northern place on the earth. p. 24.

### O

**Oath of American Citizenship** (ohth uv uh MER ih kun SIHT uh zun shihp). A serious statement that says that one will be loyal to the United States. p. 178.

**ocean** (OH shun). A very large body of salt water on the earth. p. 52.

### P

**pagoda** (puh GOH duh). A tower that is several stories high. p. 263.

**peninsula** (puh NIHN suh luh). A piece of land that sticks out into the water. A peninsula has water almost all the way around it. p. 52.

**petroleum** (puh TROH lee um). A liquid that is found in the earth, often called oil. p. 56.

**physical feature** (FIHZ ih kul FEE chur). A part of the earth. Rivers, lakes, seas, and mountains are examples of physical features. p. 5.

**Pilgrim** (PIHL grum). One of a group of people who came from England to America on a ship called the *Mayflower*, looking for a place where they could freely practice their religion. p. 195.

*plain* (playn). A large area of flat grasslands. p. 50.

*planned community* (pland kuh MYOO nuh tee). A community that is planned by a person who decides where the streets and buildings of a place should be. p. 158.

*plantation* (plan TAY shun). A very large farm or estate. p. 205.

*plaza* (PLAH zuh). A public square in a town or city. p. 290.

*Pledge of Allegiance* (plej uv uh LEE juns). A promise to be loyal to the United States and its flag. p. 182.

*pollute* (puh LOOT). To spoil by adding something. For example, rivers, lakes, and oceans are polluted by dumping trash in them. p. 69.

*pollution* (puh LOO shun). The unclean state of air, land, or water. p. 291.

*population* (pahp yoo LAY shun). The number of people in a certain place. p. 102.

*port* (port). A place where ships come and go, dropping off and picking up things to be traded. p. 229.

*precipitation* (pree sihp uh TAY shun). All the forms of water that fall to the earth. p. 78.

*presidio* (prih SIHD ee oh). A fort. p. 250.

*Prime Meridian* (prym muh RIHD ee un). The line of longitude from which other lines of longitude are measured. p. 268.

*profit* (PRAHF iht). The amount of money gained in a business deal after all expenses have been subtracted. p. 255.

*property* (PRAHP ur tee). Land, houses, or other buildings owned by people in a community. p. 171.

*prospectors* (PRAH spek turz). People who are looking for valuable minerals, such as coal or oil. p. 253.

*prototype* (PROHT oh typ). The first thing of its kind after which other things are modeled. p. 107.

*public transportation* (PUB lihk trans pur TAY shun). Transportation that moves more than one person or family at one time. p. 239.

## R

*raw material* (raw muh TIHR ee ul). A natural resource. p. 99.

*recycle* (ree SYE kul). To use again in some way. p. 173.

*renewable resource* (rih NOO uh bul REE sors). A natural resource that can be replaced if it is not used too quickly or completely used up. p. 68.

*representative* (rep ruh ZEN tuh tihv). A person who acts or speaks for others. p. 155.

*resident* (REZ ih dunt). A person who lives in a place and is not a visitor. p. 177.

*responsibility* (rih spahn suh BIHL uh tee). Something a person must do. p. 167.

*right* (ryt). Something that is owed to a person. p. 167.

*river* (RIHV ur). A long, flowing body of water. p. 51.

*robot* (ROH baht). A machine that does the work that a person usually does. p. 111.

*ruin* (ROO un). The remains of an old structure that has fallen or been destroyed. p. 290.

## rural area • tradition

**rural area** (ROOR ul ER ee uh). A place where communities are far apart and surrounded by farms and open land. p. 87.

### S

**salary** (SAL uh ree). Money paid regularly for work that is done. p. 240.

**satellite** (SAT uh lyt). An object that circles the earth, carrying special communications equipment. p. 306.

**savings** (SAY vings). Money that is kept for later use. p. 240.

**service** (SUR vihs). Work that helps other people, rather than work in which a product is made. p. 92.

**settlement** (SET ul munt). A small village. p. 12.

**shellfish** (SHEL fish). Sea animals that have a shell. p. 66.

**skyscraper** (SKYE skray pur). A very tall building. p. 242.

**slave** (slayv). Someone who belongs to another person and who has to do what that person says. p. 204.

**soil** (soil). The upper layer of the earth where plants can grow. p. 76.

**South Pole** (south pohl). The most southern place on the earth. p. 25.

**state** (stayt). A part of a country. p. 30.

**state capital** (stayt KAP ut ul). A special city where state leaders meet to decide things for all the people who live in the state. p. 30.

**suburb** (SUB urb). A community near a large city. p. 9.

**subway** (SUB way). A train that runs underground. p. 239.

**Supreme Court** (suh PREEM kort). A court made up of judges who are appointed by the President and who have the job of deciding if laws are fair. p. 157.

**symbol** (SIHM bul). A drawing on a map that stands for real places or things on earth. p. 26.

### T

**tax** (taks). Money that people pay to a government. p. 134.

**technology** (tek NAHL uh jee). The use of science in solving problems in industry. p. 286.

**teleconference** (TEL ih kahn fur uns). A conference of people in different places by means of the telephone. p. 305.

**temperature** (TEM pur uh chur). A measure of heat or cold. p. 78.

**test driver** (test DRYE vur). A driver that makes sure a car is safe. p. 108.

**thermometer** (thur MAHM ut ur). A tool that is used to measure the temperature of the air. p. 78.

**time line** (tym lyn). A scale drawing, standing for a period of time, on which dates are shown. p. 191.

**tourist** (TOOR ihst). A person who takes a trip for pleasure or learning. p. 274.

**town** (toun). A small community where people know each other. p. 9.

**town meeting** (toun MEET ihng). A meeting at which people gather to find out what is happening in their community. p. 131.

**trade** (trayd). To exchange something that is valued for something else that is valued. p. 225.

**tradition** (truh DIHSH un). Very old

beliefs and ways of doing things. p. 197.

**trawler** (TRAWL ur). A boat that uses a trawl, or net, to catch fish and shellfish. p. 66.

**tsar** (sahr). A former emperor, or ruler, of Russia.  p. 279.

## U

**urban area** (UR bun  ER ee uh). A place that includes a city and the suburbs around it.  p. 101.

## V

**veteran** (VET ur un). A person who has fought in a war.  p. 210.

**volunteer** (vahl un TIHR). A person who chooses to do important work and is not paid for it.  p. 172.

**vote** (voht). A way of choosing a leader, particularly in government.  p. 131.

## W

**wagon train** (WAG un  trayn). A line of wagons.  p. 254.

**wants** (wahnts). Goods or services that a person would like to have but can live without.  p. 240.

**watchman** (WAHCH mun). A person who once protected people and their property.  p. 233.

**weather** (WETHH ur). The way the air is at a certain time, such as sunny or cloudy. p. 76.

**wharf** (hworf) A structure that ships can lie alongside of while they load and unload goods.  p. 262.

**White House** (hwyt  hous). The building in Washington, D.C., where the President of the United States lives and works.  p. 159.

**wilderness** (WIHL dur nihs). A wild land, or an area that is unsettled.  p. 271.

**wood pulp** (wood  pulp). A mixture of cooked wood chips and water.  p. 65.

# CREDITS